36089

155 SUG

KU-176-491

Is
of
Tel

2

-9.

-3

2.
2

General editor
Peter
Herriot

New
Essential
Psychology

Life-Span
Development

Léonie Sugarman

Life-Span Development

Concepts, theories and interventions

LIBRARY
Withdrawn

Methuen

London and New York

First published in 1986 by
Methuen & Co. Ltd
11 New Fetter Lane, London EC4P 4EE

Published in the USA by
Methuen & Co.
in association with Methuen, Inc.
29 West 35th Street, New York,
NY 10001

© 1986 Léonie Sugarman

Typeset by Rowland Phototypesetting Ltd
Bury St Edmunds, Suffolk
Printed in Great Britain by
Richard Clay (The Chaucer Press) Ltd
Bungay, Suffolk

All rights reserved. No part of this book
may be reprinted or reproduced or
utilized in any form or by any electronic,
mechanical or other means, now known
or hereafter invented, including
photocopying and recording, or in any
information storage or retrieval system,
without permission in writing from the
publishers.

British Library
Cataloguing in Publication Data

Sugarman, Léonie
  Life-span development, concepts,
  theories and interventions.—(New
  essential psychology)
  1. Developmental psychology
  I. Title   II. Series
  150   BF713

  ISBN 0-416-34390-2

Library of Congress
Cataloging in Publication Data

Sugarman, Léonie, 1950–
  Life-span development.
  (New essential psychology)
  Bibliography: p.
  Includes indexes.
  1. Developmental psychology.
  I. Title   II. Series
  BF713.S84 1986   155   86-8351
  ISBN 0-416-34390-2 (pbk.)

Contents

1

Introduction: the life-span perspective

Life-span development is about every one of us. To emphasize this, I would like you to begin this book by reflecting a little on your own life. Take a blank sheet of paper and, allowing the left and right hand edges of the page to represent the beginning and end of your life respectively, draw, in the manner of a temperature chart, a line across the page to depict the peaks and troughs experienced in your life so far, and also those you would predict for the future. When finished, sit back and ask yourself some questions about this graph – your 'lifeline':

– What is its general shape? Does it continue to rise throughout life? Does it depict peaks and troughs around some arbitrary mean? Alternatively, is there a plateau and subsequent fall in the level of the curve? Is it punctuated with major or only relatively minor peaks and troughs?
– The horizontal axis represents time; but how about the vertical axis – what dimension does that reflect?
– What (or who) triggered the peaks and troughs in the graph? Why did they occur at the time that they did?

– What might have been done (or was done) to make the peaks higher and the troughs shallower? How might the incidence and height of the peaks be increased in the future? and the incidence and depth of the troughs decreased?
– What positive results emerged from the troughs and what were the negative consequences of the peaks?

It is the consideration of questions such as these that form the subject matter of life-span developmental psychology. It is to questions such as these that the present book is directed.

The lifeline which you have drawn can be thought of as a picture of your life course. A more formal definition of the life course would be 'the sequence of events and experiences in a life from birth until death, and the chain of personal states and encountered situations which influence, and are influenced by this sequence of events' (Runyan, 1978, p. 570). The concerns of life-span developmental psychology are typically broad. The area can be defined as the description, explanation and modification (optimization) of within-individual change and stability from birth (or possibly from conception) to death and of between-individual differences and similarities in within-individual change. The danger of such an umbrella definition is that it can seem to be all things to all people. Indeed, life-span developmental psychology has been criticized as just that – a 'motley and monolithic movement' in which 'everyone is invited to contribute his/her voice to the songfest without any restrictions on melody, lyrics and arrangements' (Kaplan, 1983, p. 193).

Whilst there is no necessity for life-span developmental psychology to attempt to form itself into a single intellectual body, it does need to be guided by theory, or at least by articulated assumptions. Rather than comprising a specific theory or independent body of knowledge, life-span developmental psychology constitutes a general perspective or orientation encompassing some generally agreed views. First, it assumes that the potential for development extends throughout the life span. There is no assumption that the lifeline must reach a plateau and/or decline during adulthood and old age. Secondly, it maintains that there is no single specific route that development must or should take. On the contrary, development is potentially multidirectional. Thirdly, development occurs on a number of different fronts. It would have been quite possible, and actually more accurate, for you to have drawn many lifelines, each representing a different component of the life space. For example, we might distinguish between intellectual development, physical development and social development. Of course there would be no necessity that all such curves follow a similar trajectory either within or across individuals. Finally, the life-span perspective tends to favour a reciprocal-influence model of person–environment relations. In other words, it sees both the individual and the environment as potentially influencing and being influenced by each other. It posits a changing organism in a changing context.

Each of the above tenets raises debatable points. The assumption that the potential for development continues throughout life raises the question of what we mean by development. Are we to say that change and development are synonymous? If not, then we need criteria by which to distinguish those changes which are and those which are not developmental. Thus, cognitive psychologists tend to restrict the term development to qualitative changes in cognitive organization which also meet a number of other criteria, such as being sequential, unidirectional, universal, irreversible and end-state- or goal-directed. Data on change are then examined to see whether they meet these criteria. Transporting these criteria beyond the realm of cognitive development tends to render adulthood a period virtually devoid of development since they are met by few of the life changes of the adult years. We need, therefore, to develop alternative conceptualizations of development. This is, indeed, a major task of chapter 2.

The second tenet of the life-span perspective – that developmental paths may vary – arises partly out of an expanding definition of what we mean by development and partly out of an increasing acceptance of the notion that developmental trajectories are socially and historically situated. One implication of this is that the traditional goals of research are rendered problematic (Gergen, 1978, 1980). In particular it becomes inappropriate to place great emphasis on searching for developmental theory with predictive capacity across generations. Gergen (1980) suggests that theory in the life-span domain should be directed not at enhancing prediction and control but rather at 'rendering intelligible and communicable one's experience of the world' (p. 32). Accounts of the life course discussed in chapters 4, 5 and, to some extent, 3 were selected with this in mind. Gergen further suggests that a major criterion of a theory's worth might be the extent to which it is 'generative' – that is, 'the extent to which it unsettles or challenges prevailing views within the culture and thereby points the way toward alternative solutions to existing problems, elaborates alternative forms of social action, and sustains values otherwise submerged' (Gergen, 1980, p. 32).

The third tenet of the life-span perspective – that development occurs on a number of fronts – is reflected in our subdivision of the person into various constituent parts. The lifeline which you drew earlier represented a holistic approach – attempting to depict the life course as a single dimension. A number of other holistic, diagrammatic and/or metaphorical representations of the life course have been suggested, several invoking rhythms of the natural world. Thus Levinson and his colleagues (1978) talk of the seasons of a man's life. Jung (1972), whilst also employing this image, refers to the day more than to the year. He likens the life cycle to the path of the sun – rising in the morning, reaching its zenith at midday and setting in the evening. The mid-life period is described by Jung as the noon of life. Each phase of the day/life has its own characteristics and potentialities which must not be ignored. 'We cannot live the afternoon of life according to the program of life's morning, for what in the morning was true will at evening be a lie. Whoever carries into the afternoon the law of the morning . . . must pay with damage to his soul' (Jung, 1972, p. 396).

To describe the life course, especially the life course of 'the whole person', is a mammoth task. It is easy to sympathize with the view that the concept of the whole person is an overused cliché implying 'something round, large, undifferentiated and thus difficult to manipulate, analyse, study or write about' (McCandless and Evans, 1973, p. 3). Faced with the complexity and diversity of human behaviour across the life span it is normal to seek form and order (Loevinger, 1976). Thus, Super (1976, 1980), like Jung, calls up an arc in his representation of the life span. This time, however, it is the image of the rainbow rather than the arc of the sun. The bands of colour in a rainbow are used to represent the different roles a person assumes during the course of his or her life. Figure 1.1 depicts a typical 'life-career rainbow' with the nine major roles Super considers adequate to describe 'most of the life

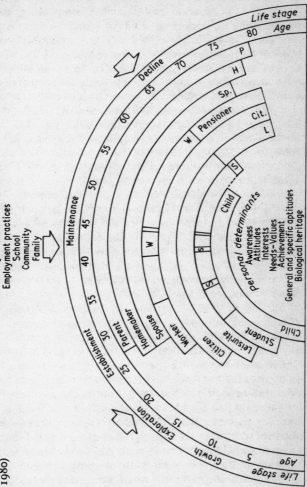

Figure 1.1
Hypothetical example
of a life–career rainbow
(Super, 1980)

Situational determinants, remote–immediate
Social structure
Historical change
Socioeconomic organization and conditions
Employment practices
School
Community
Family

Life stage
Age
80 P
75
70 H
65 Sp.
60 Pensioner
55 W
Decline
50 Cit.
45 L
Maintenance
40 W S
35 S Child
30 Parent
25 Homemaker
Establishment Spouse
20 Worker
15 Citizen
10 Leisurite
5 Student
Exploration
Growth Child
Age
Life stage

personal determinants
Awareness
Attitudes
Interests
Needs–Values
Achievement
General and specific aptitudes
Biological heritage

space of most people during the course of a lifetime' (Super, 1980, p. 283). At first the life space contains only one role, that of child; but it may at a later time contain seven or eight, as when a person is pursuing an occupation, maintaining a home, being a spouse, a parent and the supporting child of ageing parents, engaging in civic activities and following hobbies. Everyone's life-career rainbow contains some universal, some unique, and some shared but not universal features. Other roles could be identified. Not all roles depicted in figure 1.1. are necessarily occupied by all individuals. Furthermore, the sequencing of roles may vary.

Typically researchers focus on only part of the life span and the life space. The life space is generally divided into three key areas: physical-motor components; cognitive-intellectual-achievement components; and personal-social-emotional components. Such distinctions are justified on the grounds that whilst each component interacts with the other two, each also represents 'a concentration of certain behavior or developmental characteristics' (McCandless and Evans, 1973, pp. 3–4). Such a division of the life space is to be found in the majority of developmental psychology textbooks, especially those focusing on childhood and adolescence. It is a division which works less well when adulthood is the focus of attention. Then additional role-related categories are frequently introduced – marriage, career and sex-role development, for example.

The fourth tenet of the life-span perspective – the assumption of reciprocal influence – constitutes a general recognition of the impact of both the individual and the environment on development. An informative metaphor sometimes used to depict the life course is the image of a river. A river, whilst having a force and momentum of its own, is also shaped and modified by the terrain over and through which it flows. In turn, the river exerts its own influence on its surroundings. Indeed, it is somewhat artificial to separate the river from its habitat; a more accurate picture is obtained when they are considered as a single unit. None the less, for ease and clarity of conceptual analysis they may be treated as separate entities. The results of such investigations only reveal their full meaning, however, when returned to the wider perspective of the river + surroundings unit. So it is with the individual life course. We can concentrate our attention on either the person or the environment as the focus of the developmental dynamic.

However, we will gain only an incomplete picture of life-span development unless we also consider the interactions between the two.

Traditionally (see, for example, Reese and Overton, 1970) models of the person utilized by psychologists have been dichotomized between organismic and mechanistic models. Whilst the importance of both the individual and the environment in determining behaviour has generally been acknowledged, the tendency has frequently been to emphasize and focus attention almost exclusively on one or the other (Pervin and Lewis, 1978). Depending on the particular area of the enquiry, this dichotomy appears in a number of forms throughout developmental psychology (Lerner, 1976). It underlies the debates between, for example, nativism and èmpiricism; maturation and learning; heredity and environment; and innate and acquired characteristics. Whatever terms are used, the basic thrust of the issue remains the same. It is the question of nature v. nurture.

Some psychologists – the 'maturationalists' – have emphasized the part played by 'nature', with the role of innate, maturational and hereditary factors being afforded greatest attention. Alternatively, humanistic psychologists have placed emphasis on the person's ability to influence his or her life course. These approaches enshrine an organismic model of the person, with the living organism as its basic metaphor. Its central characteristic is its representation of the organism as inherently and spontaneously active; the source of acts rather than a collection of acts initiated by external forces (Overton and Reese, 1973). The environment inhibits or facilitates but does not cause development. Development occurs through the activity of the organism itself.

Another group of psychologists, notably those working from a traditional learning-theory or social learning-theory perspective have emphasized the role of 'nurture', and focused attention on the role of environmental factors as causes of development. The model of the person underlying this position has variously been termed mechanistic, reactive and passive. Its central feature is its characterization of the individual as inherently at rest. Its basic metaphor is that of the machine – naturally passive but reacting to external stimuli which are, therefore, the causes of its movement.

There is also a third model of the person able to encompass both the mechanistic and the organismic approaches. Called the

7

interactive model and described as a superordinate perspective (Reese, 1976), it is not so much a model of the person as explicitly a model of the person–environment relationship. It has several variations (Olweus, 1977; Reese and Overton, 1970), a key distinction being between what are most often referred to as the interactional and the transactional versions (Dewey and Bentley, 1949; Pervin and Lewis, 1978; Riegel and Meacham, 1978). The interactional view posits objects or elements that can be described and located independently and which act on other objects in a causal manner. Thus, we can think about a person's job description influencing the way a job is done (that is, the environmental influence) and also about the person actively working to modify the job description or, at least, the way it is enacted (that is, the personal influence). The interactional model can itself be further subdivided into different versions. One form would argue that all interactions change both organism and environment, whilst an alternative position would be that a variable might affect other variables without itself being changed by them or by the process of interaction. Although the latter position might be a theoretical possibility it is likely that most processes of interest to developmental psychologists will be of the reciprocal-action rather than unidirectional-action type (Pervin and Lewis, 1978). This model is basically a combination of the organismic and mechanistic perspectives. Both the individual and the environment are accorded (potential) causal status. The person and the environment are seen as composed of separate entities which meet and interact at an interface. Sameroff (1982) in arguing for a systems approach to development cites an example from the realm of physical handicap:

it is not a baby's cerebral palsy alone that condemns him to a low IQ, but rather the denial of entry into the educational system that could allow the child to transcend the physical handicap. And that denial is not only a function of the educational system but is also a function of a particular political system in a particular historical epoch. (pp. 85–6)

The transactional view, however, assumes relations rather than objects or elements to be primary. Person and environment are assumed to be in continuous reciprocal relationship such that it is inappropriate to think of and study them as distinct entities. The

8

transaction between the organism and the environment is seen as the most appropriate unit of analysis. Rather than being viewed as separate entities, organism and environment are seen as constituting a single life process (Gollin, 1981). Karp and Yoels (1982) apply a transactional model to life-span development when they use symbolic interactionism as the organizing framework for conceptualizing the ageing process. This also, incidentally, through the use of the term 'interaction' points to the terminological confusion that exists with regard to this model of the person. Terms are used interchangeably or differently, and alternatives to 'transactional' (notably 'relational' and 'dialectical') are also to be found. Symbolic interactionism emphasizes the meaning of objects, events, situations or processes for actors. Meaning is viewed as an emergent property of interaction between the person and the environment rather than a characteristic of either. It is not an inherent part of any one entity. The person is influenced by environmental circumstances but is capable of responding creatively. The meaning of experience is one such creative response.

Psychology, with its traditional emphasis on the individual, has developed fewer tools for analysing the environment than for analysing the person. However, Bronfenbrenner (1977), drawing heavily on the theories of Kurt Lewin, proposes a broad and differentiated model of the environment. He depicts the environment as 'a nested arrangement of structures, each contained within the next' (p. 514). Egan and Cowan (1979) present this model diagrammatically, as shown in figure 1.2. Its breadth is indicated in that it is a model which goes beyond the immediate situation or situations that contain the individual. It considers the relations within and between the different settings in which the individual operates, and also the larger social contexts, both formal and informal, in which such settings are embedded.

Employing a terminology derived from Brim (1975), Bronfenbrenner (1977) distinguishes between four environmental systems located at different levels: microsystems, mesosystems, exosystems and macrosystems.

1 A *microsystem* is 'the complex of relations between the developing person and environment in an immediate setting containing the person' (Bronfenbrenner, 1977, p. 514). The environment or setting can be delineated by a number of elements: place (for

9

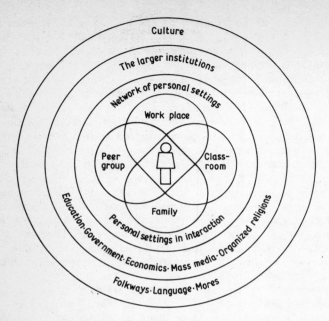

Figure 1.2 Bronfenbrenner's nested model of the environment (Egan and Cowan, 1979)

example, home, college, factory), time, physical features, activities, participants and roles. Reinert (1980), considering the microsystem of educators and students, distinguishes between personal and physical elements. It is the former that has received the greater amount of attention from psychologists. For example, Schlossberg (1981), in considering factors which influence the individual's management of change, identifies three key types of interpersonal support systems: intimate relationships, the family unit and networks of friends. Kahn and Antonucci (1980) focus on microsystems in which the individual gains social support and classifies these relationships according to the extent to which the support is role-dependent. Figure 1.3 is a hypothetical example of what such a convoy (to use Kahn and Antonucci's term) of support might look like.

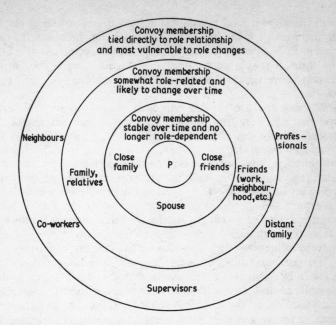

Figure 1.3 Hypothetical example of a social support convoy (Kahn and Antonucci, 1980)

2 A *mesosystem* is a system of microsystems; that is, 'the inter-relations among major settings containing the person at a particular point in his or her life' (Bronfenbrenner, 1977, p. 514). Thus, home life and work life interact when a particular career (such as in the army) results in a particular style of social life or when considerations concerning a child's education influence whether a job offer in a new location is accepted or rejected.

3 An *exosystem* is an influence system which contains microsystems, mesosystems and also specific social structures, both formal and informal, which impinge on or encompass the settings in which the developing person is found. 'These structures include the major institutions of the society, both deliberately structured and spontaneously evolving, as they operate at the concrete level' (Bronfenbrenner, 1977, p. 515). Thus, the individual is not a part

of the neighbourhood transportation system (unless, let us say, he or she works for the local bus company) but the nature of that system influences the mesosystems and microsystems of which the individual is a part. Other exosystems include the labour market, government agencies, medical services and the mass media.

4 *Macrosystems* are the blueprints of micro-, meso- and exo-systems. They are 'the overarching institutional patterns of the culture or subculture' (Bronfenbrenner, 1977, pp. 515). Carriers of information and ideology, macrosystems are generally informal and implicit, but are made explicit through a society's recorded laws, regulations and rules. They are a reflection of the values and priorities of a society. They include the principles of a society's economic, social, educational, legal and political systems. Such manifestations of a society's culture are transmitted as norms and values through exo-, meso- and microsystems to individuals, thereby influencing their thoughts, behaviours and opportunities.

To sum up, life-span developmental psychology is distinguished by its view of development as potentially lifelong, multidirectional and multidimensional, and as requiring contextual analysis. Each of these attributes has been the subject of debate, and, generally speaking, eludes one unequivocally 'best' way of representation. The further development of these points is a key function of the present book. Before this, however, some relevant issues concerning research in developmental psychology are raised.

Digression on research

The primary concern of developmental psychology has been the question of intra-individual change over time. Frequently this has taken the form of investigating age-associated changes in some aspect of psychological or physical functioning. However, it has also been suggested (for example, Baer, 1970) that age should be an irrelevant concept in developmental psychology. We should concentrate on sequences of experience rather than age-related behaviour change. Age is nothing more than the passage of time, and time on its own causes nothing. Certainly we cannot look to age as an explanation for age differences. Instead we need to look for the processes which might cause these differences. They might be the result of a normal maturation or ageing process, but we cannot automatically assume this to be the case. What we can say about cause is determined by our research design – that is, what we choose to measure, how and why.

Dimensions of developmental research

Much of chapters 3, 4 and 5 is an account of research on the life course. It constitutes but a sample of the work available. We are in danger of being swamped by the sheer quantity of material unless we can find some way of organizing it that aids its comprehension and evaluation. McCandless (1970; McCandless and Evans, 1973) offers such assistance in his discussion of four key dimensions of developmental research. These four dimensions, which describe continua along which any study of human development can be placed are: normative–explanatory; ahistorical–historical;

Table 1.1   Dimensions of developmental research (McCandless, 1970)

Normative		Explanatory
Descriptive, averages, types, frequencies	⟷	Causal relations, prediction
Ahistorical		Historical
Relations between two variables measured at same time; studies of phenomena at about same point in time; no exploration of their origins	⟷	Search in history of the organism for the origin and learning conditions of behaviour
Naturalistic		Manipulative
Organism studied under real-life, natural conditions	⟷	Conditions controlled and, if possible, placed in laboratory setting
Atheoretical		Theoretical
Designed to answer immediate problems, or substantiate informal observations, or satisfy curiosity	⟷	Deduced or induced from body of logically interrelated concepts and postulates

naturalistic–manipulative; and atheoretical–theoretical. The polar positions of these four dimensions are summarized in table 1.1. Each has its attendant strengths and weaknesses.

1 *Normative–Explanatory.* Norms are descriptions of the typical or of the average. Developmental psychologists have expended much energy on establishing age-related normative behaviour. We know, for example, about the 6-month-old's typical motor ability, the 8-year-old's typical reasoning ability and the 40-year-old's typical preoccupations. Such research provides us with an account of what, under similar conditions, we might expect to occur during the life course. It describes the 'normal' (that is, the statistically most frequent) sequence and timing of change. Such information can be of great value. The teacher who knows the average reading level of his or her class will be better able to gauge the appropriate level of instruction than one who does not. However, norms are not explanations – although developmental psychologists have sometimes been criticized for behaving as though they were: for saying, in effect, that our age causes our behaviour. Nicholson (1980) lampoons this viewpoint as reflected in age-related explanations for the human condition promulgated by popular magazines:

> Suppose, for example, you wake up one morning feeling depressed for no obvious reason. There is no need to get alarmed. It's your age that is causing it, however old you happen to be. Two? You are having problems resolving the trust-versus-mistrust psychosocial crisis. Twelve? Puberty is on the horizon. Twenty-two? Who would not be depressed when confronted by the intimacy-versus-isolation crisis which is alleged to overshadow this period of our lives? Thirty-two? You are in the middle of the first major life review, facing the painful task of deciding whether you have chosen the right partner or job. And so it goes on, . . . through the mid-life crisis, the menopause (male and female varieties), the pre-retirement era, the transition to life without work, and finally the decline through senescence and senility towards the merciful escape offered by the grave. (pp. 13–14)

The lack of explanatory power of norms becomes obvious when we seek to understand why individuals conform to or deviate from them, or when we seek to predict the life course of an individual rather than a group. To know that most people's sight begins to deteriorate during their 40s, does not help us understand why some people need spectacles at a much earlier age. It may be comforting to know that most people experience a sense of life becoming more serious towards the end of their 20s, but this does not help us to understand why this should be.

To explain we need concepts as well as data. Explanatory research is concerned with identifying concepts and developing or testing theories that will account for our findings. What factors, for example, enable some people to transcend the roles and behaviours typically prescribed for members of their sex? Why do others experience anxiety at the prospect of such sex-role deviation? Clearly such enquiry must be based on normative data – we cannot explain that which we cannot describe. Distinguishing between different possible explanations can, however, present enormous methodological problems, some of which are discussed subsequently. None the less, it is possible to locate research on a dimension which has the goal of normative description at one end and the goal of theoretically grounded explanation at the other.

2 *Ahistorical–Historical.* McCandless's ahistorical–historical dimension distinguishes studies on the basis of their degree of emphasis on the origins and factors leading to particular findings. He uses the term 'historical' to refer to the history or life course of the individual rather than the study of bygone eras. It is research which is concerned not only with behaviour at a particular point in time, but also with the origins and/or future course of that behaviour. As such, it is the standard paradigm of developmental research, namely the longitudinal study.

By contrast, ahistorical research is concerned with behaviour at one point in time only. It may well be concerned with individual differences – typically the province of differential or trait-and-factor psychologists. Thus, we may wish to identify and subsequently to measure the occupational interests of school-leavers so as to facilitate their selection of an appropriate career. In this instance our research design would be that second stalwart of developmental psychology – the cross-sectional study. Our concern may be whether, for example, individuals' interests lie in engineering, in the social sciences or in physically active pursuits. We do not necessarily wish to examine the route by which their interests came to be in a particular field or why different individuals' interest patterns should vary. Differential theorists of occupational choice, such as Holland (1973), have given some attention to the development of occupational interests, but as a secondary rather than a primary issue.

3 *Naturalistic–Manipulative*. The naturalistic–manipulative dimension refers to the circumstances under which researchers collect their data. Naturalistic research observes subjects in their natural environment. The researcher seeks to influence the subjects' behaviour as little as possible and to get as close as possible to how the subject would behave if the researcher were not there at all. At the other extreme is research located in an experimental laboratory in which the researcher seeks to manipulate or to control closely the situation under which observations are made. Control is, however, achieved at the cost of ecological validity; that is, of connection with life outside the laboratory. To know how people behave in an experimental laboratory does not necessarily help us understand how they will behave in 'real life'. Indeed, the irrelevancy of much psychological research to everyday life has frequently been the basis of critiques of the subject, especially by people working outside the discipline, but also by those working in applied areas within it. More ecologically valid, naturalistic observations may, however, be difficult and time-consuming to obtain. The behaviour of interest may not be exhibited very clearly or frequently. It will almost inevitably be embedded amongst a great deal of other behaviour. The researcher is likely to confront difficult problems of deciding what to observe and record, and then how to interpret the findings.

Much research in developmental psychology, particularly that concerned with adulthood, involves the use of questionnaires and interviews. These are clearly towards the manipulative end of the naturalistic–manipulative continuum in that the subject is asked to respond to questions devised by the researcher. However, the type of question and the extent to which the researcher wishes to restrict the response options of the subject vary enormously. At one extreme are narrowly construed questions about a particular phenomenon (for example, abstract reasoning), or closed-ended, multiple-choice questions where the researcher defines the response options as well as the questions. Then there are situations where respondents construct their own replies to set questions. Thus, moral development has been studied by presenting stories involving moral dilemmas, and then asking subjects a series of prescribed and specific questions about how they believe the situation should be resolved. At the naturalistic end of the spectrum of types of interview are those which are deliberately open-ended and non-directive. Thus, moral development could be studied by asking people to define what they mean by morality and then to describe how they resolved some real moral dilemma, rather than asking them how some hypothetical person should respond to some hypothetical situation. In the more open-ended situation interviewers seek to understand the ways interviewees see the world and to find out what issues they raise spontaneously. As a result the researcher may well be faced with the problem of lack of comparability of data across subjects. Furthermore, there is still, of course, some manipulation or directing of the subject in that the interview will have been arranged with some, if very broadly defined, purpose in mind.

4 *Atheoretical–Theoretical.* There are a number of reasons for conducting research. We may, as in normative research, wish to describe the typical course of a particular characteristic over time. Alternatively, we may have a practical problem that we wish to solve – what, for example, is the best way of helping elderly people settle into a residential home? In another instance we might wish to examine the effect of a particular intervention – what, for example, is the effect on both parties of allocating newcomers at a residential home for the elderly to an individual 'welcomer' from amongst established residents? We may, particularly if we are operating from an academic rather that a field base, wish to test a particular theory or hypothesis. The 'welcoming programme' above would not have been instigated without some hypotheses about the nature of residents' problems – loneliness, loss of social networks, loss of purpose in life, for instance.

McCandless's final dimension of research distinguishes research efforts by the extent to which they are theoretically grounded. Atheoretical research may help us manage a particular problem or describe a particular situation. It is, however, almost inevitably piecemeal since there may be no basis for connecting it to other pieces of theoretical or empirical work. Furthermore, atheoretical research is ill-equipped to handle the unexpected. If our welcoming programme for new residents were a failure we may well be hard-pressed to understand why.

It is possible to locate all of the research discussed in this book on each of the four dimensions identified by McCandless. Whilst some dimensions may vary together – descriptive research being less theoretical, historical research being more explanatory, for example – there is no logical necessity that they do so. Lerner (1976) summarizes the usefulness of McCandless's dimensions as allowing us 'to appreciate the many forms that developmental research may take, the many research emphases that may be stressed in such research, and the assets and limitations of each of these approaches to the study of psychological development' (Lerner, 1976, p. 288).

Research design

The archetypal research design in developmental psychology is the longitudinal study. A group of subjects is followed over time, with particular emphasis on changes in the characteristic under investigation. We must, however, be cautious about locating the cause for such change within the individual. Let us take a hypothetical example. Suppose we had, in 1960, begun a longitudinal study of the career patterns of a group of 20-year-olds. Further suppose that some twenty years later, when the subjects were in their early 40s, we found that the incidence of redundancy and the average time taken to secure a new job both increased. It would be naive to suppose that this could be accounted for entirely by reference to intra-individual characteristics. At the very least, the prevailing economic conditions and national level of unemployment in the 1980s as compared with 1960 would need to be considered. In other words, time of measurement should also be taken into account. Longitudinal research identifies age-related changes for that particular cohort (Nunnally, 1973), but we cannot assume them to be universal across generations or cultures.

There are other problems with longitudinal research. We need, for example, to consider the effect that prolonged participation in the research may have on the subjects. If people are regularly asked about their career plans throughout adulthood then we might reasonably expect this to influence the extent and manner in which they think about their work. At the theoretical level we may find that advances in the subject make our original theoretical perspective or subject-selection criteria seem inadequate or outmoded. Vaillant (1977) speaks of the unforgivable omission of women from the study which he joined some decades after its inception. Haan (1972) describes how data collected earlier in the study with which she worked was re-evaluated in the light of later theoretical developments. Furthermore, there will almost inevitably be some subjects who fall by the wayside in longitudinal studies – they may move home and be impossible to trace, they may die, or they may refuse to continue participating in the study. Those who do continue may not be representative of the total. At the more practical level, there may well be difficulties in securing funding for lengthy longitudinal studies, and, assuming that such funding is forthcoming, it is unlikely that there will be continuity of researchers over a twenty- or thirty-year period.

In longitudinal research the subject group remains the same and the time of measurement is varied. Reversing these characteristics produces the cross-sectional design. In this instance people of different ages are compared at the same point in time. Such a strategy is expedient. It means, to return to our hypothetical example, that we do not need to wait twenty years in order to examine the differential employability of 20- and 40-year-olds. It also obviates the need to study the same individuals repeatedly. However, it, too, has its problems. Again we must be wary of accounting for differences between the different age groups in terms of intra-individual change across time. The different groups of subjects are from different generations or cohorts and it may be this, rather than any inherent differences between 20- and 40-year-olds, that accounts for our findings. The two groups will have experienced different amounts and types of education, they will have been prepared for different worlds, with different skills and possibly different values. As with much longitudinal research, we can describe age differences, but we cannot necessarily explain them.

In order to identify possible research designs for developmental psychology in a way that would facilitate comparison of their attendant advantages and weaknesses, Schaie (1965) instigated, by proposing what he called a 'general developmental model', a long debate on research methodology (see, for example, Baltes, 1968; Baltes et al., 1978; Buss 1973, 1974; Nunnally, 1973; Schaie and Baltes, 1975). This model considers three variables that may account for behaviour change across time – age (that is, the number of years from birth to time of testing), time (that is, year) of measurement and cohort (defined by the year in which the individual was born). Of course, it must be remembered that age is only a shorthand term for the processes that it denotes. Likewise, time of measurement is a shorthand for the social and environmental conditions of influence then prevailing, and cohort differences only attain meaning in the light of a consideration of the similarities and differences in experience of the two groups.

Schaie's (1965) general developmental model can be presented as a matrix, as shown in table 1.2. Longitudinal and cross-sectional research designs can then be seen as representing particular paths through such a matrix. Longitudinal research represents a horizontal path, following, for example, a cohort of people born in 1940 over a thirty-year period as they age from 20 to 50 years. Cross-sectional research follows a vertical path through the matrix. In a particular year of testing, say 1970, it selects people from a number of different cohorts.

Schaie's model also encompasses other research designs. First,

Table 1.2   Schaie's (1965) general developmental model

Time of birth (cohort)	Time of measurement							
	1960		1970		1980		1990	
	Age in years							
1920	40		50		60		70	
		1		2		3		4
1930	30		40		50		60	
		5		6		7		8
1940	20		30		40		50	
		9		10		11		12
1950	10		20		30		40	
		13		14		15		16

there is the time-lag method, which is the last of the series of designs following a single dimension in the table 1.2 matrix. This time it is a diagonal path which crosses the matrix from left to right and from top to bottom. It examines given characteristics for people of a particular age drawn from different cohorts – how, for example, might 30-year-olds born in 1930 compare with 30-year-olds born in 1950? Differences between these two groups might be due either to time-of-measurement factors (the fact that one set of measurements were taken in 1960 and the other set in 1980) or to cohort differences (the fact that they were born in 1930 and 1950, respectively, with the consequent differences in their life experiences). If no differences are found between the two groups of 30-year-olds then it can be assumed that neither time of measurement nor cohort effects have influenced the characteristic under investigation.

To summarize, when age differences are found using each of the three research designs outlined above there exist two possible explanations for these differences which cannot be disentangled. Thus, age differences found from longitudinal studies may be caused either by the ageing process or by the conditions prevailing at the different times of measurement. Age differences found in cross-sectional research may reflect either ageing or cohort differences. Finally, differences within a particular age group identified by time-lag studies will originate in time-or-measurement and/or cohort differences.

In an attempt to disentangle the three possible explanations of age differences Schaie advocated research designs which follow a stepwise path across the table 1.2 matrix – hence its claim to be a general developmental model. Each combines the characteristics of two of the linear designs described above, and Schaie refers to them generally as sequential research designs. The cohort-sequential design, or longitudinal sequence, as it is termed by Baltes (1968), examines longitudinal sequences for two or more cohorts. In other words, it combines the characteristics of longitudinal and time-lag studies. An example from table 1.2 would be a study which sampled cells 1, 2, 3, 6, 7 and 8. The second sequential method derived from table 1.2 is the time-sequential design, or cross-sectional sequence (Baltes, 1968). It combines the time-lag and the cross-sectional designs – all ages of interest are sampled at all times of measurement. An example would be a study which examined 30-, 40- and 50-year-olds in 1970 and 1980. This would involve sampling cells 2, 6 and 10 in 1970, and cells 7, 11 and 15 in 1980. The disadvantages of repeated measures on the same individuals are avoided by selecting new samples at each time of measurement. Schaie's third sequential design, the cross-sequential method, combines the longitudinal and the cross-sectional methods, measuring all cohorts at all times of measurement. With regard to table 1.2 this would entail sampling, for example, cells 2, 6 and 10 in 1970; cells 3, 7 and 11 in 1980; and cells 4, 8 and 12 in 1990. This can, however, be viewed as merely an extended longitudinal sequence (cohort-sequential design) or an extended cross-sectional sequence (time-sequential design) depending, respectively, on whether all cells represent independent samples or whether, where appropriate, repeated measures are taken. Are, for example, the 40-year-olds sampled in 1980 (cell 11) the same group of people who as 30-year-olds were sampled in 1970 (cell 10)? Ideally the 1980 group could include some old and some new subjects – but the scope of the consequent research may be beyond the financial and staff resources of many research projects.

There has been debate as to whether sequential designs can explain as well as describe age differences. Schaie maintains that, with appropriate statistical manipulation, they can. Baltes (1968) disputes this on two counts. His first objection concerns the lack of independence in the definitions of the three parameters of age, cohort and time of measurement. Once two have been defined the third is determined automatically and Baltes (1968) argues that the 'existence of these mutual dependencies signifies that the three components do not satisfy the qualifications of three true experimental variables, namely they cannot be defined and varied independently' (p. 157). Secondly, Baltes questions Schaie's interpretation of the meanings of age, time and cohort differences. All three, Baltes argues, are aspects of the time continuum and it is unwarranted to make functional interpretations (for example, that age differences are maturation effects, or that time of measurement differences are environmental effects) of differences in these components.

Adopting the broader approach that typifies the life-span perspective brings such problems of research design to the fore. Despite their differences Baltes and Schaie agree as to the importance of psychologists' recognizing the effect that prevailing (that is, time-of-measurement) conditions and historical (that is, cohort) experiences may have on developmental processes. In other words, both advocate a contextual and historically situated study of the human life course. Indeed they go beyond this by suggesting research designs by which at least at the descriptive level, this can be achieved.

The life-span perspective: new or not so new?

A life-span perspective on human development may at first glance appear to be a recent and still embryonic phenomenon. It was not, for example, thought necessary to include a title on the subject among the thirty-six books in Methuen's original Essential Psychology series. Likewise it is doubtful whether even now modules on life-span development form a part of the core of most undergraduate psychology degrees. Set against this is the burgeoning of publications with a life-span perspective that began during the 1970s. It is this material which forms the bedrock of the present book.

Let us not, however, be overimpressed by our achievement in recognizing (assuming we do) the importance of a life-span perspective. It has in fact a long history, different aspects of which are demonstrated in a number of contemporary publications (Baltes, 1979, 1983; Charles, 1970; Groffman, 1970; Havighurst, 1973; Reinert, 1979). In the most comprehensive of these papers, Reinert (1979) charts the historical interest in life-span development from the beginning of European intellectual history (*circa* 400 BC) to the 1930s.

Reinert deals only briefly with developments from World War II to the present – an era he dubs the period of differentiation and integration. 'Differentiation' is represented by continuing specialization. We now, for example, have a large number of subdisciplines concerned with the period around birth and early infancy (Karp and Yoels, 1982). Likewise, different investigators concentrate on different aspects of the person. Any holistic quality is frequently lost.

The 'integration' of which Reinert writes is represented by the efforts of scholars within the life-span movement – most notably the contributors to the West Virginia conferences on 'Life-span developmental psychology'. Eight such symposia have been held to date, each adopting a somewhat different theme: research and theory (Goulet and Baltes, 1970); methodology (Nesselroade and Reese, 1973); personality and socialization (Baltes and Schaie, 1973); normative life crises (Datan and Ginsberg, 1975); dialectical perspectives (Datan and Reese, 1977); intervention (Turner and Reese, 1980); non-normative life events (Callahan and McCluskey, 1983); and historical and generative effects on life-span development (McCluskey, Fawcett and Reese, 1984).

Also indicative of this concern with 'integration' is the continuing series of publications on life-span development and behaviour (Baltes, 1978; Baltes and Brim, 1979, 1980, 1982, 1983, 1985). Furthermore, the first *Annual Review of Psychology* paper on life-span development appeared in 1980 (Baltes *et al.* 1980), with the second appearing four years later (Honzik, 1984). In addition, the number of textbooks taking a life-span perspective has increased markedly of late (see, for example, Ambron and Brodzinsky, 1982; Bee and Mitchell, 1984; Birren *et al.*, 1981; Craig, 1983; Schell and Hall, 1983; Turner and Helms, 1979). Finally, the past decade and a half has also seen the publication of a number of empirical investigations of the adult years or of the whole life course. Some have been the result of cross-sectional studies (for example, Gould, 1978; Levinson *et al.*, 1978; Nicholson, 1980), whilst others have been the outcome of long-established longitudinal studies (such as, Block and Haan, 1971; Vaillant 1977).

A total-life-span, total-life-space approach to human development is enjoying a revival and is slowly becoming a more integral part of mainstream psychology. With regard to the present book, an attempt to hasten this development is contained within six further chapters. Whilst the present has considered the general tenets of life-span developmental psychology and their implications, along with various design aspects of related research, chapter 2 concentrates on definitions of and orientations towards development. Chapter 3 moves on to details of change or, at times, lack of change across the life course. It focuses on the first two of McCandless and Evans's (1973) concentration points: physical-motor and cognitive-intellectual aspects of the person. Personal or personality development is covered in chapters 4 and 5. These distinctions, however, are not always clear-cut. Interaction between the individual and the environment, and between different aspects of the individual, precludes such well-defined boundaries. Furthermore, throughout chapters 3 and 4, and especially in chapter 5, the focus is primarily on the years after adolescence. This is not because of the irrelevancy of work on childhood to a life-span perspective, but because of, first, the availability of this work elsewhere (for example, Turner, 1984) and, secondly, limitations of space, which would make it difficult to do justice to the vast amount of work in the field.

In chapter 6 a somewhat different perspective on the life course is chosen. Rather than concentrating on age-related changes and stages, this chapter considers more general phenomena – how we describe, classify, respond to and cope with significant life events. In the seventh and final chapter attention turns to questions of intervention – what are the intervention implications of adopting a life-span perspective, and how might we conceptualize the myriad of specific intervention options open to us? Throughout the book your own lifeline can serve as a vantage point from which to consider the various issues raised. Occasionally you are directly encouraged to refer back to this graph of life. Explicitly in these instances, and implicitly elsewhere, it is hoped that it will serve as a link between your own concrete experience and the more abstract concepts of life-span developmental psychology.

2

Development and change

This chapter begins with a discussion of the nature and defining features of developmental change. In relation to the lifeline introduced at the beginning of chapter 1 this can be thought of as impinging on the issue of what variables the vertical dimension might represent. Two attempts to articulate the largely theoretical end point of development are outlined: Maslow's (1968, 1970) concept of the self-actualizing person and Allport's (1964) account of the mature personality. Next the form of human development is discussed. This can be thought of as addressing the question of the shape of the lifeline of a developing individual. The types of influence on the life course are then categorized and discussed. Finally, the implications of different perspectives on the life course are considered – indulging the risk of unwarranted age bias.

The concept of development

The distinguishing characteristics of developmental change have been the topic of much controversy and debate. Development is, as Van den Daele (1976) commented, a construct in search of an identity. Two symposia devoted to the question and held fifteen years apart (Collins, 1982; Harris, 1957) indicate continued concern with the issue.

'Development' is not an empirical term (Reese and Overton, 1970), although on occasions it is used as though it were (Kaplan, 1983). No matter how much data we were able to collect about the course of individuals' lives this of itself would not enable us to define what is meant by the term 'development' – unless, that is, we were to say that whatever happens across the life span or whatever happens to most people across the life span is what constitutes development. This reduces developmental psychology to an atheoretical data-collection exercise. Furthermore, an individualistic definition which says that whatever happens is development makes no judgements as to what is better or preferable. It therefore provides no guidelines for developmental intervention. Since from this viewpoint any life course is as good (developed) as any other, there are no grounds for attempting to influence it. If on the other hand a normative empirical definition of development is adopted – that is, saying that the typical constitutes development – then the implications for intervention are that people should be encouraged to be like the average. This stance represents a conflation of the 'is' and the 'ought', seeing them as synonymous.

Rather than emerging in some self-evident way from empirical data, the concept of development requires the initial postulation of assumptions, underlying premises or value judgements as to its defining characteristics. These standards of comparison precede empirical observation, which may even then only provide indirect evidence. Thus, cognitive structures are only inferred from data, and changes in cognitive organization are not directly observable.

From the perspective of cognitive psychology something like the learning of new words would not, on its own, constitute development. Development would take the form of formulating new, more advanced ways of manipulating verbal concepts which also met the criteria, mentioned in chapter 1, of being sequential, unidirectional, and so on. Such a restrictive or 'hard' definition of development has repeatedly been rejected as inappropriate for the array of aspirations and orientations to be found in the life-span movement (for example, Baltes and Willis, 1977; Brim and Ryff, 1980) as well as being unable to account for data relating to the adult years when these are seen as times of developmental potential (Baltes *et al.*, 1980).

It is not, however, appropriate to substitute a straightforward quantitative concept of development for this complex qualitative formulation. In the same way that development is more than any old change across time it is also more than any old change in amount. With some behaviours – such as learning new words – it is an increase in amount that would be defined as development, and with other behaviours – such as aggressive outbursts – it would probably be a decrease. Moreover, such changes in amount would be contextually evaluated. Thus, efforts on my part to improve my vocabulary might initially be applauded as indicating personal or intellectual development. However, if I were to continue learning three new words a day for five years it is unlikely that this alone would be sufficient to merit the term 'development'. I would, perhaps, need to be using these words in a more elegant or creative manner in order to be seen as continuing to develop. In other words, a qualitative criterion would be invoked. Whether such a change would actually represent a cognitive reorganization which was also sequential, unidirectional, etc., is, of course, quite another question.

The construct of development centres on some notion of improvement. Changes in amount and in quality are evaluated against some implicit or explicit opinion as to what constitutes the 'good' or the 'ideal'. In other words, postulates concerning the nature of development are being made. We begin with a definition of development and then examine data to see whether they meet our criteria. The definition of development precedes rather than arises from the data. Thus, for example, whether or not it is viewed as development when young people challenge the received wisdom of their elders depends on what we mean by the term. Opinions on such matters can vary. Value judgements are involved.

How, then, should we proceed with the task of defining development? A good place to begin is by following Kaplan's (1983) advice to distinguish clearly between development as an ideal process and the realities of what actually happens during the course of a life. Development 'pertains to a rarely, if ever, attained ideal, not to the actual' (Kaplan, 1983, p. 188). With this in mind, empirical studies can then furnish data concerning the extent to which individuals do or do not develop and may provide information concerning factors that facilitate or impede development.

Secondly, development is better thought of as a process than as a state. Thus, we ask not whether a person has reached some ideal end state or *telos*, but how near that person is to it and whether he or she is moving in its direction. Furthermore, if we adopt a view of the person as a constantly changing organism in a constantly changing environment then even if such an ideal were reached it would not be a final achievement. The organism and, indeed, the environment, would inevitably change, thus rendering the achievement out of date and in need of modification. In this vein, Kaplan (1983) defines development as movement in the direction of perfection, although he acknowledges that what we mean by perfection is neither transparent nor easy to articulate. None the less, from, in particular, the area of humanistic psychology have emanated a number of expositions if not of perfection, then at least of what Jourard (1974, p. 28) calls 'man at his best'. They constitute ways of being which, to quote again from Jourard (1974, p. 1), 'surpass the average'. A far-from-complete list of such accounts would include the fully functioning person (Rogers, 1961), the self-actualizing person (Maslow, 1970), the healthy personality (Jourard, 1974), the mature personality (Allport, 1964), and the concepts of self-empowerment (Hopson and Scally, 1981) and positive mental health (Jahoda, 1958; Birren and Renner, 1980).

Two of these concepts are summarized below: Maslow's self-actualizing person and Allport's mature personality. They serve to demonstrate that such concepts are not easily articulated. In some instances (for example, Maslow, 1970; Jourard, 1974) whole books have been devoted to their exposition. Each of these concepts comprises a number of constituent parts rather than a single entity. Furthermore, these conceptualizations are not mutually exclusive, competing alternatives. There are many similarities between them. They draw upon each other for their articulation. Later authors cite earlier ones as sources. Some of the terminology is identical. They each offer different ways of expressing basically similar sentiments.

Maslow's (1968, 1970) self-actualizing person

Maslow, in effect, conceived the pinnacle of development as self-actualization – that is, 'the full use and exploitation of talents, capacities, potentialities, etc.' (Maslow, 1970, p. 150). His theory is a theory of motivation. We are motivated to satisfy a range of hierarchically organized basic needs, with the need for self-actualization existing at the head or apex of this hierarchy. The demands of lower-order needs must be at least partially met before we are motivated to address ourselves to those higher up the hierarchy.

Typically a person's hierarchy of needs is organized as shown in figure 2.1. The most basic needs are, first, those for physiological well-being and, secondly, those for safety. Their fulfilment requires adequate nourishment, rest and shelter, and a sense of security and stability. If any of these needs is unmet, the individual will usually be dominated by them.

When both physiological and safety needs are reasonably well

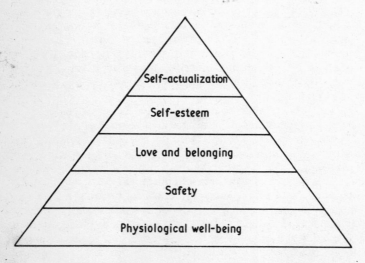

Figure 2.1   Maslow's hierarchy of needs

satisfied, the individual's needs for belongingness and love become apparent. These needs represent a hunger for affectionate relationships, for contact with others and for a place in our society. They include both the need to give and the need to receive love. The fourth level in Maslow's hierarchy comprises self-esteem needs: the need, first, for a stable, firmly based, usually high evaluation of oneself (that is, self-respect) and, secondly, for the esteem of others. 'Satisfaction of the self-esteem need leads to feelings of self-confidence, worth, strength, capability, and adequacy, of being useful and necessary in the world. But thwarting of these needs produces feelings of inferiority, of weakness, and of helplessness' (Maslow, 1970, p. 45).

Finally, if physiological, safety, love and esteem needs are all satisfied, self-actualization needs can manifest themselves. Whilst the route to their satisfaction varies greatly across individuals, Maslow was able to identify traits that tended to characterize self-actualizing people. From the study of people who seemed to be operating successfully at this level he identified fifteen characteristic traits:

1 *Accurate perception of reality.* Self-actualizing (S-A) people perceive people and events accurately. Being good judges of character, they are less influenced by 'their own wishes, hopes, fears, anxieties, their own theories and beliefs, or those of their culture group' (Maslow, 1970, p. 154).

2 *Acceptance of self and others.* S-A people recognize and accept the frailties of human nature. They are able to accept themselves and their shortcomings and, whilst not self-satisfied, are therefore free of unnecessary guilt, shame and anxiety. They are concerned about discrepancies between what is and what might be, but do not fret over that which cannot be changed.

3 *Spontaneity.* Maslow describes S-A people as relatively spontaneous in their behaviour and very spontaneous in their inner life, thoughts and impulses. Their inner system of beliefs is based on fundamentally held principles rather than conventional wisdom. However, they have no wish to hurt others unnecessarily, or to contest every triviality with which they disagree. Thus they will comply with conventional rituals and ways of behaving they believe to be unimportant, but persistently debate those issues they see as being of vital concern.

4 *Problem-centring.* In contrast with the introspection and self-

centredness of insecure people, S-A people focus on problems outside themselves. Moreover, these problems are seen in the widest possible frame of reference. Customarily problem-centredness is manifested in a life's mission – a task or endeavour which the individual feels a duty and responsibility to fulfil.

5 *Detachment.* S-A people are emotionally self-sufficient. They tolerate and may positively value solitude and privacy to a greater degree than the average person. Frequently able 'to remain above the battle, to remain unruffled, undisturbed by that which produces turmoil in others' (Maslow, 1970, p. 160), they may appear aloof and reserved. Applying this detachment to their own lives, S-A people will tend to accept misfortunes with greater calmness and serenity than is usual. Maslow describes them as able to retain their dignity in undignified surroundings and situations.

6 *Autonomy.* A general characteristic of S-A people is their relative independence of their physical and social environment. They can remain true to themselves in the face of pressure to do otherwise. They are not dependent on culture or on other people for their main satisfactions in life. Rather, they depend for their development and continued growth on their own potentialities and latent resources. They may value the good opinion and affection of others, but they are not dependent on it.

7 *Continued freshness of appreciation.* As a result of their close and uncluttered relationship with reality, Maslow (1970) suggests, S-A people can continue to gain 'ecstasy, inspiration and strength from the basic experience of life' (p. 163). A sight, a sound, a fleeting moment of beauty can all continue to thrill in the same way as when first experienced. Such sensations are not taken for granted and can therefore be repeatedly re-experienced. S-A people do not take their blessings for granted, nor do they undervalue them. Their subjective experiences are rich and exciting, not stale and boring.

8 *Mystic or peak experiences.* A frequently encountered characteristic of S-A people is the intensification of emotions such that they become strong, chaotic and widespread enough to be described as mystic or peak experiences. During such experiences the sense of self is temporarily transcended as it becomes lost amid feelings of ecstasy, wonder and awe. The sense of self emerges strengthened from such experiences and to some extent changed.

9 *Gemeinschaftsgefühl.* Maslow uses this German word to

describe the empathy and identification S-A people feel with the human race. It is an unconditional, positive regard which persists despite recognition of the shortcomings of fellow human beings, and despite the fact that on occasions these shortcomings may enrage, exasperate or sadden.

10 *Characteristic interpersonal relations.* S-A people are likely to have close relationships with only a few other people and these people themselves are likely to be more self-actualizing than the average. Such relationships are likely to be deeper and more profound than those experienced by non-S-A people. With others S-A people are likely to be tolerant, pleasant but somewhat distant, reserving harsh treatment for those they deem hypocritical, pretentious or pompous.

11 *Democratic character structure.* S-A people seem less aware of and less influenced by a person's social, educational and racial background than non-S-A people. Rather, others are evaluated on the basis of 'character, capacity and talent' (Maslow, 1970, p. 168). However, whilst according to any individual what Maslow describes as a certain minimum quantum of respect, S-A people also possess a strong sense of right and wrong. They are more likely than the average person to take a stand against that and those they believe to be evil or wrong. In this sense they are 'less ambivalent, confused, or weak-willed about their own anger' (Maslow, 1970, p. 168) than are non-S-A people.

12 *Definite moral standards.* Maslow's S-A people live by firmly held, although sometimes unconventional, notions of right and wrong. Believing that 'means' are as important as 'ends' they choose ways of behaving on the basis of ethical or moral standards rather than expediency.

13 *Philosophical sense of humour.* S-A people do not make or find funny humour which is hurtful, distasteful or based on another's inferiority. Rather, their humour is philosophical. It will often have an educative purpose beyond providing transient amusement and will focus on the foolishness and pretensions of human nature generally. More likely to produce a wry smile than a hearty laugh, S-A people may be viewed by others as somewhat serious and sober.

14 *Creativeness.* Maslow found that S-A people were, without exception, creative – not necessarily in the sense of being a genius, but rather in the sense that they had either regained or never lost

'the naive and universal creativeness of unspoiled children' (Maslow, 1970, p. 170). This is a creativeness which Maslow sees as the consequence of the characteristics listed above: having a greater freshness, penetration and efficiency of perception, and being more spontaneous and natural than is average.

15 *Cultural transcendence.* Whilst complying with many of the superficial conventions of their culture S-A people resist enculturation. Their yielding to convention is casual and perfunctory and is not based on profound identification with a particular culture. They are more likely to show a calm concern with long-term cultural improvement than an active impatience or moment-to-moment discontent.

Maslow presents self-actualization as, in principle, an achievable state although, in reality, probably attained by less than 1 per cent of the population (Maslow, 1968). He distinguishes between deficiency motivation and growth motivation, meaning that we might be motivated either to restore deficits or to strive towards the kinds of experience that characterize the S-A person. Whilst acknowledging that not all lower-order needs are necessarily deficiency-motivated, Maslow (1968, 1970) has elaborated most fully the distinction between deficiency-motivated love (D-love) and growth- or 'being'-motivated love (B-love). Rowan (1976), however, has extended this analysis to all levels in Maslow's need hierarchy, offering examples of both deficiency-motivated behaviour and growth- or, to use Rowan's term, abundance-motivated behaviour.

Deficiency-motivated behaviour can be seen as being designed to re-establish equilibrium – bringing the person 'up to par' as it were. Growth-motivated behaviour, by contrast, takes the person above the norm of experience – putting him or her 'on top of the world' could be a colloquial way of expressing it. Frequently the experiences derived from growth-motivated behaviour are ends in themselves. The experience rather than any tangible outcome is what matters. Rowan's extension of growth-motivated behaviour to all levels in the need hierarchy renders self-actualization a dynamic process of development potentially within the experience of the majority, more than an ultimate and frequently distant goal.

Maslow's definition of self-actualization as the pinnacle of development also serves to demonstrate the concept of development as a theoretical postulate rather than an empirical construct. Having made the value judgement that self-actualization is the highest stage and the goal of development our task then becomes the plotting of progress towards that end point. Other cultures and other historical epochs may well challenge such an individually based definition of optimum human functioning (Sampson, 1977). A different end point might be achievable through a very different route. Also, Maslow does not claim that the hierarchical sequence of basic needs is either inevitable or universal. Though figure 2.1 indicates the most usual ordering of basic needs, he found a number of exceptions. The most common deviation was for self-esteem to be more important than love. Maslow found this reversal of the hierarchy generally to be based on the assumption that it is those who are self-confident and powerful (that is, high in self-esteem) who are most likely to be loved. Thus, such people are not in fact valuing self-esteem *per se*. Rather, 'they seek self-assertion for the sake of love rather than for self-esteem itself' (Maslow, 1970, p. 52).

Maslow observed several other systematic deviations from the typical need hierarchy. In some highly creative people the need to create may override all other needs. People who have suffered great deprivation may subsequently be satisfied if only their most basic needs are met. Maslow sees the psychopathic personality as one in which love needs have been permanently lost. Finally he cites the ability of some people to stand up for their ideals and beliefs in the face of marked deprivation with regard to lower-order needs. He sees this as grounded in an early experience of high-need gratification – 'people who have been made secure and strong in the earliest years, tend to remain secure and strong thereafter in the face of whatever threatens' (Maslow, 1970, p. 53).

Allport's (1964) mature personality

Maslow's fifteen characteristics of the S-A person comprise a somewhat unwieldy list. Based on the work of, amongst others, Jahoda (1950), Erikson (1959) and Maslow (1970), Allport (1964) offers a description of what he terms the mature personality. He delineates six dimensions or criteria of maturity – a number selected somewhat arbitrarily to give an account which is neither too fine nor too coarse. The person of mature personality will have a widely extended sense of self; be able to relate warmly to others in both intimate and non-intimate contexts; possess a fundamental emotional security and self-acceptance; perceive, think and act with zest in accordance with outer reality; be capable of self-objectification – of insight and humour; and live in harmony with a unifying philosophy of life.

1 *Extension of the sense of self.* Allport's first criterion of maturity requires the person to participate fully in some significant realm of human activity such as work, study, family, hobby, politics or religion. The involvement must be meaningful as well as active. It entails extending a part of oneself into a sphere of involvement and incorporating that activity into the self. It entails 'ego-involvement' as well as 'task involvement'. It is analogous to the life mission Maslow sees as emanating from the problem-centredness of S-A people.

2 *Warm relating of self to others.* Allport identifies two quite different types of warmth that characterize the mature person: intimacy and compassion. The capacity for intimacy comes with self-extension. Mature personalities are able to share themselves with others and to love without 'placing iron bonds of obligation' (Allport, 1964, p. 286) on the loved one, be it spouse, child, lover or friend. Through compassion or fellow feeling this respect and appreciation is directed to humankind in general. It implies a recognition and unpatronizing acceptance of the imperfections of others and develops through an extension of the recognition of one's own deficiencies. Within the criterion compassion Allport also incorporates tolerance and Maslow's notion of the democratic character structure.

3 *Emotional security.* A fundamental prerequisite for emotional security, Allport's third criterion of maturity, is self-acceptance; that is, the recognition and tolerance of both one's strengths and one's weaknesses. Self-acceptance involves applying compassionate (but not self-satisfied) judgements to oneself whilst at the same time striving to fulfil one's potential. The emotionally secure person is emotionally poised – acknowledging but not being overwhelmed by emotional experiences. He or she also possesses frustration tolerance – the ability to accept and handle frustration. Emotional security is also manifested in a willingness to take calculated risks – possibly with caution, but without panic. It also

allows one to express personal convictions and feelings without fear but with consideration for the feelings and convictions of others. As Allport (1964) says: 'Such a sense of proportion is not an isolated attribute in personality. It comes about because one possesses integrative values that control and gate the flow of emotional impulse' (p. 288).

4 *Realistic perception, skills and assignments.* The mature person is in touch with reality, not distorting it to fit his or her particular needs or fantasies. As well as accurately perceiving reality the mature person possesses appropriate skills for solving real (that is, objective) problems. Furthermore, mature personalities are able to immerse themselves in tasks, becoming problem-centred and 'losing' themselves in their work. This can also be seen as a version of self-extension.

5 *Self-objectification.* The realistic perception of mature people extends to themselves; that is, they possess self-insight or self-objectification. They have the ability to see themselves (nearly) as they are – both strengths and imperfections. Allport (1964) sees a true sense of humour and, in particular, the ability to laugh at oneself as a key concomitant of self-insight: 'The man who has the most complete sense of proportion concerning his own qualities and cherished values is able to perceive their incongruities and absurdities in certain settings' (p. 293). The opposite of self-objectification is affectation. Whilst most of us will try to present ourselves in the best light the mature person is not deluded by such self-aggrandizement: 'Insight and humor keep such egotism in check' (p. 294).

6 *Unifying philosophy of life.* Allport's final criterion of maturity is the development of a unifying philosophy of life, 'a clear comprehension of life's purpose in terms of an intelligible theory' (p. 294). Such a philosophy gives direction to life and embodies a coherent values stance. It identifies for the individual 'what things are sacred and of ultimate value' (p. 301). It constitutes an integrated sense of conscience or moral obligation.

In the commentary on his dimensions of maturity Allport (1964) acknowledges many of the general points made earlier in this section. He recognizes that 'the distinctive richness and congruence of a fully mature personality are not easy to describe' (p. 276). He also believes it to be 'questionable whether we should ever expect to find in the flesh a paragon of maturity' (pp. 276–7).

None the less, as he also says, some people do 'lead lives far closer to this ideal than do others' (p. 283).

The form of human development

The self-actualizing and mature personalities are both descriptions of an end product, albeit a dynamic rather than a static one. They are not in themselves statements about how such a condition is reached. They are not, in other words, statements about the shape and form of the life course of a developing person. The preference of Kaplan (1983) and others (for example, Hopson and Scally, 1981) for considering development as a process rather than an end state suggests that such issues should be considered. Indeed, they have not been ignored. Debates concerning the form of development have centred on the processes of change, stability and, to a lesser extent, chance. Gergen (1977) distinguishes different orientations to development according to which of these processes is given priority. In so doing he provides a useful framework, employed in the following section, with which to discuss alternative perspectives on the form of human development.

The ordered-change orientation to development

Probably the dominant orientation within recent developmental psychology, the ordered-change template assumes development to be constituted by 'patterned or orderly change across time' (Gergen, 1977, p. 144). The regularity is frequently manifested in the form of stages – like the concept of development, a much discussed issue.

It has frequently been pointed out that, again like the concept of development, 'stage' can mean a number of different things in developmental psychology (Bijou, 1968; Brainerd, 1978; Kohlberg, 1973b; Wohlwill, 1973). Thus Kohlberg (1973b) distinguishes three uses of the term – as a biological-maturational, a sociocultural and a cognitive-structural concept. The biological conception of stage reflects a growth-maintenance–decrement model of development. Growth or maturation is seen as being complete by early adulthood, from whence the processes of stabilization and/or decline take over. A lifeline shaped like an inverted, splayed-out 'U' would reflect this model of development. It is also implicit in arclike metaphors of the life span. The gradient of the slopes could indicate the rate of development and decline, with the length of the upper plateau indicating the extent of the stabilization phase.

Such a conception of development is controversial only if it is presented as the whole picture. A biological concept of stage ignores the sociocultural context in which the individual lives and the impact of this context on both the life course and our definition of development. Thus we also have a sociocultural conception of stage which recognizes that 'a culture (responding in part to maturational events) outlines a rough sequence of roles or tasks from birth to death, and adaptation to this task sequence leads to age-typical personality change' (Kohlberg, 1973b, p. 498). Kohlberg further distinguishes between two sociocultural conceptions of stage – the age-linked social-role and the developmental-task conceptions. The first of these – the age-linked social-role definition of stage – focuses on the part biological, and part socially constructed roles the individual is called upon to fulfil. Within family development a typical series of stages would be: couple with no children; couple with young children; couple with older children; the 'empty nest'; grandparenthood; widowhood. Clearly biological factors place some very broad limits on the timing of such stages but both the more precise timing and the way in which the roles are fulfilled are largely matters of social convention.

The developmental-task notion of stage focuses on those things a person needs to learn at a particular point in the life cycle in order to be judged by others and by himself or herself as being reasonably happy and successful. Havighurst (1972), one of those who has been most active in elaborating the concept and defining the tasks associated with different life stages, describes the developmental tasks of life as 'those things that constitute healthy and satisfactory growth in our society' (p. 2). Midway between 'an individual need and a societal demand' (p. 2), the developmental-task concept 'assumes an active learner interacting with an active social environment' (p. 2). Havighurst (1972) distinguishes a third source of developmental tasks in addition to those arising from physical maturation and from the cultural pressures of a society, namely 'the desires, aspirations, and values of the emerging personality' (p. 6). More often than not developmental tasks arise 'from combinations of these factors acting together' (Havighurst, 1972, p. 6).

The social-role conception of stage leaves unanswered the question of whether or which stage sequences constitute development. It describes the typical. By contrast, the developmental-task conception of stage leads to descriptions of what one needs (or ought) to do. Thus Havighurst operates on an (implicit) definition of development as changes which result in the individual becoming or remaining 'reasonably happy and successful'. He recognizes that developmental tasks are culture-bound, thus pointing to their value-laden basis.

Like the biological conception of stage the concept of socioculturally defined sequences of roles and tasks is readily accepted. Views may vary, however, regarding the universality and immutability of such stages and also regarding the relative importance of biological, social and individual factors.

Finally there is the cognitive-structural conception of stage. Only qualitative changes in competence, assumed to result from changes in underlying cognitive structure, are considered to reflect stages. Quantitative changes are assumed to be 'changes in performance rather than changes in structural competence' (Kohlberg, 1973b, p. 498). Thus, although there are decrements in the speed and efficiency of immediate memory and information processing with age, such quantitative changes are not taken to imply a regression in the logical structure of the individual's reasoning process. Cognitive-structural stages refer to changes in structure which result in changes in competence and are reflected in qualitatively new patterns of response. Such responses differ from their predecessors in form or organization, not merely in their content.

Moreover, cognitive-structural stages do not occur randomly. They form an invariant sequence which may be speeded up, slowed down or stopped by cultural factors, but not changed. In addition, such stages are hierarchical. Later (or higher) stages integrate earlier (or lower) stages into their structure. In other words, later stages are more advanced, not merely different. Such stages could be represented on a lifeline as a series of rising steps like a staircase. The uprights between the steps (that is, between the stages) would be sloping rather than vertical since the transition between stages is gradual rather than sudden. Distinct stages can, however, be identified. They represent structured wholes – that is, they balance and unify interrelated behaviours, concepts or skills. They can, therefore, be depicted on the lifeline as horizontal plateaux.

Unlike the biological and sociocultural concepts of stage, the cognitive-structural (or cognitive-developmental) concept of stage has been highly controversial. Bijou (1968) criticized the stage concept for being, in effect, an intellectual straightjacket which stunts divergent theorizing and research. Instead of investigating all possible factors which may affect behaviour, energy is directed at establishing 'whether certain behaviors do, in fact, occur at a particular stage as claimed and, if so, whether their onset can be modified' (Bijou, 1968, p. 422). More recently Brainerd (1978) questioned the explanatory power of cognitive-structural stages on the grounds that it is circular, viz: 'children do X because they are in stage two. We know they are in stage two because they do X.'

Both Bijou (1968) and Brainerd (1978) call for stage criteria based on what the former terms 'empirically defined biological, physical and social interactions' (Bijou, 1968, p. 423). This would make it similar to the social-role concept of stage. However, as Wetherick (1978), one of the commentators on Brainerd's paper, points out, Brainerd's and others' empiricist conception of science can be, and has been, challenged. Furthermore, as has already been argued, data alone cannot give us a definition of development. Bijou's criticism of the narrow perspective of developmental psychology does, none the less, have some validity. However, the answer need not merely be to become more empirical. This would do no more than substitute one unduly narrow perspective for another. It may be more fruitful to view the cognitive-structural definition of stage as only one way of conceptualizing development – useful but limited.

The stability orientation to development

A second major approach in developmental psychology has focused on stability rather than on change. It has shunned the transitory and attempted to identify the consistent. I suspect that most of us as children were asked what we wanted to be when we grew up. Probably some readers of this book are still being asked and do not feel they know the answer. The assumption that this is an answerable question denotes a stability orientation to development.

Developmental psychologists have traditionally adopted an ordered-change orientation to childhood and a stability orientation to adulthood. Freud is the classic example of this. His main stages of psychosexual development occur within the first six years and are critical determinants of adult personality. Likewise Piaget restricts his four stages of cognitive development to childhood and adolescence, although it has been proposed (Arlin, 1975, 1977) that there is a fifth stage of cognitive development achieved in adulthood.

Stability does not imply the total absence of change, however. In the same way as the ordered-change orientation to development includes different concepts of stage and different descriptions of development, so too does the stability orientation include different kinds of stability (see, for example, Kagan, 1980; Mortimer *et al.*, 1982; Wohlwill, 1980). Thus, we can distinguish between structural invariance, level invariance, process stability, ipsative stability and normative stability.

Structural invariance refers to 'continuity in the nature of the phenomenon under investigation' (Mortimer *et al.*, 1982, p. 266). It concerns the extent to which the construct of interest continues to comprise the same dimensions. It is a qualitative concept, referring to nature rather than amount. Structural invariance is demonstrated empirically by similarity over time in the factor structure of a construct such as intelligence or personality.

In contrast to structural invariance, *level invariance* is a quantitative concept, referring to 'persistence in the magnitude or quantity of a phenomenon over time' (Mortimer *et al.*, 1982, p. 266). Level invariance is premised upon structural invariance in that it would be nonsensical to talk about constancy in the amount of a phenomenon whose nature had changed. Thus, level invariance with regard to personality implies not only similarity of factor structure from time 1 to time 2, but also similarity in the level of each component of personality within the individual. Level invariance is often what is meant when we talk of constancy or lack of change since this is what it does represent at the individual level. However, it may be accompanied by, for example, a change in the individual's relative position with regard to others and/or with regard to the typical progression of that attribute. These changes would represent lack of normative and process stability, respectively.

Process stability, or regularity of form of change (Wohlwill, 1980), refers to the extent to which the course of development of a particular attribute is consistent across individuals and the extent to which a particular individual conforms to that typical pattern. Thus, the development of mobility in infants demonstrates high process stability, passing through the stages of sitting, crawling, standing and walking. Occasionally individuals may deviate from such a pattern by, for example, substituting 'bottom shuffling' for the more usual crawling stage. Much of the ordered-change orientation to development is concerned with identifying the course of processes which are consistent across individuals.

Ipsative stability refers to the 'persistence of a hierarchical relation between complementary dispositions within an individual' (Kagan, 1980, p. 32). It refers to the degree of consistency in the relative strength of an individual's attributes. It would be shown, for example, in the similarity of an individual's pattern of occupational interests over time.

Whilst ipsative stability makes within-individual comparisons, *normative stability* compares across individuals. It refers to constancy of relative position, to the 'preservation of a set of individual ranks on a quality within a constant cohort' (Kagan, 1980, p. 32). Thus, children who are small relative to their peers at the age of 11 are likely to remain so at 18 even though all will have grown to some extent.

To reiterate, stability does not necessarily imply lack of change. For example, structural invariance allows for changes in level. Level invariance may be accompanied by ipsative and/or normative instability. With regard to process stability, attributes may change, but in a specified way. With ipsative and normative stability the absolute amount of an attribute may change but not its relative position with regard to, respectively, other attributes of the individual and the same attribute in other members of a consistent comparison group.

In the area of personality a distinction can be made between traits and states, with proponents of a stability orientation to development arguing that whilst individuals' behaviour and more

transient characteristics (that is, states) may change, the underlying personality structure or traits remain the same. There have
been numerous cross-sectional investigations of the relation
between aspects of personality and age using objective and,
frequently, standardized personality inventories, which have produced notably inconsistent results (Neugarten, 1977). In any case,
such studies cannot, on their own, answer questions about the
consistency of personality – they are concerned with the identification of age differences which may or may not reflect age
changes. Longitudinal and follow-up studies of personality traits
generally support notions of consistency (for example, Block and
Haan, 1971; Haan and Day, 1974; Terman and Oden, 1959;
Woodruff and Birren, 1972), but some (such as Neugarten and
associates, 1964) are suggestive of change. Again, though, these
studies can be criticized on methodological grounds, as summarized in chapter 1 (Nesselroade and Baltes, 1974). They may also
employ measuring instruments which are too crude and imprecise
to pick up age changes and/or whose validity for adults has not
been established (Mischel, 1969; Neugarten, 1977).

Thus, whilst debate continues both as to the validity of a trait
approach to personality development (see, for example, Schaie
and Parnham, 1976) and as to the stability of such traits across
time, it is generally agreed that situationally determined personality states may show substantial variations according to the
individual's environmental circumstances. These conclusions are
supported by the findings that whilst the changes of adulthood
may be substantial they tend to be less universal and less systematic than those of childhood. This, in turn, brings us to Gergen's
(1977) third perspective on development, and one which focuses
on random or chance influences on the life course.

The aleatory-change orientation to development

Like the first orientation to development discussed by Gergen
(1977), the aleatory-change approach focuses explicitly on
change. However, it rests on the assumption that, far from being
orderly and predictable, 'there is little about human development
that is "preprogrammed"' (p. 148) – 'We enter the world with a
biological system that establishes the limit or range of our activities
but not the precise character of the activities themselves' (p. 148).

It is proposed that the 'precise character' of our life course is highly dependent on a variety of environmental factors – economic, geographic, social, class, political, and so on.

So far this argument concerning the aleatory change perspective is congruent with the sociocultural concept of stage – an ordered-change orientation to development. The aleatory orientation does not however focus on the regularity of role or behaviour sequences emerging from person–environment interactions. Rather it emphasizes how specific environmental influences vary across time and culture. The life courses of individuals are, therefore, neither universal nor invariant. Your life course – your lifeline – will differ from that of your parents and grandparents simply by virtue of your having lived through different historical eras. For each of you the nature and timing of the transition from education to employment will be different as a result of changes in the education system, with its gradual raising of the school-leaving age, and in the occupational structure of society. Other outcomes of a society's progression, such as improved medical care or the decreasing importance of the extended family, will also exert their influence. Thus, any individual life course must be located within a particular historical era.

The very categories we use to divide up the life course have changed across time. Karp and Yoels (1982) document how, associated with such factors as industrialization, increased longevity and extended education, the meaning, number and age span of discernible life stages have varied. It would seem that in the Middle Ages childhood as a distinct age grouping did not exist (Aries, 1962). Those whom we now call children were viewed simply as small-scale adults. It was only when work became divorced from the home and the young spent an ever increasing time at school that childhood (with its tasks of play and education) became a phase distinct from adulthood (with its overriding task of work). At the other end of the life span, people may now spend twenty or so years retired from work. With medical advances and generally improved living conditions, resulting in more people living to a healthy old age, it may be that more stages (sequences) will be identified and elaborated for the later years of life. We are so familiar with stages such as childhood, adolescence and middle age that it is easy to assume that they have always been meaningful divisions of the life span. The aleatory-change orientation to development reminds us that these categories and/or their meanings are not immutable.

In addition to differences associated with a society's 'advancement' or 'progression', the lives of different generations will be influenced by the experiencing of different significant social and political events such as wars and economic depressions. These, too, contribute to the shape and form of a particular life. However, the lives of different generations do overlap, so that you, your parents and/or your children may all experience a particular event. The event's impact will, however, vary depending on the point in the individual's life span at which it occurs. Thus, a war is experienced very differently by young children, by men of fighting age and by the old, who may have recollections of previous hostilities. Likewise, unemployment and economic recession mean one thing to the young person who has not yet begun to develop an occupational identity, and something different, although there may also be similarities, for the worker with twenty or so years' experience of a particular trade or profession.

Finally, we have random influences rather than those resulting from the time and social circumstances in which, by chance, the individual lives. Thus, we might move to a new area of the country or be involved in a car accident at virtually any age. Taken across many generations these two examples are influenced by the historical era in which we live. The population is generally more geographically mobile than it was – gone, at least in our society, are the days when people moved no more than a few miles from their birth place throughout the whole of their lives. Likewise, involvement in car accidents clearly could not predate the invention of the internal-combustion engine. For contemporary generations, however, such events are not systematically associated with any particular age.

Thus, life-span developmental psychology cannot hope to produce a definitive and everlasting picture of the life course. It is concerned with a changing individual in a changing society. It must accept that any account can represent only a temporary truth. Its most enduring products are likely to be concepts, models and theories which promote explication of the constancies and the changes, the universals and the particulars, of human development.

Types of life-course influences

Baltes *et al.* (1980) offer an explanation of development capable of accounting for both ordered and aleatory change. They distinguish between normative age-graded, normative history-graded and non-normative influences on the life course. *Normative age-graded influences* are biological and environmental determinants of development, such as many aspects of physical development and of a society's age-graded socialization events, which have (in terms of onset and duration) a fairly strong relationship with chronological age. Thus, we all tend to go to school or reach our peak of physical strength at about the same age. In terms of the stability orientation to development, such phenomena can be said to show a high degree of process stability.

Normative history-graded influences on life-span development are biological and environmental determinants which have a strong relationship with historical time rather than chronological age. They are shared by most members of a society at a particular point in time but not, or not in the same way, by members of preceding or subsequent generations. They give rise to the dubbing of eras as the 'swinging sixties' or the 'roaring twenties'; the 'industrial' or the 'technological' age. History-graded influences make the past an uncertain and unreliable guide to the future, especially in times of rapid social change.

Finally, *non-normative influences* or systems of change are biological and environmental influences that do not, for most individuals, occur in any normative age-graded or history-graded manner. They are thus particularly compatible with the aleatory orientation to development. It is possible, however, that over time non-normative events may become normative. The incidence of married women in employment is a case in point. At one time most women gave up their job on marriage. Now this is highly unusual. Datan (1983) details such progressions: 'the exceptional becomes the scarce, the scarce becomes the infrequent, the infrequent becomes the acceptable, and finally the acceptable becomes the norm' (p. 41). Similarly, socially grounded normative events may, over time, become non-normative. Datan suggests that such transformations involve a qualitative as well as a quantitative change – the event (in the non-normative to normative progression) becomes acceptable, not merely usual. So, for example, when unemployment in a community is 'exceptional' or 'scarce' those individuals without work may feel isolated and be condemned. As unemployment increases a point is reached where the belief that everyone could find a job if they tried hard enough is no longer tenable. It becomes patently obvious that there is not enough work to go round. When this occurs a quantitative change has triggered a qualitative change. Both the way unemployment is evaluated and its probability of occurrence have been altered.

The three systems of influence – normative age-graded, normative history-graded and non-normative – act and interact to produce, when mediated through the individual, life-span development. Baltes (1979; Baltes *et al.*, 1980) speculates as to the possibility of these three classes of influence exhibiting distinct life-course profiles, as shown in figure 2.2.

It is suggested that normative age-graded influences might predominate during childhood and show a second, but lesser, peak in old age. In childhood there are significant age-graded

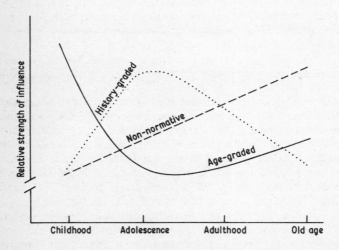

Figure 2.2 Prototypical profiles of relative impact of influences on development across the life course (Baltes *et al.*, 1980)

influences stemming from both biological maturation and educational/socialization events. The suggestion of another peak in advanced old age is far more tentative, but is suggested by, for example, evidence of a 'terminal drop' in intelligence (Riegel and Riegel, 1972) shortly before death.

Currently there is scant empirical evidence for a prototypical life course profile of normative history-graded influences. Baltes *et al.* suggest, however, that such influences might peak during the adolescence/early-adult period on the grounds that the nature of the transition to adulthood is one particularly susceptible to sociocultural factors.

With regard to the life-course profile for non-normative events the evidence is even more scarce. None the less, Baltes *et al.* speculate that their relative impact might increase steadily throughout the life course. They deduce this in part from the greater heterogeneity in the life courses of adults in comparison with children, which, in turn, might result from the overall weakening of age-graded and history-graded influences. Furthermore, they suggest that significant life events may have a relatively greater impact on the life course of adults than on that of children. Such profiles of influence as shown in figure 2.2 suggest it is as appropriate for researchers of child development to look for age-graded patterns of development as it is for researchers of adult development to examine the impact of major life events.

The importance of different orientations to development

The variety of orientations to development detailed above does more than cause confusion among psychology students and debate among academics. It impinges on the everyday life of each of us. Thus, we hold contradictory, generally unarticulated and possibly misinformed assumptions about the life course. For example, 'stability' is frequently taken to mean 'static' although, as was shown earlier, all forms of stability (as defined by Kagan, 1980; Mortimer *et al.*, 1982; and Wohlwill, 1980) do allow for some change. If we none the less apply this 'stability = static' orientation to adulthood, then we are unprepared for post-adolescent disruptions and change. The assumption of stability as permanence can be so ingrained and taken for granted that when we experience upheavals during adulthood it is ourselves rather than the assumption that is blamed. We do not conclude that the stability assumption is wrong when we need to change careers in mid-life. Rather, we express anger at the injustice of the continual need to change and/or decide that there is something amiss with ourselves.

Coexisting with this notion of adult fixity are equally implicit and unquestioned assumptions concerning the age-appropriateness of various behaviours (Hopson and Scally, 1980a). That is, we adopt a change as well as a static–stability orientation. Suppose a couple fall in love and want to get married. How would you feel about this if they were 16? How would you feel if they were 26, or 36? What if they were 76 – how would you feel then? The chances are that the couple who were 26 would be perceived as most 'normal'. The 16-year-olds would be considered too young and immature. There might be relief and pleasure that the 36-year-olds had (at last) found someone to settle down with – pleasure perhaps tinged with concern lest it was the wish no longer to be single rather than their true compatibility that was the spur. As for the 76-year-olds, if both were single or widowed it might be viewed as rather sweet and charming. If divorce and remarriage were involved, with the couple making no secret of their sexual interest in each other, then the whole episode might be viewed with distaste. In short, our evaluation of an event may be significantly influenced by the ages of the parties involved. On the one hand we see adulthood as a period of changelessness, but on the other hand we see as different the roles, tasks and behaviours associated with, let us say, the 30s and the 60s.

A society's views concerning age-appropriate behaviour comprise its age-grade system (Neugarten and Datan, 1973). Aspects of this system may be institutionalized – as when upper and/or lower age limits are set for such activities as school attendance, voting eligibility and retirement. Most aspects of a society's age-grade system will however be consensual rather than formal – as the example concerning age of marriage shows (although there is, of course, a legal minimum age for marriage).

In either case, a society's age grade system is a reflection of its social and cultural values. Furthermore, it is a normative system, by which is meant that most people feel some degree of pressure to conform to its dictate and do, indeed, generally conform. It constitutes 'a prescriptive timetable for the ordering of life events'

(Neugarten, 1977, p. 45). We operate in relation to a 'social clock' (Schlossberg *et al.*, 1978) which enables us to state whether we were 'early', 'late' or 'on time' for any number of significant life events – viz. 'I was late taking my A-levels because of glandular fever when I was sixteen' or 'I had my children early so that I could delay starting my career until after they were at school.'

The pattern of timing of life events significantly influences our self-esteem and self-concept. Whilst some age deviations are applauded (for example, passing A-levels at 16 or completing the London Marathon at 60), generally speaking to be 'off time' is to invite criticism and social sanction. Deviations from age norms by ourselves as well as by others are generally evaluated negatively. Thus we may feel ourselves to be failures if we have not found a steady job by the age of 25, become a parent by our mid-30s, obtained two promotions by the age of 40, or whatever.

Age bias

Age is a ubiquitous concept in developmental psychology. It is used either as the main or as a subsidiary criterion in anchoring virtually all accounts of change over the life course – including those summarized in the next three chapters. Such categorization of people and processes according to age can serve some useful functions – it facilitates the organization of knowledge, individuals and society, and provides a framework in relation to which we can order much of our daily lives. None the less, because of its centrality, its limitations or dangers – which revolve around its obscuring of individual differences – are worth reiterating and elaborating. Age itself is not a cause of change or an explanation of behaviour. It is a marker of stages in a sequence – a shorthand term for the underlying processes of concern. Age norms are inevitably averages, with many, if not most, individuals deviating from them to some degree. Furthermore, age norms describe the typical, not necessarily the ideal.

A significant role for life-span developmental psychology lies in the identification and control of unwarranted age bias – that is, erroneous assumptions made about people purely on the basis of their age (Schlossberg *et al.*, 1978). Age bias is premised on the belief that 'because we know a person's age, we can with fair accuracy predict his/her abilities, values, interests, and behaviour'

(Schlossberg *et al.*, 1978, p.4). Troll and Nowak (1976) distinguish three consequences of age bias: age restrictiveness, age distortion and negative attitudes. Age restrictiveness limits the ages at which certain behaviours, attitudes or values are deemed acceptable, and also defines those attributes which are considered appropriate. Age distortion refers to erroneous assumptions about the characteristics of a particular age group and, in particular, to disparity between attributions made, on the one hand, by those older or younger and, on the other hand, by those who are members of an age group itself. Negative attitudes refer to unfavourable generalizations about members of any one age group. Life-span developmental psychology, with the attention it gives to establishing age-associated changes and characteristics, runs the risk of promoting or perpetuating such prejudicial judgements. In order to avoid this we must be scrupulous in looking past the age variable to the individual beyond, and strive, in the words of one commentator, 'to develop a society that encourages people to stop acting their age and start being themselves' (Ponzo, 1978, pp. 143–4). We must remember that categorizing people may also stigmatize them, thereby making it harder for them to reach their full potential. 'Categorizations, as they are applied to people, must be constantly shaken up and questioned' (Schlossberg *et al.*, 1978, p. 10).

Such sentiments are appropriate ones with which to embark on chapters 3, 4 and 5 – a consideration of the nature of the life course.

3

The life course: physical and cognitive changes

The present chapter is concerned with aspects of physical and cognitive functioning and, in particular with whether, how and in what ways these processes change with age. Bee and Mitchell (1984) summarize the bodily changes associated with ageing in five words: smaller, slower, weaker, lesser, fewer. However, such objective attributes are not the whole story. Whilst there is evidence from young adulthood onwards that we are growing older it may be many years before this becomes important in our everyday life. We may not need to perform at peak levels outside the experimental laboratory. We have gained experience and can learn to compensate for many gradual declines associated with age. Corso (1975) concluded that education, experience and intelligence can all help to maintain normal sensory and perceptual functioning. Functional age (Birren, 1969) may indeed be more meaningful than chronological age. It refers to an individual's level of capacity relative to others of his or her age for functioning in a given human society.

As important as our objective performance level is our

subjective assessment of such achievements. It is quite possible at the psychological as well as the physical level to suffer a disability without being disabled by it. A two-way process operates. On the one hand physical and cognitive changes have an impact on our goals, values and priorities, and on the other hand our goals, values and priorities influence the evaluative meaning we attach to the age-related changes we experience. Such evaluations are associated with our sense of identity and with the goals, values and priorities of the society in which we are embedded. Thus, there is in the present chapter a recurring concern not only with objective changes in functioning and/or performance, but also with the individual's response to these changes and the meaning afforded them. Discussion is organized around the first two of McCandless and Evans' (1973) 'concentration points' or components of the person: physical-motor components and cognitive-intellectual components. Each of these is further divided into three sections: the former into changes in appearance, psychomotor performance and perception; and the latter into learning and memory, intelligence and cognitive development, and moral reasoning.

Physical-motor components of the person

Changes in appearance

Middle age frequently heralds a number of bodily changes which affect appearance (Kleemeier, 1959). There is generally an increase in body weight – something which is viewed unfavourably since it is an increase in size alone and is unlikely to increase the functional or social capacity of the individual. The weight gain is particularly rapid for middle-aged women. The increased weight is not spread evenly over the body but tends to be concentrated around the body's trunk rather than its extremities, giving rise to what is commonly known as the middle-age spread.

Height decreases slightly over the latter part of life (Kleemeier, 1959). A postural slump or stoop may, however, have a more marked effect on appearance as the 'cumulative effect of years of poor posture is now accentuated by the shrinkage of muscles, a decrease in the elasticity and an increase in the calcification of the ligaments, the shrinkage and hardening of tendons, and the flattening of the vertebral discs' (Stevens-Long, 1979, p. 328).

Skin becomes thinner, less elastic, wrinkled and dry (Rossman, 1977). Hair greys and is lost. Lungs, kidney, intestinal tract, muscles and the heart all begin to function less effectively and/or deteriorate (Rockstein, 1975). There is some decrease in bone mass (Garn, 1975).

For most people these changes are gradual rather than sudden. Of course there may be exceptions, heart attacks and strokes probably being the most obvious examples. However, in the main these changes do not constitute psychosocial transitions – they fail to meet the criterion (Parkes, 1971) of occurring over a relatively short period of time. They demand of us continual minor rather than once-and-for-all major adaptations. Very often it is our attitude and reaction to these changes that is of more importance than the changes themselves. The man who can start learning the piano, for example, when his cricketing days are over may fare better than his friend who continues to watch forlornly from the boundaries.

A song of earlier years offered the advice to 'stay young and beautiful if you want to be loved'. It captures the sentiments of a society which values youth and physical attractiveness. It suggests that it is only the young who are beautiful. The retention of youthful looks is a major industry directed especially at women. Indeed there is something of a double standard for men and women. Women learn that physical attractiveness is a valuable asset. The fact that they are losing this asset can markedly decrease self-esteem. The maturing man, however, may be viewed as distinguished. Increased occupational, community or political status, for example, may compensate for physical decline. The women's movement in particular has sought to encourage women to accept their bodies rather than attempting to adhere to some hypothetical ideal. Likewise, the chapter entitled 'Bodies are beautiful' in Kastenbaum's *Growing Old* (1979) emphasizes that old does not automatically mean ill and argues that age-related changes can alter beauty without spoiling it. He subtitles his book *Years of Fulfilment*.

Psychomotor performance

The most pervasive and marked change in motor performance that comes with age is in speed (Welford, 1959, 1977). We become slower – particularly in large movements made at maximum speed and in smaller movements involving dexterity and co-ordination for which the individual cannot prepare in advance. For the latter type of movement the slowing in performance is largely due to longer decision times and more cautious monitoring of performance. Demand for speed seems harder for older people than demand for moderate physical effort. Two factors will, however, tend to offset age changes in fine motor performance (Welford, 1980): accuracy will tend to increase as speed decreases, and there will be a greater benefit from practice and familiarity.

Perception

New perceptual concepts are acquired, elaborated and refined throughout infancy and childhood. These are not discussed here. For a concise and straightforward account of perception in children the reader is referred to Bower (1977). More detailed accounts are to be found in several sets of readings – for example, in Cohen and Salapatek (1975a, 1975b); Oates, (1979); Pick (1979). Over the life span many perceptual processes follow a growth–maintenance–decline curve. Age-related changes in the perceptual processes of vision, hearing, taste and smell, cutaneous sensitivity and touch, and pain are briefly summarized here. All are discussed at greater length in Birren and Schaie (1977). Corso (1971) offers a useful briefer review.

Vision. There are a number of age-related changes in vision (Fozard *et al.*, 1977). Visual acuity (the ability to discriminate the components of a visual display) declines progressively with age from about the 40s (Corso, 1971), especially where lighting is poor or there is low contrast between figure and ground. The effect, which can be mitigated to some extent by increased intensity of lighting, is that we need to be nearer objects in order to see them properly. Visual accommodation (focusing vision through changing the shape of the lens) becomes slower and less efficient. Spectacles can reduce this difficulty. Dark adaptation is slower in old people, meaning that it takes longer to adjust when moving from well-lighted surroundings to semidarkness. Tolerance for glare, as for example when one moves from a darkened room into bright sunlight, also diminishes with age. In late adulthood colour vision may also be affected as a result of yellowing of the lens.

Hearing.   Hearing is affected by a variety of age-related changes in the auditory system, such as thickening of the eardrum, accumulation of fluid in the middle ear (which also commonly affects young children), hardening of the ossicles (the bones of the middle ear) and degeneration of the structures of the inner ear. Hearing loss begins by the early 30s for most men and the late 30s for most women. The most common hearing impairment involves the reduced ability to hear and discriminate, in particular, high-pitched sounds (above 1000 cycles per second). From the 60s onwards this can often have a marked effect on a person's ability to perceive speech. Other impairments can include tinnitus (ringing in the ears) and recruitment (a condition which results in low-intensity sounds appearing quieter but high-intensity sounds appearing as loud as previously) (Welford, 1980).

Taste and smell.   In comparison with vision and audition the perceptual processes of taste and smell have been little studied. Furthermore, the tendency in much of the research that has been done to focus on ability to discriminate concentrations of substances (that is, identifying just noticeable differences) means that these modalities have not been examined at their best (Engen, 1977). It is suggested that we are better at discriminating between qualitatively different substances and that research should, therefore, emphasize preference rather than sensitivity.

There is no conclusive evidence that taste sensitivity changes with age, and odour sensitivity would appear to remain very stable. There does seem to be an increased aversion for bitter tastes with age, and changes in odour preference have been found, although these tend to occur earlier rather than later in life. Engen (1977) suggests that it may be factors such as disease, smoking and the effect of sex hormones rather than age that produce changes in taste and smell.

Cutaneous sensitivity and touch.   There is only patchy and fairly limited data concerning age-related changes in cutaneous sensitivity. The general picture has tended to be one of declining sensitivity, but this is not an inevitable concomitant of growing old. Such losses as do occur may be the side effects of disease, injury or circulatory insufficiency (Kenshalo, 1977). With regard to touch sensitivity it would seem that changes, if any, are minimal. There does, however, appear to be agreement that vibratory sensitivity frequently decreases with age. The degree of loss varies across different parts of the body. It seems, for example, to be more severe in the lower than the upper limbs. The temperature at which maximum thermal comfort is experienced seems to remain more or less constant, although the ability to regulate temperature in response to extreme environmental conditions appears to be impaired in the elderly (Kenshalo, 1977).

Pain. Older people appear to have a higher pain threshold (that is, they are less sensitive to pain) than younger people. However, it has also been found that older people may be less willing to report a sensation as painful. If, as seems possible, they want to be more sure of pain before reporting it, this may partly account for the apparent increase in pain threshold after the age of 60 (Botwinick, 1978). Furthermore, pain is more than a sensory phenomenon (Kenshalo, 1977). The way it is experienced is influenced by cognitive and motivational factors such as anxiety and expectation.

Taken overall the pattern with regard to perceptual functioning 'seems to be one of relative maintenance of function until late middle age with decline in later life' (Botwinick, 1978, p. 153). However, adults perform sets of perceptual functions in conjunction with one another and, as has been pointed out, may well be able to compensate for losses in any one particular area. Touch, smell and sound may for example, all be used to supplement vision in the identification of objects. Experience teaches us where steps, uneven pavements and the like are to be found, and we can learn where to proceed cautiously rather than assume we will see such hazards. Likewise we can learn to listen carefully to conversations in noisy places. Such changes as do occur may affect our sense of identity, in particular as to whether we see ourselves as youthful, middle-aged or old. In a society where youth is valued over old age it is likely that these indicators of ageing will, like age-related changes in appearance, be experienced and evaluated negatively.

Cognitive-intellectual components of the person

Learning and memory

Craik (1977) defines learning as 'the acquisition of general rules and knowledge about the world' and memory as 'the retention of specific events which occurred at a given time' (p. 385). However, the two processes cannot be fully differentiated. Something cannot be remembered unless it has previously been acquired (learned) and, likewise, we cannot know that something has been learned unless it is also remembered. Most reviews of the area address both processes (for example, Botwinick, 1978; Botwinick and Storandt, 1964; Hartley *et al.* 1980; Schonfield, 1980; Smith, 1980; Walsh, 1983). Those which purportedly focus on either learning (Arenberg and Robertson-Tchabo, 1977) or memory (Craik, 1977; Fozard, 1980) will typically also incorporate the other to some extent.

In what Kalish (1982) calls an old warhorse from the stable of geriatric humour we have one elderly person saying to another, 'I understand that three things happen when people age: their memory begins to slip . . . and I forget the other two.' Many older people do indeed experience a decline in their ability to learn and/or remember, and whilst they are certainly capable of learning (it is possible 'to teach old dogs new tricks') there is also evidence that the elderly do not on average perform as well as younger people in standard laboratory studies of learning and memory.

There is no simple explanation for these findings. They are the outcome of a number of factors. We already know, for example, that older often means slower. The elderly are especially likely to perform poorly in situations where speed is of the essence. They may also be more cautious, being less likely to guess if they do not know an answer. Perhaps fear of failure is greater than desire to succeed. It is also more likely that the elderly will be suffering from health problems such as cardiovascular disease which adversely affect performance on learning (and other) tasks. There is evidence indicating that older people are less likely to organize material in such a way as to facilitate learning. Furthermore, older people may have had less experience than younger people with the types of material and task typically used in learning experiments. Tasks may also be seen as meaningless or irrelevant, and this may reduce the motivation to learn.

Memory is generally seen as comprising the stages of acquisition, storage and retrieval. Considerable effort has been expended in attempting to establish whether memory decrements in old people reflect a deficiency in mainly the first or the third of these processes. In the first the information is simply not available in memory and in the third it is available but not accessible at the time of recall (Hartley *et al.*, 1980). In studies of retrieval capacity the typical research strategy has been to compare the performance of older and younger subjects on recognition or cued-recall tasks (both assumed to be low in retrieval demands) and on free-recall tasks (which are assumed to maximize retrieval demands). Some earlier studies did find greater age differences under conditions of free recall (for example, Schonfield and Robertson, 1966), suggesting that age-related memory deficits represented primarily problems of retrieval. Later studies have also demonstrated age differences in performance on recognition tasks, with Erber (1974) suggesting that task difficulty is important and that the tasks used in earlier studies may have been too simple to reveal any age differences in ability. Hartley *et al.* (1980) question the tenability of the original assumption that acquisition and retrieval can be studied independently. Arguably this is a point at which attempts to isolate and study smaller and smaller facets of the human subject becomes dysfunctional. The nature of the material and the method of its acquisition influence the efficiency of its subsequent retrieval. The two processes of acquisition and retrieval are interdependent and are best thought of as such.

A second line of enquiry has been to look for age differences in different types of memory. Following Waugh and Norman (1965) a distinction is generally made between primary and secondary memory. 'Items in primary memory are still in conscious awareness; they may be maintained in primary memory by a process of rehearsal and this process also serves to transfer information about the items to the more commodious and permanent second memory system' (Craik, 1977, p. 387). Many findings suggest that, provided the material does not require reorganization, the functioning of primary memory is more or less unimpaired in the elderly. It does however appear that there are age decrements in secondary memory, especially with more complex recall tasks.

Intelligence and cognitive development

Whitbourne and Weinstock (1979) define adult intelligence as 'the overall integration of the basic cognitive processes of perception, psychomotor reactions and learning with the higher-order cognitive processes of conceptualization, reasoning and abstract symbolization' (p. 44). The quantitative, or psychometric, approach to conceptualizing intelligence views intellectual ability as a synthesis of various abilities, each separately measurable through standardized tests. Thus, the two subscales of the Wechsler Adult Intelligence Scale (WAIS) (Wechsler, 1955) – verbal and performance – each comprise a number of separate tests. Examples of the verbal tests are information (a measure of factual knowledge), vocabulary, comprehension, digit span (recall of lists of digits) and arithmetic. Performance tests include picture completion, object assembly and picture arrangement (so that the series of pictures tells a story). Performance on the various tests (assumed to be a reflection of ability) may change with time, thus in effect indicating an increase or decrease in intelligence.

In contrast to this approach, qualitative approaches to the development of intelligence give primary attention not to level of performance, but rather to the ways in which problems are tackled and conceptualized. Changes in intelligence are, therefore, denoted by changes in the typical cognitive strategies employed by the individual in problem-solving situations. In the present discussion such changes, primarily those which do or might occur during adulthood, are treated after possible age-related changes in quantitative or psychometric intelligence have been considered.

Quantitative' intelligence. Older adults tend to perform less well than younger adults on psychometric tests of intelligence. This of itself does not, however, prove that intelligence declines with age. It may be that the older adults have had less education and experience with the type of items to be found in intelligence tests and that this contributes to their lower performance. Factors which adversely affect their performance in tests of learning and memory may have a similar influence on intelligence-test performance. If the tests are completed under severe time constraints, the lower performance of the elderly may reflect their slower pace of working – their longer reaction time and greater unwillingness to guess, for example. Would we really be prepared to say that intelligence is synonymous with speed of response? Again, health problems may impair performance. Furthermore, most intelligence tests were developed for use with children or young adults, perhaps to predict future educational or occupational attainment, and their relevance for an elderly population must be questioned. The ambience of examinations and tests in which school children and students are immersed may be alien to the older person. He or she may lack the motivation or competitive drive to perform optimally in such settings.

With regard to the psychometric measurement of intelligence the distinction between performance and competence must be borne in mind. The harrowing picture of the stroke victim whose mind is clear but whose ability to speak and communicate is severely impaired perhaps demonstrates this distinction most vividly. It would seem probable that it is for the older person that ability demonstrated in performance is least likely to be an accurate reflection of that theoretical abstraction, 'true' ability or competence. In other words, apparent age differences in intelligence may be the result of measurement error – artefacts of the research method and data-collection instruments. Since the 1970s research and reviews of intelligence and ageing (for example, Botwinick, 1977; Schaie, 1980; Willis and Baltes, 1980) have paid great attention to such possibilities and have attempted to untangle the complex interconnections between such factors as performance, experience, motivation and health. They still conclude that 'decline in intellectual ability is clearly part of the aging picture' (Botwinick, 1977, p. 580) but their analyses are more refined than previously. Intelligence, even as measured by psychometric tests, is not a unitary concept and attention has been directed at identifying the rate, degree and time of onset of any age-related changes in performance that do occur in its various components.

Distinctions have also been made among the kinds of decline occurring at different ages, and individual differences have been taken into account. Declines occurring before the age of 60 are likely to be pathological rather than normal (Schaie, 1980) – the result of illness or disease. During the late 50s and early 60s decrements are also more likely to occur in individuals who are living in relatively undifferentiated or socially deprived environments. Between the early 60s and the mid-70s there is for some people in some abilities what has been called a normal decline (Schaie, 1980). The extent of the between- and within-individual differences indicates that we must look for differential or heterogeneous rather than homogeneous patterns of ageing (Willis and Baltes, 1980). It seems reasonable that we should seek to understand and explain individual differences in patterns of cognitive functioning with age rather than search for universal age trends.

Beyond the age of 80 decrement is the rule for most individuals. We need, however, to distinguish between age decrements and what Schaie (1980) calls intellectual obsolescence. The former refers to declines in intellectual ability which are concomitants of the impairment of ageing bodily processes. The latter refers to lower performance by elderly in comparison with younger subjects due to 'their differences in experiential backgrounds and other population characteristics which have changed across generations' (Schaie, 1980, p. 274). The distinction is important since it is likely to be intellectual obsolescence that is most readily amenable to rectification through formal and informal educational interventions.

Cognitive development. Qualitative approaches to changes in intellectual functioning are concerned with changes in mental structure or in the cognitive strategies employed in thinking and problem solving; that is, they are concerned with cognitive development. This approach is epitomized in the work of Piaget (see, for example, Phillips, 1981; Piaget, 1970). The focus of attention has generally been the childhood years, on the assumption that by early adulthood cognitive strategies, whilst they may still be further refined and improved, do not change sufficiently to warrant the proposition of further stages of development. Thus, Piaget's theory of cognitive development comprises four main stages, with the final stage beginning to emerge at around the age of 11. The first or sensorimotor stage extends through approximately the first two years of life, during which interactions with the environment are dominated by sensory (for example, seeing and hearing) and motor (such as sucking, touching and grasping) actions. Piaget divides the sensorimotor stage into six substages, with the most significant transition occurring between the fifth and the sixth substages.

At the sixth and final substage of the sensorimotor period the child starts manipulating internal representations of objects. This lays the foundations for Piaget's second or pre-operational stage of cognitive development, which lasts from about the age of 2 to the age of 6 or 7. During this time the child develops the ability to use symbols (for example, mental images of objects) and, as language develops, verbal representations of objects and events.

Another feature of the pre-operational stage is centration – the focusing on only one dimension of an object or situation at a time. A perceptual manifestation of this would be when a sausage of plasticine is rolled thinner and longer, and the child, attending only to the length, thinks it has become bigger. Another form of centration is egocentrism – having difficulty or being unable (opinions differ) to see objects or situations from other than a personal perspective. The ability to focus on even one dimension is, however, a significant achievement and enables the child to perform simple classifications of objects according to a single dimension such as shape, colour or size.

Piaget's third stage, that of concrete operations, lasts from about 6 to 11 or 12. It is characterized by the development of an understanding of the law of conservation, by decentration and by seriation. Comprehension of the law of conservation involves the realization that the mass, weight and volume of an object remain the same (are conserved) despite changes in their shape or physical arrangement. Decentration is the ability to focus on more than one of an object's dimensions at a time. This enables, for example, objects to be classified hierarchically. That is, objects of the same shape may be classified by size and colour, and different objects by, let us say, shape and size. Seriation is the increasing ability to order objects according to some quantified or perceptual appearance such as relative size or relative brightness.

This third stage is termed the stage of concrete operations because the child can perform these tasks only when the objects can be seen and manipulated. Beginning to emerge at about the age of 11 is Piaget's fourth and final stage of cognitive development – the stage of formal operations. It is indicated when the young person begins to employ abstract reasoning, denoting the ability to distinguish the form of a problem from its specific content. Its main characteristics include the use of logical, abstract thinking in the solving of problems and the ability to apply concepts to different and hypothetical situations.

Piaget acknowledges that formal reasoning continues to develop through adulthood, but formulates no distinct fifth stage of cognitive development. Of particular interest in the context of the present discussion, however, is the fact that at least three suggestions for an additional stage, emerging during adulthood, have been proposed. Arlin (1975, 1977) suggests a problem-finding stage; Riegel (1973) a stage of dialectical operations; and Schaie (1977–8) a reintegrative stage. These are briefly discussed below.

Arlin's (1975) problem-finding stage. Of the three proposals for adult cognitive development to be discussed here Arlin's (1975, 1977) is most closely related to Piaget's theory. She distinguishes between two aspects of Piaget's formal-operations stage – a convergent problem-solving and a divergent problem-finding aspect – and addressed the question of whether they are substages of a single stage or whether problem finding meets the criteria for a distinct fifth stage.

Arlin investigated problem finding by asking subjects to generate interesting questions about an array of objects. The questions were categorized in relation to Guilford's (1956) hierarchy of types of question. Questions concerning basic information (for example, 'How many objects are there?') or classification (for example, 'Can these objects be grouped according to colour?') were interpreted as concrete rather than abstract questions and directed at problem solving rather than problem finding. Questions about relations ('Is the hole in object A the same size as object B?') or systems ('Can you make such-and-such a shape using objects L, M and N?') were interpreted as evidence of formal reasoning (that is, of Piaget's fourth stage). However, only questions about transformations ('What could you change object X into?') or implications ('What is the meaning of displaying objects in such-and-such a way?') were seen as evidence of problem-finding cognition.

Arlin found that formal operations were a necessary precondition for problem finding, but that not all subjects who demonstrated formal operations demonstrated problem finding. She tentatively concluded, therefore, that problem finding did constitute a fifth stage of cognitive development. This conclusion has, however, been disputed. Fakori (1976) argues that problem finding exists in Piaget's stages of concrete and formal operations, that consistency of sequencing is of itself insufficient grounds for positing a distinct stage, and that problem finding is not as distinct from problem solving as, say, concrete operations are from formal operations.

Riegel's (1973) dialectical operations stage. Riegel (1973) characterizes Piaget's theory as emphasizing the removal of conceptual contradictions. The child is initially content with making contradictory judgements about, for example, the relative mass of two balls of plasticine. During the stages of concrete and formal operations thought becomes increasingly noncontradictory. In other words, it becomes logically consistent. Riegel, however, argues that cognitive development does not stop here.

The mature person needs to achieve a new apprehension and an effective use of contradictions in operations and thoughts. Contradictions should no longer be regarded as deficiencies that have to be straightened out by formal thinking but, in a confirmative manner, as the very basis of all activities. In particular, they form the basis for any innovative and creative work. Adulthood and maturity represent the period in life during which the individual knowingly reappraises the role of formal, i.e. noncontradictory, thought and during which he may succeed again (as the young child has unknowingly achieved in his 'primitive dialectic') to accept contradictions in his actions and thoughts ('scientific dialectic'). (Riegel, 1975, pp. 100–1).

The developmental task of being an adult does not, in Riegel's view, demand or require the exorcism of contradictions, merely their temporary resolution. It requires the ability to live with complexity and tolerate a high level of ambiguity. This is achieved, Riegel argues, not through a higher or more advanced form of logical reasoning, but through a different form of cognition which facilitates a new understanding and effective use of contradictions in operations and thought. This dialectical-operations stage of cognitive development is achieved through intuitive thought – that is, through insight and understanding based on hunch, sensing and immediate apprehension rather than reasoning – which Riegel sees, like logical thought, as making a significant contribution to intellectual growth.

Riegel (1973) proposes that an individual operating at any of Piaget's developmental levels may progress directly to its corresponding mode of dialectical operations, reaching, thereby, a more mature stage of thinking. In its fullest form Riegel's fifth stage comprises the ability to operate in the dialectical fashion at all Piagetian levels, as shown in figure 3.1.

Schaie's (1977–8) model of life-span cognitive development. Schaie's (1977–8) model of cognitive development centres on age-related changes in environmental demands on the individual which

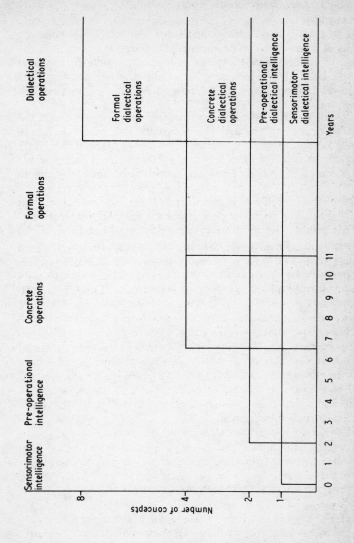

Figure 3.1 Riegel's (1973) model of cognitive development

result in a series of stages, as shown in figure 3.2. The sequential stages are acquisitive, achieving, responsible, executive and reintegrative.

The first, or acquisitive, stage is the one which has been the focus of most of the work on intellectual development. It is the stage of childhood and adolescence, during which the environmental press (from, for example, schools and parents) is on the acquisition of ever more complex cognitive structures more or less as an end in itself.

On leaving the educational system the young person enters the second, or achieving, stage. The environmental press requires the young person to use the acquired problem-solving abilities in a goal-directed way to facilitate the achievement of independent social functioning. From now on cognitive abilities are means to ends.

Having achieved role independence the individual is ready for the next stage of cognitive development – accepting the responsibility for others (in the family unit and/or at work). Experiential demands on the person require him or her to become less self-centred and to take the needs and demands of others into account. Adaptive cognitive processes during this stage include greater flexibility, consideration in problem solving of the implications for the whole family unit, and the ability to integrate

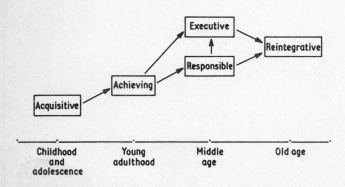

Figure 3.2   Schaie's (1977–8) model of life-span cognitive development

solutions to immediate real-life problems with longer-term goals.

For some individuals a further, executive, stage may occur during middle age. It is characterized by an environmental press which results in their assuming responsibility for larger social systems – whole departments and organizations rather than small work groups, for example. To meet this need cognitive strategies must be developed which enable the manipulation and integration of complex and hierarchical relationships.

Whereas the acquisitive stage represents 'What should I know?' Schaie characterizes the fifth and final phase of cognitive development as addressing the issue of 'Why should I know?' He calls it the stage of reintegration. It is a stage which accounts for cognitive behaviour during the latter part of life, 'when the extent of societal involvement and responsibility relaxes and when biological changes may indeed once again impose constraints on cognitive functioning' (Schaie, 1977–8, p. 134). Environmentally programmed role requirements are reduced through occupational retirement, the relinquishing of responsibility for children, and so on. The withdrawal from such roles is frequently described as disengagement, but Schaie argues that 'the cognitive response is not that of disengagement at all, it is one of achieving more selective attention to cognitive demands which remain meaningful or attain new meaning' (Schaie, 1977–8, p. 136).

Arlin's problem-finding stage and Riegel's stage of dialectical operations can both be seen as requiring divergent and innovative rather than convergent and logical thought. Schaie (1977–8) in his final or reintegrative stage focuses on the role of the individual in selecting which problem-solving situations to respond to on the basis of the 'meaning and purpose within the immediate life situation of the individual, or within the more cosmic interests of selected older individuals who exemplify what folk myth describes as the "wisdom of old age"' (p. 135). In taking this position Schaie is straying into the realm of values – personal and societal – and their impact on cognitive processes. In cognitive psychology the role of values and value systems has been extensively studied under the rubric of moral reasoning. It is to this topic that attention now turns, through an account of the contrasting theories of Lawrence Kohlberg and Carol Gilligan.

69

Moral reasoning

Kohlberg's stages of moral development. Moral reasoning is concerned with the types of thinking employed by older children and adults in the face of moral and ethical dilemmas. In his work on the development of cognitive structures Piaget (1932) investigated the development of moral reasoning as well as the development of reasoning about concrete, physical objects. It is, however, Kohlberg's research and writings on the topic (1963, 1969, 1973a, 1978, for example) that have been most widely disseminated. Like Piaget, Kohlberg is concerned with how rather than what people think. In particular, he focuses on the reasons people give for their moral judgements. Subjects are presented with a series of stories in which one or more individuals are faced with a moral dilemma. For example, one story concerns a man who could not afford to buy the drug that would save his wife's life, and so he stole the drug from the pharmacist who would not give it to him without payment. Was the man justified in stealing the drug? If caught, should he be punished? Was the pharmacist justified in wishing to earn a fortune from the drug which he had developed? Which is worse, stealing or allowing one's spouse to die? From subjects' responses to questions such as these Kohlberg identified three distinct levels or stages of moral reasoning, each comprising two substages. The three main stages are those of preconventional, conventional and post-conventional thought. Like Piaget, Kohlberg sees all individuals as passing through these stages in invariant order, irrespective of their social and cultural environment.

1 *Pre-conventional thought.* External criteria, such as whether or not the behaviour is going to be punished, form the basis of moral judgements at this earliest stage. In the first substage, the punishment and obedience orientation, the child acts so as to avoid punishment. In the second, instrumental-relativist, substage the child acts to gain personal rewards as well as to avoid punishment. The child might engage in an exchange of favours – 'I'll scratch your back if you scratch mine', one might say.

2 *Conventional thought.* As the name suggests, the touchstone of the child's moral reasoning at this stage shifts from the personal consequences of behaviour to the definitions of what is 'right', as evidenced by key reference groups such as the family, the peer

group or the nation. The child places prime importance on conformity and loyalty. During the first substage, the 'good boy–nice girl' orientation, the child's reference group is the people actually in contact with the child who have the power to reward or punish behaviour. Good behaviour is defined as that which pleases other people. In judging an act, intention is considered for the first time; that is, a misdeed is worse if committed on purpose than if committed accidentally or with good intentions. During the second substage, the law-and-order orientation, the frame of reference shifts from emotionally significant others to societal institutions such as the school, the church or the law. Duty and respect for authority are primary concerns, and good behaviour is that which obeys authority and maintains social order.

Between the second substage of the conventional-level reasoning and the first substage of the post-conventional level the individual may pass through an intermediary phase of moral development. It is characterized by a questioning of the societal definitions of right and wrong which had previously been accepted so unreservedly. Originally Kohlberg saw this challenging of conventional moral norms, which may, unlike the other stages, be omitted, as a regression to the instrumental-relativist orientation. Subsequently, however (Kohlberg, 1973a; Kohlberg and Turiel, 1973), he has reinterpreted it as representing self-realizing rather than selfish functioning on the grounds that it involves a general rather than a self-centred questioning of morality.

3 *Post-conventional thought.* Recognizing the discretionary nature of social conventions and laws, the individual develops during the post-conventional stage personal standards of behaviour which are independent of the views of other people and external authority, and which may or may not conform to conventional standards. Its two substages comprise the social-contract orientation and the conscience, or universal ethical principle, orientation. The first of these substages is marked by a strong social conscience, with the welfare of the majority being the key criterion by which actions are judged. Commitment and obligation are felt towards freely agreed contracts. Social orders and rules which are imposed and which disadvantage large sections of society are challenged.

At the level of the universal ethical principle, actions are judged on the basis of personally chosen, but universal, ethical principles.

People assume personal responsibility for their actions. Justice and reciprocity retain great significance, but it is accepted that deviation from conventional ideas of goodness can be justified in the face of violations of the individual's sense of morality. Originally Kohlberg believed that this stage was reached by the end of adolescence. Later he was to relax his views, seeing moral development as potentially continuing during adulthood, and this final stage as 'a theoretical construction suggested by the writings of "elite" figures like Martin Luther King, and not an empirically confirmed developmental concept' (Kohlberg, 1978, p. 86).

Gilligan's (1982) different voice. Gilligan (1982) challenges Kohlberg's definition of the highest level of morality as being based on an ethic of justice. The origin of Gilligan's thesis lies in her experience of listening to men and women, but particularly women, talk about both real and hypothetical moral dilemmas. She observed a way of talking about the relationship between the self and others that was different from that described and defined as development in a number of the critical studies cited elsewhere in the present book – in particular Kohlberg, but also others such as Levinson *et al.* (1978) and Vaillant (1977). Gilligan described this alternative way of talking as a different voice – identified by theme, but found empirically to be strongly, although not absolutely, associated with women rather than men.

The essence of the different theme articulated by Gilligan resides in the centrality accorded to questions of relationships, responsibilities and care in situations of choice and moral dilemma. The sequential elaboration of these concepts forms a developmental trajectory distinct from that depicted in models based on studies of men. It centres on the development of attachment rather than separation, its polar opposite. Gilligan finds that women tend to see the world in terms of connectedness, and may consequently find isolation frightening, whereas men, who tend to see the world in terms of autonomy, are threatened by intimacy. Recognition of the significance of intimacy and relationships with others, which Levinson and others observe as dawning on men during midlife, 'is something women have known from the beginning' (Gilligan, 1982, p. 17). Gilligan describes the elaboration of this knowledge as the development of the ethic of care. She identifies three distinct stages, each separated by a transitional period.

1 *Care for one's own survival.* The initial focus in Gilligan's developmental sequence is on caring for oneself in order to survive. The individual feels isolated and not connected to others. The self is, therefore, of sole concern. There is no conflict between one's own needs and those of others because only the former are recognized. Dilemmas exist only when ones own needs or wants are in conflict. Development is denoted when this perspective comes to be viewed as selfish. This marks the transition to stage 2, with the transitional issue centring on a developing awareness of the inevitable connection or attachment between the self and others, and the responsibilities that this implies.

2 *Care for others.* Recognizing the earlier perspective as selfish expresses a new insight into the connection between self and other which is evidenced by the concept of responsibility. It is, however, a self-sacrificing definition of responsibility in which good is equated with caring for others. It is a caring which takes as its touchstone the avoidance of hurting others. In such a situation the needs of the other are met but the needs of the self are excluded, or else are recognized only at the cost of guilt. It conforms to the image of the responsive and subservient woman subsuming her needs to those of husband and children. Another developmental transition is triggered when, and if, such denial to the self of that care which is extended to others comes to be perceived as an inappropriate imbalance.

3 *Care for integrity.* The concept of care, having previously been defined as not hurting others, is complicated by recognizing the legitimacy of care for oneself. The tension between selfishness and responsibility (or between responsibility to self and responsibility to others) is addressed through attending to the dynamics of relationships. Thus, care remains the principle on which judgements are made, but it is now a principle which extends to the self, based on the insight that self and other are interdependent. To deny legitimacy to the needs of the self is, because of this interdependence, eventually to harm others as well as the self. It would thus be inconsistent even with a principle of care directed solely at others. Concepts of selfishness and responsibility to others are mediated through an understanding of the dynamics of social interaction. General notions of rights and justice are tempered by contextual factors – by the details of a particular situation.

73

Gilligan contrasts the theme of morality based on the ethic of care with the theme of morality based on the ethic of justice, as exemplified by Kohlberg's work. She sees it as a morality concerned with relationships rather than rights. 'While an ethic of justice proceeds from the premise of equality – that everyone should be treated the same – an ethic of care rests on the premise of nonviolence – that no one should be hurt' (Gilligan, 1982, p. 174). The principled conception of human rights that Kohlberg sees as the pinnacle of moral development is founded on the 'human being's right to do as he pleases without interfering with somebody else's rights' (Kohlberg, 1973a, pp. 29–30). It is orientated towards individual autonomy, impartial judgement and behaving in an objectively fair and rational way. From a moral perspective which rests on the concept of care and mutual responsibilities such a stance can appear unsatisfactory, potentially justifying indifference and unconcern. On the other hand, the alternative – which looks to what is left out in a supposedly objectively fair assertion of rights and to who is hurt by such a resolution – can appear inconclusive and diffuse from a moral perspective based on rights. Gilligan conceives maturity as a combination of both, a dialogue between fairness and care premised on 'the realization that just as inequality adversely affects both parties in an unequal relationship, so too violence is destructive for everyone involved' (Gilligan, 1982, p. 174). Thus, Gilligan identifies two developmental routes. One, typically followed by men and well articulated by theorists of the life cycle, has separation as its organizing principle and rights as its yardstick. The other, typically followed by women and accorded only a secondary role in most accounts of development, centres on attachment and responsibility. Maturity combines both.

The question remains of why the definitions of morality and the routes to maturity should be differentially associated with men and women. Gilligan, following Chodrow (1978), sees the origins of this as lying in women's virtually universal responsibility for early child care. There is greater similarity and continuity between mother and daughter than between mother and son. The boundary between self and other is thus more blurred for girls and more distinct for boys. That is, attachment is a more prevalent aspect of this relationship for girls whilst separation is for boys. This sets the stage for a continuing female development around the theme of

74

connection and relationship, and a continuing male development based on separation and individuation. Gilligan is not saying that men's and women's development and world views are inevitably different, but that their experience places them in closer proximity to one version than to the other. Moreover, to date, only one voice – that of men – has been heard at full volume. Women's voice needs to be heard also, and accorded an equal place alongside men's.

In discussing Gilligan's work we have crossed the indistinct boundary between cognition and personality. As such, we have strayed towards McCandless and Evans's (1973) third concentration point: personal-social-emotional aspects of the person. These topics are discussed more fully in chapters 4 and 5. With regard to the present chapter, we have seen how bodily functioning tends to follow the growth–maintenance–decline pattern so often taken as the prototype of all human development. The rate and magnitude of growth, the age of peak, the length of the maintenance phase, the rate of decline will all, however, vary across both functions and individuals. For children, their physical development will often make other advances possible, whilst the activities of the elderly are frequently limited by their physical frailty and reduced stamina. It is generally during middle age that the accumulation of initial declines becomes apparent to the individual. He or she will, however, usually be much older before being restricted to any great extent. Many of the physical declines initiated in middle age will continue throughout later life and some will accelerate.

With regard to cognitive functions, and especially those involving significant aspects of the self or ego (as in both Riegel's and Schaie's models of cognitive development and both Kohlberg's and Gilligan's theories of moral development), the lifeline may follow one of a number of trajectories during adulthood and old age. It may, like the lifeline for bodily functioning, follow an overall growth–maintenance–decline path. Alternatively, it may continue more or less on a plateau, or – and this is the hope – it may continue to rise until the end of the life span, thereby indicating continued development or growth. These varying routes for the lifeline during the second half of life constitute the main topic discussed in the following two chapters.

4

The life course: personality and personal development

Kenneth Gergen, cited in chapter 2 for his analysis of different orientations to development (Gergen, 1977), discusses elsewhere (Gergen, 1978, 1980) the role of theory in life-span developmental psychology. Traditionally the functions of social theory are described in terms of facilitating understanding, prediction and control. Gergen questions the appropriateness of the last two of these functions when the total life span is under consideration. The inevitable transhistorical and transcultural variability in the nature of a 'typical' life course, combined with the power of significant life events to change the course of an individual's life, makes prediction a risky and somewhat pointless goal. With regard to the function of control, it is more general process theories rather than more specific content theories that are likely to prove of greater utility. Gergen (1980) does, however, see understanding as a central function of life-span developmental theory:

> Given the press of an ever-changing sea of ambiguous events, the individual may frequently search for a means of determin-

ing 'what there is' and 'why'. Theory offers a means of dissecting the flux; through theory the rough and tumble of passing experience is rendered orderly. Theory furnishes an essential inventory of what there is and ideally satisfies the individual's quest for why the units of the inventory are related as they are. In this way, theory furnishes a satisfying sense of understanding, along with terms enabling the individual to communicate this understanding to others. (p. 50)

Here, then, is one reason for developing accounts of personal experience across the life course. Given the variable and ever-changing nature of life courses, there will be a continuing need for new, or at least updated, accounts.

Ideally, new theories will offer fresh insights and perspectives. Ironically, however, the more convincing such a new perspective is and the more generally it becomes accepted the more it is in danger of becoming, in Gergen's view, a millstone around the neck of those in search of understanding. In becoming generally accepted a theory is in danger of being taken for granted and of being seen as a complete and immutable account of reality – precisely those characteristics which Gergen argues we should not look for in life-span developmental theories. Having first served to sensitize us to new phenomena, a 'popular' or 'successful' theory can then blind us to what lies beyond its boundaries. Thus, Freudian theory, having vividly drawn to our attention the sexuality of children and the significance of early experience, blinded us to the developmental potential of the adult years. Gergen sees, therefore, a continual need for new theories to counter the myopia induced by established accounts of reality. He suggests (Gergen, 1978) a further criterion against which to evaluate social theories, namely, their generative potential; that is, 'their capacity to challenge the guiding assumptions of the culture, to raise fundamental questions regarding contemporary social life, to foster reconsideration of that which is "taken for granted," and thereby to furnish new alternatives for social action' (p. 1346).

Gergen argues not only for the continual need for new theories, but also for the need for several of them. Since, as was argued in chapter 2, concepts of development are theoretical and value-laden, each represents only one of a number of possible perspectives or viewpoints. We need, therefore, multiple theories, each viewing the phenomena of concern from a somewhat different standpoint or with a somewhat different focus.

The accounts of the life course presented in this chapter bring into focus what McCandless and Evans (1973) term the personal-social-emotional aspects of the person, and were selected because of the generative potential that they contained at the time of their postulation. In particular, they each challenged the concept of adulthood as a period devoid of change and development. Generative potential has, by definition, built-in obsolescence. So, too, has any one account of the life course. In the chapter that follows, therefore, two more recent accounts of the adult years are presented. Of course these, likewise, cannot be the final words on the subject. With time they too may become taken-for-granted accounts, and thereby obscure alternative perspectives from view. In this chapter we consider the work of Charlotte Bühler, Erik Erikson and Robert Havighurst. In chapter 5 we look at the work of Daniel Levinson and Roger Gould.

Bühler's stages of biological and psychological development

Charlotte Bühler's career spanned some forty years. She began publishing articles during the 1920s and produced her original book on the course of human life in German in 1933 (Bühler, 1933). She continued to research and publish in America, having left her native Vienna during the 1930s. The book edited jointly with Fred Massarik (Bühler and Massarik, 1968) represents the most complete and up-to-date discussion of her views. In addition to editing the volume she contributed eight of the twenty-four chapters, either alone or in collaboration with various co-authors.

Whilst Bühler's work concentrates on psychological development she considers this in conjunction with the biological life cycle since, so she argues, it is the two of them together that furnish the life course with a definite, phasic form. The underlying biological structure of life provides a 'ground-plan' comprising, first, a period of growth, or progression; secondly, a period of 'stationary growth' during which the organism's power to maintain itself and develop is equal to the forces of decline; and, thirdly, a period of decline. The duration of each phase varies according to environmental circumstances and the particular index of ageing that is employed. Combining physical ability with reproductive ability as criteria, Bühler produced a more refined five-phase model of the life cycle to which she assigned approximate chronological ages, as shown in table 4:1.

Whilst recognizing that no exact parallel exists between biological and psychological development, Bühler used this biological ground plan as the basis of her phasic account of psychological development. This account has three themes: (1) the varying range and number of experiences available to an individual over the life span (encapsulated in the expansion–restriction model); (2) the individual's role in determining and fulfilling personal goals (the self-fulfilment model); and (3) the ways the individual strives to achieve the twin goals of maintenance and change (the basic-tendencies model). These three models are described below.

1 *The expansion–restriction model.* Most closely resembling the biological curve is Bühler's expansion–restriction model of events, experience and attainments (Bühler, 1935). In the first part of their lives people are concerned with the enlargement or expansion of their opportunities, activities, knowledge, and so forth. Then comes a period in which a high point is reached. This is maintained but not exceeded, although losses are repeatedly replaced. Thus, whilst being a 'steady' period, it is not static. Finally, however, either willingly or unwillingly a period of restriction follows in which positions and activities are lost or relinquished and not replaced, associations become more limited,

Table 4.1 Bühler's biological curve of life

Age	Physical ability	Reproductive ability
0–15	Progressive growth	No reproductive ability
15–25	Progressive growth	Onset of reproductive ability
25–45/50	Stationary growth	Reproductive ability
45/50–65/70	Beginning decline	Loss of reproductive ability in women
65/70–death	Continuing decline	Possible loss of reproductive ability in men

ambitions lessen, and so on. This curve lags behind the biological curve in that it rises more slowly, culminates later and falls later. Achievements, activities and events in what Bühler terms 'spiritual factors' predominate. The achievements curve for diplomats and philosophers culminates much later, for example, than it does for fashion models and footballers.

2 *The self-fulfilment model.* Bühler defines an effective person as someone who leads a goal-directed life, striving for what she calls self-fulfilment or self-actualization. Basic needs become transformed into life goals and, ideally, 'ultimate purposes'. She assumes an active, intentional and potentially creative person, with effective individuals gradually accepting increased responsibility for their lives and pursuing self-determined 'ultimate purposes'.

Bühler developed a five-phase, normative life-course model with regard to the self-determination of life goals. The first phase, from birth until the age of about 15, predates the self-determination of life goals. During this time the notion of life goals is hardly ever visualized. A second phase, between the ages of approximately 15 and 25, constitutes the phase of tentative and experimental self-determination. Young people gradually realize that their life 'belongs' to them, that it has a beginning and an end, and that they can, and do, determine its goals. Thirdly, between the ages of about 25 and 45 to 50, is the phase of more specified and definite self-determination of life goals. Fourthly, from the age of about 45 until about 60 to 64, comes the phase of self-assessment and review of past activities. The evaluation is in terms of fulfilment or failure and provides the framework within which individuals orient themselves to the future. Finally, from the age of about 65 onwards, occurs a period primarily of experiencing fulfilment, failure or resignation. However, healthy and strong individuals may still set themselves new goals or renew efforts to achieve previously set goals.

Although these stages of self-determination do not directly parallel the underlying biological structure of life there is some relation between the two profiles. There is concordance of age boundaries between the two schemes, and the first phase of the biological sequence and the model of self-determination each represents growth or expansion. It is with regard to the final stage that the two models may deviate significantly. This final phase need not, in the self-determination model, be a period of decline. Bühler argues that there are a greater variety of living styles in this fifth phase than in any other. It may continue to be a time of goal-setting and fulfilment. The link with biological life cycle remains, however, since such activity is premised upon the continuance of health and strength.

3 *The basic-tendencies model.*   No person is ever fully balanced or fully integrated and this imbalance is seen by Bühler as the cause of development. However, she does not see the establishment of balance (homeostasis) as the organism's sole goal. Rather she adopts the view that maintenance (the re-establishment of balance) and change (the promotion of imbalance) are two equally basic tendencies in human life. Furthermore, she proposes that maintenance and change are each addressed in two ways – making four basic tendencies in all. Maintenance is achieved through the restitution of deficiencies and the upholding of the system's complex internal order. These are the manifestations of the basic tendencies towards need satisfaction and the upholding of internal order. Change is achieved through adaptation and production, which are the outcome of the basic tendencies towards self-limiting adaptation and creative achievement respectively. Bühler offers definitions of these tendencies (Bühler and Massarik, 1968) as follows:

Need satisfaction is the pursuit of any kind of tension-reducing satisfiers, be they physical, emotional or intellectual. *Self-limiting adaptation* is a person's tendency to adapt his or her behaviour to that of others and to the given circumstances. It is manifested in the self-restraint that emanates from the desire to belong and to participate. *Creative expansion* is the tendency to advance in the world and to change it creatively through actions or through physical or mental productivity. It includes the behaviour by which an individual extends his or her influence and productions – the bearing of children, the establishment of a business, the writing of a book, for example. *Upholding the internal order* involves different ordering principles which work towards the unity of personality and behaviour. 'These principles are first found in the coordination of movements; a little later in the organization of activities; still later in the operation of such integrating principles as goals, ideals, and those self-assessments which fall under the heading of what generally is called "conscience"' (Bühler and Massarik,

81

1968, pp. 93–4). This is the most complex of the four basic tendencies.

Whilst there are assumed to be individual differences in the extent to which one or other of these four tendencies predominates it is also assumed that all tendencies are present at and are utilized from birth. However, Bühler also hypothesizes a sequential relative predominance of the different tendencies during the life cycle. Thus, the drive of newborn infants is primarily directed towards need satisfaction. They must, however, adapt themselves, extend themselves and co-ordinate their behaviours at least to some small degree if they are to satisfy their needs. Self-limiting adaptation develops and predominates during the childhood learning process. Creative expansion reaches its zenith during adolescence and early adulthood as individuals move into a wider world. The self-assessment of middle adulthood probably reflects a desire to restore inner order and represents the predominance of the tendency to uphold inner order. Old age again represents the time of greatest potential individual differences. Some old people will regress and allow need-satisfaction tendencies to predominate whilst others will try to accept a self-limiting adaptation which is forced upon them. Others will be able to continue their creatively expansive activities, whilst still others will emphasize the upholding of internal order by reminiscing and assessing their lives. In other words, any of the four basic tendencies may predominate in the period of old age.

Bühler's normative models of the fluctuating predominance of different basic needs does, like the expansion–restriction model and the self-determination of goals model, bear a relation to the basic biological ground plan. There is, again, the underlying sequence of growth, maintenance and, sometimes, decline. There are other links between these three models, some already alluded to. Need satisfaction and self-limiting adaptation predominate during the period prior to the self-determination of life goals. Self-determination goes hand in hand with creative expansion. Likewise, the tendency towards the upholding and re-establishment of internal order is associated with the period of self-assessment. Both the self-determination and basic-tendencies models reflect the general shape of the expansion–restriction model.

In short, Bühler's three models reflect a concern with development as a lifelong process and the use of the life span as an integrative framework, whilst together they bear witness to the multidimensional and multiform nature of development. She does adopt an interactive view of the person, although this is sometimes hidden behind the humanistic emphasis on the person rather than the environment as the locus of the developmental dynamic. She pays only lip service to the importance of context in her theoretical statements, although she does incorporate it more thoroughly into her analyses of particular life histories. She is not concerned with transhistorical changes in the nature of the life course. Her models are rooted in a biological plan which is implicitly assumed to be universal across time as well as environment. None the less, the influence of her work has been wide and is evident in the writings of several authors who have subsequently worked in the field of life-span development.

Whereas the biological model of growth–maintenance–decline underpins the expansion–restriction model and may be the developmental trajectory followed by the curve of self-fulfilment, it is the epigenetic principle which underpins Bühler's basic-tendencies model. It is, however, in the work of another emigré to America, Erik Erikson, that the best-known application of the epigenetic principle across the total life span is found. Deriving from the discipline of embryology this principle states that 'anything that grows has a ground plan, and out of this ground plan the parts arise, each part having its time of special ascendency, until all forms have arisen to form a functioning whole' (Erikson, 1980, p. 53). It is to Erikson's theory that our attention now turns.

Erikson's theory of psychosocial development

Whilst Freud and Piaget may be the authors most widely cited when child development is the focus of psychologists' attention, Erik Erikson holds pride of place when the whole life span is considered. Beginning with the publication of *Childhood and Society* in 1950 (revised in 1963), Erikson has made a significant and lasting contribution to the field. His work spanned over thirty years, with some of his earlier writings (Erikson, 1959) being reissued more than twenty years after their original publication (Erikson, 1980). His eight-stage theory of psychosocial development remain the most widely known and widely quoted account of the life cycle in the social science literature.

Erikson's model is of a changing individual operating in a changing society. As the individual develops society places new demands on him or her; demands to which the ego must adapt. Each new demand provokes an emotional crisis, the successful resolution of which leads to the development of a new 'virtue' or 'vital strength'. This development does not occur in a random manner or order. Rather, it occurs in accordance with the epigenetic principle. Thus, ego development is a cumulative process occurring in accordance with a timetable. Erikson depicts this timetable as a series of eight psychosocial tasks or crises as summarized in table 4.2. Although the crises are presented as a series of polar opposites they in fact represent dimensions rather than alternatives. Thus, the outcome of the first stage can range from basic trust to basic mistrust; the outcome of the second stage from a strong sense of autonomy to a profound sense of shame and doubt, and so on. Whilst each task has a period of ascendency they all exist in some form throughout life and may, therefore, be addressed at other times as well. Thus, whilst failure to deal adequately with a task during its period of ascendency is damaging to the ego's development, this damage is not entirely irrevocable. As development proceeds it becomes more complex. As each new task is addressed earlier resolutions are also questioned. The struggles of yesteryear may, for better or worse, be fought again.

Erikson sees the tasks or struggles of both previous and present generations as being enshrined in a culture's social institutions. In other words, there is a cultural manifestation of each stage of individual development. These institutions impinge on the individual, thereby influencing both the specific form and the outcome of the crises. Development is a function of both individual and cultural factors – hence Erikson's description of his theory as a theory of psychosocial development and of his tasks as psychosocial tasks. The cultural manifestations of the psychosocial tasks are indicated on the right-hand side of table 4.2. Erikson has not explicated this aspect of his theory as fully as he has the stages of individual development. It is, however, summarized in the appendix to *Identity and the Life Cycle* (1980) and can be gleaned from his discussions of the psychosocial stages. Erikson's eight stages of psychosocial development are now outlined.

Table 4.2 Erikson's stages of psychosocial development

Age (approx.)	Stage	Crisis	Potential new virtue	Societal manifestation
0–1	Infancy	Basic trust v. Basic mistrust	Hope	Religion and faith
1–6	Early childhood	Autonomy v. Shame and Doubt	Will	Law and order
6–10	Play age	Initiative v. Guilt	Purpose	Economics
10–14	School age	Industry v. Inferiority	Competence	Technology
14–20	Adolescence	Identity v. Role confusion	Fidelity	Ideology
20–35	Young adulthood	Intimacy v. Isolation	Love	Ethics
35–65	Maturity	Generativity v. Stagnation	Care	Education, art and science
65+	Old age	Ego integrity v. Despair and Disgust	Wisdom	All major cultural institutions

1 *Basic trust v. Basic mistrust.* During the first year of life infants learn to trust or mistrust the predictability of their environment. Through the experience provided by their major care-givers they learn whether they can depend on their needs for food, warmth and other forms of comfort being met. It is during this time as well that the beginnings of trust in oneself are learned as the infant comes to trust his or her body to cope with its necessary functions – breathing, feeding, digestion, elimination. Thus, in addition to a reasonable trustfulness of others, a sense of basic trust also implies a reasonable trust and confidence in oneself. Erikson sees this as manifested in the willingness and ability to allow the major care-givers out of sight without suffering undue anxiety or rage – an achievement which is dependent on a sense of inner certainty as well as outer predictability. In other words, it is dependent on a rudimentary sense of ego identity.

The cultural institution which Erikson sees as deeply related to the matter of trust is that of religion or, more generally, of faith. Individual trust becomes at this level a common faith, and individual mistrust a commonly formulated evil. If it is not derived from religion, basic faith must be derived from some other source – fellowship, productive work, social action, scientific pursuit or artistic creation, for example. Erikson's theory links generations when he argues that without such faith an adult is unable to nurture and support the infant's developing sense of trust.

2 *Autonomy v. Shame and Doubt.* During the second and third year of life children become more mobile and, thereby, more independent. They need no longer be content with what others bring to them, but can move about the world and choose how and with what they interact. However, their sense of discrimination is as yet untrained. They do not know what is possible and what impossible; what is safe and what is dangerous. Without protection and guidance the child will experience repeated failure and ridicule, which foster feelings of doubt and shame rather than bolster the child's sense of autonomy and independence. Excessive as well as insufficient control also leads to a thwarting of the child's sense of autonomy, promoting instead a sense of inadequacy.

The goal of this stage is to attain self-control without loss of self-esteem. Being made to see oneself as inadequate makes one ashamed. There are limits to the amount of shaming one can bear.

Too much, and the outcome is either defiant shamelessness or a determination to get away with things unseen. Thus, to develop a healthy sense of autonomy, the child must be given both choice and protection, and must experience a reasonable balance between freedom and control. At the societal level concerns about the balance between freedom and control are to be found in debates concerning law and order and the relationship between obligation and rights. Likewise, a society's resolution of these issues is to be found in its system of laws, rules and regulations, and its mechanisms for the disciplining of transgressors. As with the crisis of trust v. mistrust the question of autonomy v. shame may be revived in adulthood. If adults experience relationships with individuals and institutions which undermine their sense of autonomy this also undermines their ability to provide their children with an appropriate balance between freedom and control.

3 *Initiative v. Guilt.* A sense of autonomy gives the child the sense of him or herself as a person. Through the crisis of initiative v. guilt children begin to explore the question of the kind of person they are going to be. Being able now to move around independently and vigorously in (almost) the same way as adults, children can begin to imagine themselves being as large as adults and fulfilling adult roles. Largely through imitative play with other children they begin to explore possible future roles for themselves. In particular they play with the idea of what it would be like to be like their parents.

Erikson defines initiative as a truly free sense of enterprise. Its manifestations at the societal level are found in a society's economic structure and endeavour. Initiative is largely governed by conscience – a self-dependence which in turn makes the individual dependable. With the development of conscience also develops the potential for guilt. 'The child now feels not only ashamed when found out but also afraid of being found out. . . . Moreover, he begins automatically to feel guilty even for mere thoughts and for deeds which nobody has watched' (Erikson, 1980, p. 84). Whilst being a cornerstone of individual morality a child's conscience may be overburdened by adults. When this happens initiative may be thwarted. Instead of developing a sense of purpose – the new virtue that results from successful resolution of this crisis – the child may learn to constrict him or herself to the

87

point of general inhibition, or may become excessively good and obedient, or may develop 'deep regressions and lasting resentments because the parents themselves do not seem to live up to the new conscience which they have fostered in the child' (Erikson, 1980, p. 84).

4 *Industry v. Inferiority.*   Erikson (1980) summarizes the convictions around which personality crystallizes during the early part of the life cycle. At stage 1 (trust v. mistrust) there is the belief that 'I am what I am given'. At stage 2 (autonomy v. shame) this becomes 'I am what I will'. At stage 3 (initiative v. guilt) the child comes to believe that 'I am what I can imagine I will be'. At the fourth stage (industry v. inferiority), this becomes transformed into 'I am what I learn'. At this stage the child is involved in learning to use the physical and intellectual tools of his or her society. In other words, the society's technology (the societal manifestation of this crisis) is now imparted to the child. Through his process the child, ideally, learns industry. That is, he or she learns to adjust to 'the inorganic laws of the tool world' (Erikson, 1980, p. 91).

The risk at this stage is the development of a sense of inadequacy and inferiority rather than industry. This may result from the insufficient resolution of preceding conflicts. Perhaps the child still wishes to remain tied to the apron strings of home, or else is still comparing him or herself with parents and feeling guilty about personal shortfalls. Alternatively, or as well, feelings of inferiority may result from the child being unable to learn or being prevented from learning the set of specific skills needed for effective functioning in that society. Another danger is that of overexaggerating the role and importance of technology and technological competence. In accepting work (or industry) as more or less the only obligation and 'what works' as the only criterion of value, a person or society will become a slave of technology rather than its ruler.

5 *Identity v. Role confusion.*   It is for this fifth stage, the adolescent identity crisis, that Erikson is best known. Rapid physical growth and hormonal changes (described by Erikson as a physiological revolution) marking the attainment of genital maturity combine with awareness of tangible adult tasks ahead to produce a questioning of 'all samenesses and continuities relied on earlier' (Erikson, 1963, pp. 252–3). The search is for a new sense of continuity and sameness. Questions of sexual and, in our society,

occupational, identity are paramount. In the struggle the c. earlier years may need to be fought again.

Successful resolution of this crisis leads to a sense of ego identity – 'a conviction that one is learning effective steps toward a tangible future, that one is developing a defined personality within a social reality which one understands' (Erikson, 1980, p. 95). Ego identity is premised upon, but is more than, the virtues marking successful resolution of earlier stages – hope, will, purpose and competence. It is a reworking of such attributes into a more coherent set of values and beliefs to which the individual feels commitment and loyalty. It is a state of flux between the morality of childhood and the ethically principled adult. The resulting new virtue is fidelity and its cultural manifestation is in a society's ideology.

The danger of this stage is identity diffusion or role confusion – uncertainty about who one is and what one is to become. To counteract such uncertainty or to bolster a still fragile sense of identity the young person may temporarily overidentify with a clannish subgroup of peers and/or particular cults or individuals. The development of a negative (self-destructive) or socially un- acceptable identity may be preferable to no identity. Thus, the young person may cling to an identity of addict, delinquent or football hooligan if more attractive alternatives seem unavailable.

6 *Intimacy v. Isolation (distantiation and self-absorption).* Having achieved and developed some confidence in his or her separate identity, the young adult is now able to risk destroying this individuality by fusing it with another's. This fusing is achieved through intimacy – the capacity to commit oneself to 'concrete affiliations and partnerships and to develop the ethical strength to abide by such commitments, even though they may call for significant sacrifices and compromises' (Erikson, 1963, p. 255). Love is the potential new strength to be developed at this stage. At the wider level the resolution of this crisis is to be found in a society's explicit or, more often, implicit ethical standards.

Intimacy calls for self-abandonment. The often painfully ac- quired sense of identity is thereby put at risk. In order to take such a risk the individual must have some confidence that his or her ego will remain intact. If the threat of ego loss is too great the individual will avoid potentially intimate relationships, leading to a deep sense of isolation. Intimacy involves rising above and beyond

the risk of prolonging the self-absorption
adolescent is high. For some, intimacy may be
to the crisis of identity, harnessing one's identity
rather than struggling to fashion an independent
s own. In such a situation, however, one is
ing always an unequal partner and placing on that
rden of providing a sense of identity for two people.

At t. t in Erikson's sequence of crises the age boundaries
dividing the different stages start to become extremely unclear.
For example Havighurst (1973) sets the end of the intimacy v.
isolation stage at the age of 40, whilst Turner and Helms (1979)
place it at 34, and Bee and Mitchell (1984) as early as 25. This is
doubtless due in no small part to Erikson's general reticence about
the tasks of the 30s – Vaillant (1977) describes him as leaving an
uncharted period of development between the 20s and the 40s.
Vaillant himself, in his own contribution to a longitudinal study of
students of good academic standing in a competitive American
college, identifies an intermediate stage of career consolidation
occurring between Erikson's crisis of intimacy and the one which
follows – namely, that between generativity and stagnation. He
also points to the sequence of identity, intimacy, career consolidation, and generativity found by other American studies of adult
development (for example, Block and Haan, 1971; Levinson *et al.*,
1978; Oden and Terman, 1968). During their early 30s, Vaillant
(1977) found his subjects to be 'too busy becoming, too busy
mastering crafts; too busy ascending prescribed ladders to reflect
upon their own vicissitudes of living' (p. 202). By their mid-30s
they were itching 'to step into the driver's seat' (p. 202). Such a
self-centred preoccupation tended, by the age of 50, to be
replaced with a much greater concern for those working with and
for them – in other words, a generative concern, the focus of
Erikson's next psychosocial stage.

7 *Generativity v. Stagnation.* Erikson's seventh crisis, and the
second one he locates during the years of adulthood, is between
generativity and stagnation. Finding expression most usually
through the experience of parenthood he defines generativity as
'primarily the interest in establishing and guiding the next generation' (Erikson, 1980, p. 103). It is not synonymous with parenthood, however. Indeed Erikson suggests that difficulties in the
parenting role may stem from the retardation of or inability to

achieve generativity with its consequent virtue of care. Likewise, parenthood is not the only mechanism for achieving generativity. It may also be expressed through other forms of creativity and altruistic concern. At the societal level generativity is evidenced most clearly through education although 'all institutions codify ethics of generative succession' (Erikson, 1963, p. 259).

More than any other of his psychosocial stages Erikson's crisis of generativity v. stagnation serves to demonstrate the inter-dependence of generations.

> The fashionable insistence on dramatizing the dependence of children on adults often blinds us to the dependence of the older generation on the younger one. Mature man needs to be needed, and maturity needs guidance as well as encouragement from what has been produced and must be taken care of. (Erikson, 1963, p. 258)

Failure to attain generativity will lead, Erikson argues, to stagnation and personal impoverishment. The care that, to be growthful, needs to be directed towards one's child or other creation, may instead be turned inwards. The individual becomes (or remains) self-centred; in effect being like his or her own child and possibly succumbing to early physical or psychological invalidism.

Vaillant (1977), in addition to pinpointing a stage of career consolidation between the crises of intimacy and generativity, also found evidence in his study of another phase, this time occurring between the crisis of generativity and the final struggle identified by Erikson between integrity on the one hand and despair and disgust on the other. Vaillant described this intermediary phase as a tension between 'keeping the meaning' and rigidity. He sees it as characterizing the decade of the 50s, a time during which a new generation is beginning to take over: 'As this happens, rigidity interferes with Generativity' (Vaillant, 1977, p. 231). Vaillant found rigidity to be denoted by efforts on the part of his subjects to ensure the perpetuation rather than the replacement of their own culture and values, and by their experiencing of mild regret about aspects of the direction in which they saw society heading. The positive side of this rigidity was shown in his subjects' concern with 'keeping the meaning' – their efforts to teach what they themselves have learned to others who can perpetuate that which is of worth in society and continue the attempt to accomplish goals which will not be attained in the lifetime of those now into middle age. 'Passing on the torch' and exposing his children to 'civilized values' was how one of Vaillant's subjects described this stage. Another positive aspect of the rigidity of this phase was denoted by the men's clearer and seemingly enduring sense of their own identity – they believed they knew who they were, and the best adjusted felt, correctly or otherwise, that they had found their niche in society. Vaillant saw this stage of keeping the meaning v. rigidity as a precursor of Erikson's final stage of development – the struggle of ego integrity v. despair and disgust.

8 *Ego integrity v. Despair and Disgust.* Erikson describes an integrated ego as the ripe fruit of the seven earlier stages. It is attained through resolution of the crisis of integrity v. despair. Lacking a clear definition, Erikson points to several indicators of ego integrity. It is indicated by an acceptance of one's life for what it has been and a freedom from the burden of excessive regret that it had not been different. It also involves an acceptance that one's life is one's own responsibility. Ego integrity involves a willingness to defend the dignity of one's own life style whilst at the same time experiencing a sense of comradeship with people of other times, cultures and walks of life. There is a recognition of the value of other ways of expressing integrity, but this is not seen as threatening or incompatible with one's own version. There is also a recognition of the smallness of one's own place in the universe – the realization that 'an individual life is the accidental coincidence of but one life cycle with but one segment of history' (Erikson, 1980, p. 104). Successful resolution of this final psychosocial crisis leads to the emergent virtue of wisdom. Rather than being embodied in a cultural organization, integrity permeates, or not, all a society's major institutions and mores.

Lack or loss of accrued ego integration leads to despair. This is often revealed in a fear of death and expresses the feeling that life is too short to alter anything. One cannot start a new life or plan to do things differently next time. Despair may be hidden behind a show of disgust – a contemptuous displeasure with particular institutions and people. This in turn signifies the individual's disgust with him or herself.

Although remaining firmly within the psychoanalytic tradition, Erikson's focus of attention differs from Freud's in a number of significant ways. First, Erikson focuses on the conscious self (the ego) whereas Freud's attention is directed primarily at the unconscious drives or instincts (the id). Secondly, he sees the personality as developing throughout life, whereas Freud viewed the course of adulthood as having been largely set by the events of early childhood. Thirdly, and in contrast to Freud's emphasis on the biologically based components of psychosexual development, Erikson concerned himself with the social, cultural and historical determinants of personality development. He recognized that both his and Freud's theories were the outcome of the historical era and social milieu in which each worked. Thus, Freud worked in a society which needed liberation from sexual repression, whereas he, Erikson, operated in an environment (namely America in the middle years of the twentieth century) where questions of identity – of 'who am I and what am I to become?' – were of central concern. The integrating theme in Erikson's work is the transformation of ego identity. This in turn pointed to a concern with issues of ego rather than the id. The goal of the ego is survival in the real world, adapting to reality. Since this reality is largely socially constructed, concern with the ego also implies concern with the role of society in individual development.

Erikson's theory has not, however, been without its critics. At times he overemphasizes the symbiotic relationship between individual development and societal progress and, as a consequence, has been criticized for promulgating a conformist theory which is excessively supportive of the status quo (Roazen, 1976). Objection has also been made (Buss, 1979) to Erikson's 'sometimes naive and accepting attitude toward the family' (p. 327). In fact Erikson's attitude to the role of social institutions in general and the family in particular is ambivalent rather than uncritically laudatory, although as Buss (1979) points out he does tend to defuse critiques as soon as he makes them. Buss (1979) also points to a major value assumption in Erikson's work – namely that 'psychological growth and health is possible only to the extent that the individual is not out of step with society' (p. 328). This demands an unduly benign view of society, denying that the social reality may be psychologically and/or physically repressive, alienating or constricting. Under such conditions, argues Buss, the valid and healthy response may be shame and doubt rather than autonomy, guilt rather than initiative, identity diffusion rather than identity, and so on. Buss thus disagrees with Erikson's view of integrity as the culmination of development when it includes acceptance of the inevitability of one's life as it has been: 'Integration of the individual into society is not an absolute to be unquestioningly sought after. . . . Unqualified acceptance of one's total life history, and by implication of the external forces that have helped to shape that life, is too heavy a price to pay for the comfort of integration' (p. 329). This criticism highlights in concrete fashion the value-laden nature of definitions of development.

Havighurst's developmental tasks

Also based on the epigenetic principle and related to, although more concrete than, Erikson's concept of psychosocial tasks, is the idea of developmental tasks. Elaborated most fully by Robert J. Havighurst, the idea has also been utilized by several others, most notably by Daniel Levinson and his colleagues (1978), at least as far as adult development is concerned. Havighurst's publications (for example, Havighurst, 1953, 1982) span an even longer period than Bühler's and Erikson's. His most comprehensive exposition of the concept of developmental tasks is to be found in *Developmental Tasks and Education*. Published originally in 1948, this book was reprinted many times and revised in 1971 (Havighurst, 1972).

A developmental task is defined as 'a task which arises at or about a certain period in the life of the individual, successful achievement of which leads to his happiness and to success with later tasks, while failure leads to unhappiness in the individual, disapproval by the society, and difficulty with later tasks' (Havighurst, 1972, p. 2). The developmental tasks of a particular group of people arise from three sources: physical maturation; cultural pressure (the expectations of society); and individual aspirations or values. Some tasks will result primarily from one source whilst others will result from the interaction of any combination of physical, cultural and psychosocial factors. Thus, learning to walk is primarily the result of physical maturation. Learning to read, by contrast, occurs primarily in response to the cultural pressure of a society. Since the timing and degree of this pressure can vary across societies there will be a corresponding variation in the timing and importance of the developmental task of learning to read. Havighurst sees the personality, or self, as emerging from the interaction of organic and environmental forces. However, as it evolves, the self becomes a force in its own right capable of directing the individual's subsequent development. Thus, Havighurst sees both choosing and preparing for an occupation, and achieving a scale of values and philosophy of life, as developmental tasks arising primarily from the personal motives and values of the individual. Given his definition of the self, however, there is inevitably some cultural (that is, environmental) implication in such tasks as well.

The identification of developmental tasks is seen largely as an empirical issue. Havighurst (1956) conceives of three possible procedures for discovering and defining them – observation, questioning and introspection. In the first procedure people are observed and inferences made concerning what their principal developmental concerns are at any one age. It is a process of discovering what they are 'working at', to use Havighurst's phrase. The second procedure, that of asking people what their chief concerns and interests are, is distinguished by assuming that people are conscious of their developmental needs and willing to talk about them. In the third procedure social scientists in effect question themselves – reflecting on their own past and present life, thereby identifying their principal developmental motives.

Havighurst utilized all these procedures directly and, combined with a scouring of social science literature, used the data to pinpoint 6 to 9 developmental tasks for each of six age periods as shown in table 4.3. Being both empirically defined and relatively concrete, Havighurst's notion of developmental tasks provides a coherent framework for portraying the specifics of a life course. Reinert (1980) further describes such lists of tasks as 'a kind of culturally specific guidance system' (p. 17), pointing to their normative role as a series of goals which individuals in a society are motivated or persuaded to pursue, and against which they are evaluated, as well as their role as a description of the 'typical'. Havighurst's approach is, however, descriptive rather than explanatory. He identifies the physical, cultural and individual origins of developmental tasks, but does not specify what conditions and properties of these sources spur or inhibit motivation to address them.

The concrete and empirical nature of the developmental tasks detailed by Havighurst confer disadvantages as well as advantages. These characteristics limit the general applicability of any one list

Table 4.3   Havighurst's developmental tasks

Stage	*Developmental tasks*
Infancy and early childhood	Learning to walk Learning to take solid foods Learning to talk Learning bowel and bladder control Learning sex differences and sexual modesty Forming concepts and learning language to describe social and physical reality Getting ready to read
Middle childhood	Learning physical skills necessary for ordinary games Building wholesome attitudes towards oneself as a growing organism Learning to get along with peers Learning an appropriate masculine or feminine role Developing basic skills in reading, writing and calculating Developing concepts necessary for everyday living Developing conscience, morality and a scale of values Achieving personal independence Developing attitudes towards social groups and institutions
Adolescence	Achieving new and more mature relations with peers of both sexes Achieving a masculine or feminine role Accepting one's physique and using the body effectively Achieving emotional independence of parents and other adults Preparing for marriage and family life Preparing for an economic career Developing an ideology (a set of values and an ethical system that guide behaviour) Desiring and achieving socially responsible behaviour

Stage	Developmental tasks
Early adulthood	Selecting a mate
	Learning to live with a marriage partner
	Starting a family
	Rearing children
	Managing a home
	Getting started in an occupation
	Taking on civic responsibility
	Finding a congenial social group
Middle age	Assisting teenage children to become responsible and happy adults
	Achieving adult social and civic responsibility
	Reaching and maintaining satisfactory performance in one's occupational career
	Developing adult leisuretime activities
	Relating to one's spouse as a person
	Accepting and adjusting to the physiological changes of middle age
	Adjusting to ageing parents
Later maturity	Adjusting to decreasing physical strength
	Adjusting to retirement and reduced income
	Adjusting to the death of one's spouse
	Establishing an explicit affiliation with one's age group
	Adopting and adapting social roles in a flexible way
	Establishing satisfactory physical living arrangements

of developmental tasks since it will inevitably be socially, culturally and historically specific – a consequence of the potential lack of transcultural and transhistorical generality of accounts of the life course. At the more general level Havighurst's concept of developmental tasks is content-free, thus making it a feasible candidate for transcultural and transhistorical transposition. Daniel Levinson and his colleagues, whose work is discussed in the next chapter, are amongst those who have used this concept most extensively.

The three researchers whose work has been the focus of attention in the present chapter are important precursors of the current interest in life-span development. Between them they demonstrate to a greater or lesser extent the tenets of life-span developmental psychology identified in chapter 1. The first and fourth tenets – the belief that the potential for development extends throughout life, and the adoption of a reciprocal influence model of person–environment relations – are core features of Bühler's phasic account of psychological development, Erikson's psychosocial crises and Havighurst's developmental tasks. At first glance Bühler, Erikson and Havighurst each seem to violate the second tenet of life-span developmental psychology – namely that there is no specific route that development must or should take – in that each does offer a view of ideal or optimum development. Thus, Bühler talks of the self-determination of life goals, Erikson of the attainment of integrity, and Havighurst of fulfilling tasks which facilitate further development and bring personal happiness and societal approval. However, each schema also allows – Havighurst's less so than the others' – for variation in the specific route through which these objectives are achieved. Bühler, through her deliniation of three models of psychological development, enacts most explicitly the third tenet of the life-span perspective – that development occurs on a number of fronts. However, Erikson, like Bühler, developed his theory in the belief that aspects of development were not included in prevailing accounts. Havighurst, with his identification of three sources of developmental tasks, implicitly acknowledged different facets of development, or developmental fronts.

In addition to their commonalities, the theories of Bühler, Erikson and Havighurst each have their own focus of attention and make their unique contribution. Bühler's is a theory of self-realization, Erikson's a theory of psychosocial development, and Havighurst's a theory of socialization (Staude, 1981). Bühler stood apart from her contemporaries in emphasizing a core self in personality which is orientated towards purpose and meaning, and which contrasted strongly with the prevailing scientific milieu of objectivity and detachment. Erikson was unique amongst the three in the emphasis he gave to the interdependence of generations – with the old needing the young as much as vice versa. Havighurst, in his turn, was concerned to develop life-span developmental psychology as an applied and relevant discipline. He believed that researchers should concern themselves with significant and possibly controversial problems such as mid-life career change; perception of ageing by the self, the family and the community; personality change in the context of declining health and vigour; and the attitudes towards death held by people of different ages. In the chapter that follows we can see how two contemporary researchers have built upon the foundations laid by such predecessors as these.

5

Adulthood

Adulthood is the longest phase of the life course and yet, until recently, it has been the least researched. Levinson *et al.* (1978) described the nature of adulthood as 'one of the best kept secrets in our society, and probably in human history generally' (p. ix). As a phase it is typically denoted by a combination of physiological and chronological criteria.

> The phase of adulthood covers the timespan between the emergence of the individual from adolescence to the onset of senescence and the advanced aging process. Chronologically, this phase varies considerably among different cultures, but in the highly complex structure of Western civilization it usually covers the era between 21 and 70. (Dewald, 1980, p. 35)

An alternative, or additional, definition of adulthood relates to the characteristic psychosocial or developmental tasks of different eras. These might be specific and concrete tasks such as those described by Havighurst (1972) or more abstract and general episodes such as those in Erikson's (1980) sequence.

Whilst capable of delimiting a general phase, chronological, physiological and developmental task criteria are inadequate for distinguishing adults from non-adults (Whitbourne and Weinstock, 1979). Chronological age as a criterion appears superficially to have the virtue of simplicity. However, on closer examination, problems become apparent. Legally adulthood is achieved at the age of 18. It used to be 21, but in Britain this was lowered on 1 January 1971 by three years. Did this mean there was a cohort of individuals aged 18, 19 and 20 who overnight became more grown-up – more adult? Of course not. There remain many individuals over even the age of 21 who would not be considered adult in their behaviour. Thus, identifying an official start to adulthood is an arbitrary business. In any case, whilst the attainment of such a status brings with it certain rights and responsibilities (suffrage, for example), there is in most areas of life a more gradual assumption of the trappings of adulthood.

Establishing an upper age limit to adulthood is even more problematic. Eligibility for a retirement pension is the nearest we come to having an official criterion. Again, though, this is arbitrary. The five-year difference in age of eligibility between men and women was not introduced because women were believed to be 'old' at 60, but men not until 65. Rather, it was based on the assumption that husbands would be approximately five years older than their wives and that they could, with such an arrangement, retire at approximately the same time. A greater problem in using chronological age as a cut-off criterion for adulthood, however, stems from the enormous individual differences in physical, psychological and social functioning that prevail during the 60s and 70s – the decades where a cut-off point is most likely to be sought, at least by those who have not yet attained that age. People in their 80s might, with some justification, object to being thought of as no longer adult.

There is clearly more to being adult than chronological age. Used in this sense chronological age is typically employed as a rough indicator of a combination of physiological, physical and mental functioning. Whilst there will undoubtedly be differences between the functioning of, say, a 75-year-old and a 25-year-old there will also be wide individual differences. Moreover, the multiplicity of possible explanations for individual and age-related differences discussed in chapter 3 further mitigate against the use of such indicators as criteria for adult status.

Equally problematic as a set of criteria for defining adults is the achievement of age-appropriate or life-stage-appropriate developmental tasks. Like chronological age, they suffer from the difficulty of not giving the whole story. The first four of Havighurst's developmental tasks of early adulthood are concerned with establishing a marriage and a family, and yet we would surely not wish automatically to deny the status of adult to those people who remain single and/or childless. Clearly there is yet more to what we mean when we talk of someone being adult.

Whitbourne and Weinstock (1979) propose that the fundamental criterion by which we distinguish adults from nonadults is psychological in nature. When we think of an adult or of adultlike behaviour we are usually referring 'to qualities of personality exhibited in words and actions' (p. 4). Whitbourne and Weinstock, after Rappaport (1972), refer to these global qualities as psychological maturity. Involving the ability to shoulder responsibilities, make logical decisions, empathize with others, cope with minor frustrations and accept one's social role, this concept of maturity is consistent with both Maslow's concept of the self-actualizing person and Allport's description of the mature personality (see chapter 2).

We have commented on criteria for delimiting adulthood as a phase and for distinguishing between adults and nonadults or, at least, between adultlike and nonadultlike behaviour. It is, however, a third line of inquiry that is the main concern of the present chapter: namely, how is adulthood experienced? To answer this it is necessary to move to more detailed, in-depth and experientially based narratives of the life course. Two such accounts are related in the present chapter. Both emanating from North America during the 1970s, they capture the concern with adult development and with the normative crises of adulthood that emerged with particular force during that decade. It is not coincidental that they emerged at the time they did. The ability to tolerate ambiguity and manage change is an increasingly important life skill. An awareness of the psychological upheavals we might reasonably expect to experience during our adult years is an important basis for such a skill. It is towards this end that the following accounts are offered. Each study is the outcome of similar interests, but they are investigated using different methods and against different disciplinary backgrounds. The first (Levinson *et al.*, 1978), the work of an interdisciplinary team led by a social psychologist, is an in-depth study of a small sample of men from various occupations. The second investigation (Gould, 1978, 1980) was conducted by a group of psychiatrists and researchers. They first observed and isolated age-related preoccupations of psychiatric outpatients in group therapy, and then checked their findings through a questionnaire study of a large sample of non-patients. The findings of both research groups are described and discussed below.

Daniel Levinson's evolving life structure

The work conducted by Daniel Levinson and his colleagues at Yale University (Levinson *et al.*, 1978) is directed at the general question: 'What does it mean to be an adult?' It comprises a multidisciplinary, in-depth study of forty men drawn from four different occupational groups (business executives, university biologists, industrial workers and novelists). When the sample was selected in 1969 the age range of the subjects was from 35 to 45 years. Data was collected primarily through what the researchers call 'biographical interviewing'. It was an approach to interviewing which aimed to combine aspects of the research and the clinical interview. Whilst certain topics had to be covered, the interviewer was sensitive to the feelings expressed by the interviewee and attempted to follow themes in a way that had meaning for him – following rather than leading him through them. Each man was seen between 5 and 10 times over a period of 2 or 3 months. Most interviews lasted between 1 and 2 hours. All interviews were tape-recorded and subsequently transcribed. This yielded an average of 300 pages of transcript for each man.

The pivotal concept in Levinson *et al.*'s (1978) work is that of the individual life structure – 'the underlying pattern or design of a person's life at a given time' (p. 41). The concept is used to explore 'the interrelations of self and world – to see how the self is in the world and the world is in the self' (p. 42). The life structure is considered from three perspectives: the individual's sociocultural world; the ways in which the person draws upon or ignores the self in everyday life; and the person's participation in the world, the transactions between self and world. Levinson *et al.* see the life structure as evolving through a series of alternating stable (structure-building) and transitional (structure-changing) phases which give an overall shape to the course of adult development – to 'the seasons of a man's life', to use the title of the book describing the research. Whilst each structure-changing period has features in common with all other transitional periods (and similarly with regard to the stable periods), each has specific tasks reflecting its place in the life cycle and distinguishing it from the other transitional and stable phases. Levinson *et al.* (1978) depict these various periods diagrammatically, as shown in figure 5.1. It is in some ways unfortunate that this diagram has become the most widely reproduced and widely known aspect of Levinson *et al.*'s work since it does little more than indicate the demarcations of the various seasons which, as the researchers are at pains to point out, are merely averages. Whilst acknowledging the existence of indi-

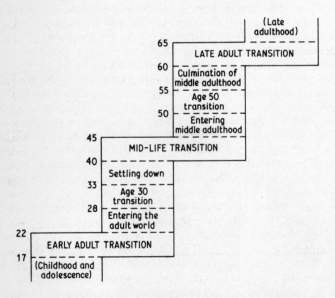

Figure 5.1 Developmental periods in early and middle adulthood (Levinson *et al.* 1978)

vidual differences with regard to the timing of the different stages the researchers also maintain that the variation is contained within fairly narrow limits – 'probably not more than five or six years' (Levinson *et al.*, 1978, p. 19).

The seasons of adulthood

The *early adult transition* (EAT) is a developmental bridge between the era of childhood and adolescence on the one hand, and of adulthood on the other. The sense of self that developed during pre-adulthood must be reappraised and modified. Separation is a key theme – separation from our pre-adult world, in particular from our family of origin. Outwardly it is denoted by such phenomena as increasing financial independence, moving out of the family home and entering new, more autonomous and responsible roles. Internally it involves increasing differentiation between self and parents, great psychological distance from the family, and reduced dependency on parental support and authority. A second theme is the forgeing of initial attachments to the adult world – exploring its possibilities, imagining oneself as a participant in it, and making and testing some preliminary identities and choices for living.

The next phase, that of *entering the adult World* (EAW), is a structure-building rather than a structure-changing phase. The tentative basis for adult life established during the EAT is tested, refined and consolidated. The overall goal is 'to fashion a provisional structure that provides a workable link between the valued self and the adult society' (Levinson *et al.*, 1978, p. 57). This goal is approached through work on two primary yet antithetical tasks. The first task is to explore possibilities. It requires that we keep options open, avoid strong commitments and maximize the alternatives. The second task is to create a stable life structure. In contrast to the first task this requires that we make choices and commitments. These are most likely to concern choice of occupation and/or spouse (see, also, Havighurst's (1972) developmental tasks). It also entails the development of life goals (see, here, the work of Bühler (Bühler and Massarik, 1968)) and the establishment of a more organized life. This task fulfills our desire for stability, order and roots. Levinson *et al.* maintain that whilst work on one of these two tasks may predominate, the other is never totally absent. If the emphasis is very strongly on the first task the young person's life will have a transient, rootless quality. If the second predominates the risk is that commitments are made on the basis of insufficient exploration of alternatives.

The *age thirty transition* (ATT) provides an opportunity to change our first life structure. We can work on its flaws and limitations. It is heralded by the sensation that life is losing its provisional quality and is becoming more serious. There is a feeling of time pressure – the belief that if we want to change our life we must do so now, for soon it will be too late. Levinson *et al.* found that whilst some of their subjects had a fairly smooth ATT most experienced some degree of crisis at the time. It tended to be a period of moderate or high stress.

During the *settling down* phase the second life structure which began to take shape at the end of the ATT is consolidated and built upon. The major goal 'is to "settle for" a few key choices, to create a broader structure around them, to invest oneself as fully as possible in the various components of the structure (such as work, family, community, solitary interests, friendships) and to pursue long-range plans and goals within it' (Levinson *et al.*, 1978, p. 139). As with the EAW phase, the period of settling down is characterized by two tasks which are potentially contradictory, although this is less marked than in the earlier instance. The first task is concerned with consolidation – with establishing one's niche in society. It entails a deepening of roots, an anchoring of oneself more firmly in one's family, occupation and/or community. The second task is concerned with advancement – with progression within the stable structure that is the fruit of labour performed on the first task. Levinson *et al.* use the imagery of the ladder (remember, also, Vaillant's (1977) stage of career consolidation) to describe this process. At the same time, however, they emphasize that they use the term 'advancement' in its broadest sense: 'building a better life, improving and using one's skills, becoming more creative, contributing to society and being affirmed by it, according to one's values' (Levinson *et al.*, 1978, p. 140).

A distinction is made between the earlier and the later parts of the settling down phase. The latter is dubbed the time of *becoming one's own man*, which reduces to the evocative acronym BOOM. It marks a period of special emphasis on the struggle to be more fully one's own person that is found at many ages. It concerns our desires and efforts to be more independent and self-sufficient, and less subject to the control of others. Levinson *et al.* also, however, see a contradiction here since the man (and all their subjects were male) seeks affirmation in society as well as freedom from its pressures and blandishments. It may become a time of severe conflict and difficulties. External circumstances may be restrictive and damaging to self-esteem. Particularly in the work situation people may feel constrained by organizational rigidity and by those who have territories to maintain and protect from the heir assumptive. At the same time the wish for advancement and affirmation may make the man particularly susceptible to social pressure. The individual distress will often take the form of feeling held back – 'of being oppressed by others and restrained by his own conflicts and inhibitions' (Levinson *et al.* 1978, p. 145). But Levinson *et al.* see the difficulties as lying deeper than that. They are confounded by the resurgence of unresolved pre-adult conflicts triggered by the effort involved in BOOM. This boy–man conflict is, however, seen as a step forward. It provides the opportunity to resolve the conflict more completely. In identifying this dynamic Levinson *et al.* are arguing along similar lines to Gould's (1978, 1980) analysis of adult development as the substitution of a childish with a more adult view of reality.

At around the age of 40 Levinson *et al.* see a new period getting under way. The concerns about not advancing sufficiently, or gaining too little affirmation, independence and seniority, which characterize the period of BOOM, give way to a different type of issue. This marks the onset of the *mid-life transition* (MLT). Levinson *et al.* identify three main tasks for this era. The first two are analogous to those of the other transitional phases – first, the termination of one life structure and, secondly, the initiation of another. The third task is unique to the mid-life period. It involves continuing the process of individuation began during the BOOM phase. As this occurs

> the person forms a clearer boundary between self and world. He forms a stronger sense of who he is and what he wants, and a more realistic, sophisticated view of the world: what it is like, what it offers him and demands from him. Greater

individuation allows him to be more separate from the world, to be more independent and self-generating. But it also gives him the confidence and understanding to have more intense attachments in the world and to feel more fully a part of it. (Levinson *et al.*, 1978, p. 195)

There are echoes here of the last two of Erikson's psychosocial crises. Levinson *et al.* make reference to these, to Jacques's (1965, 1980) emphasis on the issue of coming to terms with one's own mortality, and to Neugarten's (1965) identification of growing 'interiority' as a basic process of the mid-life period. Also acknowledged are the roots of many of these concepts in the work of Jung (1972), who placed the age of 40 at the meridian of his arc of life and saw the mid-life as marking the onset of a new effort at individuation.

By this stage Levinson *et al.*'s sample size is much reduced. The majority of their subjects had not yet reached the end of the mid-life transition. However, through follow-up interviews with most participants some two years after the initial contact, through further detailed interviews with four men chosen for more intensive study, and through casual and minor contacts with some of the other men, data were obtained on the lives, after the age of 45, of fifteen subjects aged between 42 and 45 at the beginning of the study. Thus, the evidence for the next stage, that of *entering middle adulthood* (EMA), is more sketchy than for earlier ones. The researchers were, however, able to pinpoint several of its features.

The distinction between the MLT and the stage of EMA is, again, the distinction between a structure-changing and a structure-building period. Thus, the MLT ends when, between two years either side of the age of 45, the individual reduces the amount of energy devoted to reappraising the past and attempting to reintegrate the polarities of the mid-life period. Instead, the main tasks become the making of crucial choices, giving these choices meaning and commitment, and building a life structure around them. Levinson *et al.* found that sometimes a man was able to slip fairly readily into the last two of these tasks, but that almost always the choices themselves proved a major difficulty. Generally the research participants needed most of the EMA period to establish the choices on which to build the new life structure.

During the MLT, having reappraised the past, the man may, as he enters middle adulthood, make several significant moves to detach himself from his previous life structure. Marital separation, job resignation, termination of significant personal relationships, and home relocation are all examples cited by Levinson *et al.* of how a man might enact such detachment. Such choices 'create a space within which he may succeed in improving his life, but he may find himself temporarily – and unhappily – suspended within this space until he can go on to make some positive choices and start the restructuring' (Levinson *et al.*, 1978, p. 279). The restructuring process itself comprises many steps and can be beset with many setbacks. Options must be determined and explored. Preliminary choices must be made, implemented and evaluated. Some may not work out and may have to be abandoned – sending the man back to the drawing board, as it were.

The EMA period continues so long as the individual's predominant task remains the building of a satisfactory life structure. Irrespective of whether this goal has been successfully achieved, the phase ends when attention shifts from structure-building to a new transition. Levinson *et al.* label this next phase the *age fifty transition* although their sample has not yet reached the age when they can provide data to flesh out its characteristics. Likewise, whilst Levinson *et al.* include periods entitled the *culmination of middle adulthood* and the *late adult transition* in their schema of developmental periods (see figure 5.1), they do not yet have sufficient empirical evidence to discuss them in detail. None the less, they are confident that whilst each of these periods will have its distinguishing features, it will also demonstrate, as appropriate, the general characteristics of a structure-building or a structure-changing phase.

Levinson *et al.* (1978) can, on the data they had available, take their analysis of the specific characteristics of the different eras of life no further. They define the function of their concept of eras as providing 'a contour map, as it were, within which to examine the terrain of early and middle adulthood and to specify the developmental tasks that must be met' (p. 330). As well as this, however, they identify three more general sets of tasks which characterize the whole of adult development or, at least, traverse several different eras. The first of these, building and modifying a life structure, has provided the framework for the discussion so far. The other two are discussed below. Working on single components of the life structure is the set of developmental tasks particularly representative of early adulthood. Developmental tasks associated with becoming more individuated are symptomatic of middle life.

The developmental tasks of early adulthood

The specific content or concerns of Levinson *et al.*'s eras are enshrined in the various, and usually contradictory, developmental tasks which they identify as characterizing each period. The different periods are not, however, presented as totally separate entities. Thus, the period from the onset of the early adult transition to the end of the age thirty transition is described as the novice phase of adulthood. Levinson *et al.* identify common tasks which run through the whole of the novice phase and which are essential to the process of entry into adulthood. Since work on a task is uneven rather than steady, and is not necessarily synchronized with work on other tasks, it is through analysis of developmental tasks that the flavour of a particular life is captured.

The four tasks distinguishing the novice phase of adulthood are: forming a 'Dream' and giving it a place in the life structure; forming mentor relationships; forming an occupation; and forming love relationships, a marriage and a family. In addition Levinson *et al.* identified a fifth task, forming mutual friendships, which was notable for its absence from the life work of their participants. Each of these developmental tasks is now briefly considered.

1 *Forming and living out 'the Dream'.* An individual's life course is strongly influenced by factors such as family, class, subculture and social institutions. It is also affected by attributes of the individual – such things as values, abilities, efforts, anxieties and goals. Levinson *et al.* identified another factor that was crucial in early adulthood – 'the Dream'. A key developmental task of early adulthood is to give the Dream a clearer definition and to find ways of living it out.

> In its primordial form, the Dream is a vague sense of self-in-adult-world. It has the quality of a vision, an imagined possibility that generates excitement and vitality. At the start it is poorly articulated and only tenuously connected to reality, although it

may contain concrete images such as winning the Nobel Prize or making the all-star team. It may take a dramatic form as in the myth of the hero: the great artist, business tycoon, athletic or intellectual superstar performing magnificent feats and receiving special honors. It may take mundane forms that are yet inspiring and sustaining: the excellent craftsman, the husband-father in a certain kind of family, the highly respected member of one's community. (Levinson *et al.*, 1978, p. 91)

Implicit in the notion of a developmental task is the idea that it can be performed either well or poorly. If young people are unable to accommodate their Dream into the initial adult life structure to at least some extent then the Dream may fade and die, and with it the person's sense of vitality and purpose. Levinson *et al.* found that many of their subjects experienced a conflict between a life direction in which their Dream could find expression and another which was quite different. Pressure may come from parents, for example, or from external constraints such as lack of money or opportunities. Personal characteristics of the individual – for example, competitiveness, lack of confidence or special abilities which suggest a life course incompatible with the Dream – may also hinder its implementation. Levinson *et al.* argue that those who build an initial adult life structure around their Dream have a better chance of attaining personal fulfilment. Those whose life structure is a betrayal of their Dream 'will have to deal later with the consequences' (Levinson *et al.*, 1978, p. 92).

2 *Forming mentor relationships.* Levinson *et al.* describe an effective mentoring relationship as one of the most complex and developmentally important relationships a person can have in early adulthood. They also conclude that most men receive less than perfect mentoring and that the situation for women is probably worse still. The mentor, where there is one, is generally 8–15 years – that is, half a generation – older than the protégé. This is not always the case, but with a greater age gap the likelihood is that the older person will represent a parental rather than a mentoring figure. It is likely that someone who is closer to the same age as the protégé will not be perceived as a person of greater relevant experience and seniority, or as a responsible and admired older sibling – both of which are key features of a mentor.

When available, a mentor may perform a range of functions for a protégé. These include being a teacher and, thereby, enhancing the young person's skills and intellectual development; serving as a sponsor who, through the use of influence, facilitates the young person's entry and advancement; welcoming, as a host and guide, the initiate into a new occupational and social world, and providing an entrée to its values, customs, resources and members. Through the evidence of personal virtues, achievements and life style a mentor may be an exemplar and role model. Direct assistance may be proffered in the form of counsel and moral support in times of stress. Developmentally, according to Levinson *et al.*, the most important function of the mentor is to support and facilitate the realization of the protégé's Dream – believing in the young person, sharing in and giving blessing to the youthful Dream, helping in the definition of the newly emerging self in its newly discovered world, and creating a space for the young person to work towards establishing a reasonably satisfactory life structure in which the Dream has a place.

Levinson *et al.* argue that, by its very nature, a good mentoring relationship is a temporary phenomenon. At least in the medium term, it is not perceived as totally satisfactory. A mentor who was a permanent figure would be confirming the younger person to a position of immaturity rather than facilitating the protégé's move towards maturity. Ideal mentors, in effect, do themselves out of a job. A relationship between mentor and protégé may remain, but it must change if it is to continue to facilitate the development of both parties. A peer relationship is 'the ultimate (though never fully realized) goal of the relationship' (Levinson *et al.*, 1978, p. 99).

3 *Forming an occupation.* Levinson *et al.* make a useful and important distinction between the concept of choosing an occupation and forming an occupation. The latter constitutes a recognition that career choice is more than a once-and-for-all decision; rather it is 'a complex, social-psychological process that extends over the entire novice phase and often beyond' (Levinson *et al.*, 1978, p. 101). No matter how definite the first career choice seems to be Levinson *et al.* found that it usually turned out to represent only a preliminary definition of interests and values. A strong occupational commitment made in the early 20s without sufficient exploration of all possible options or of personal preferences is often regretted later. On the other hand, a young person

may struggle for years to transform interests into occupation. The sequence of occupational formation is frequently not the steady, single-track progression that it is often assumed to be. However, if a firm commitment is never made, or perhaps not made until the late 30s, then the individual is deprived of what Levinson *et al.* describe as the satisfaction of engaging in enduring work that is suitable for the self and valuable for society.

4 *Forming love relationships, a marriage and a family.* Levinson *et al.* emphasize that, as with the task of forming an occupation, the task of forming a marriage and family is an extended process which continues through the novice period and often much longer. It is a process which begins long before and continues long after the marker events of marriage and the birth of a first child. First a man must develop the capability of having adult peer relationships with women. Levinson *et al.* recognize that a man's love relationships with women may take many forms and fulfil many functions. They argue that the ideal relationship for fostering his development is one where the woman is able to support and animate his Dream, if necessary allowing him to project onto her his own feminine side. When this occurs the man's Dream often serves as a vehicle for defining the woman's pursuits as well. 'The big challenge for her comes in the thirties and forties: her husband and children need her less and offer her less, and she must then form a more distinctive identity of her own' (Levinson *et al.*, 1978, p. 110). The roles of husband and father may be best fulfilled if the man is allowed and able to live out both the masculine and the feminine sides of himself. The achievement of this may well be one of the crucial tasks of the mid-life period.

Although Levinson *et al.*'s attitude to the marital relationship appears chauvinistic, relegating the wife to the role of supporter of the husband's Dream, they do make the point that the couple can only form a lasting relationship if it furthers the woman's development as well as the man's. They argue that if the woman's Dream involves an identity more distinct than one based on the roles of wife and mother, then to build a life structure that contains both persons' Dream is a heroic task – 'and one for which evolution and history have ill prepared us' (Levinson *et al.*, 1978, p. 110).

5 *Forming mutual friendships.* Levinson *et al.* found their subjects, in adulthood, to have few intimate male friends of the kind they recalled fondly from their childhood and youth. Nor did they

seem to develop intimate nonsexual relationships with women. None the less the researchers considered friendship to be a valuable attribute of adulthood. They wondered as to the reasons for its rarity and expressed concern as to the consequences of its absence from adult life.

The tasks associated with working on different single components of the life structure, and typifying the early years of adulthood, continue to demand and receive attention during the middle years. However, they become, argue Levinson *et al.*, subordinate to another set of concerns – those associated with the process of becoming more individuated.

The component parts of mid-life individuation

Levinson *et al.*'s third and final set of developmental tasks relates to individuation – already discussed as a distinguishing feature of the mid-life transition. They see it as being addressed through the confrontation and reintegration of four polarities concerned with: young/old; destruction/creation; masculine/feminine; and attachment/separateness. These are each considered below.

1 *Young/Old – the major polarity*. We think of children as young and of the elderly as old. And yet these concepts are only tangentially related to chronological age. At every point in our life we are both young and old. The 3-year-old is 'too old' to have a dummy. The 59-year-old is 'too young' to have a Senior Citizen's travel pass. Levinson *et al.* describe the separation and reintegration of the young and old within us as the major polarity to be resolved during human development. It is an inherent part of every transitional period. And yet during the mid-life period there is an added dimension since then this recurring dynamic coincides with the chronological middle of the life course. The young/old polarity is experienced with special force. The man feels that 'the Young – variously represented as the child, the adolescent and the youthful adult in himself – is dying. The imagery of old age and death hangs over him like a pall' (Levinson *et al.*, 1978, p. 213). The beginning of physical decline documented in chapter 3 intensifies this sense of losing touch with one's youth. Responsibility for our ageing and dying parents adds further force for, once they are gone, it is our turn next. At work we are no longer 'up and coming' – that term is now applied to those

who joined after us. These indicators of our own mortality are so painful to bear, maintain Levinson *et al.* (1978), because of our wish for immortality – 'one of the strongest and least malleable of human motives' (p. 215).

In order to resolve the young/old polarity during the mid-life Levinson *et al.* (1978) argue that a 'man must begin to grieve and accept the symbolic death of the youthful hero within himself' (p. 215) and discover 'how he might be a hero of a different kind in the context of middle adulthood' (p. 215). This requires that the man relinquish his illusion of immortality – something that can be achieved during the mid-life transition provided his development has not already been too impaired. The challenge is to develop a wiser and more mature middle-aged self that is 'still connected to the youthful sources of energy, imagination and daring' (p. 217). Awareness of personal mortality becomes less devastating as it is placed in the context of human generational continuity. From a firmer sense of individuality concern can turn outward from the self towards the generations that will follow: 'Slowly the omnipotent Young hero recedes, and in his place emerges a middle-aged man with more knowledge of his limitations as well as greater real power and authority' (p. 218).

2 *The Destruction/Creation polarity.* Growing realization of our own mortality heightens our awareness of destruction as a universal process. This recognition intensifies the wish to be creative – 'to bring something into being, to give birth, to generate life' (Levinson *et al.*, 1978, p. 222). One aspect of the mid-life task is to find an appropriate outlet for this creative urge. As with the young/old polarity both sides of the destruction/creation polarity are particularly salient and evident during the mid-life period. We become aware of what has been sacrificed or destroyed as we strove to create the life structures of early adulthood – what we ourselves have hurt or destroyed and, in turn what, or who, has been destructive of us. Another component of the mid-life task is, therefore, to come to terms with our guilt concerning our destructiveness towards others and our rage concerning their destructiveness towards us.

3 *The Masculine/Feminine polarity.* In our society, as in most, there has traditionally been a splitting along gender lines such that men are 'masculine' and women are 'feminine'. Whilst the social pressures to maintain such a distinction may now have diminished

somewhat, they are still significant. During early adulthood men are likely to have emphasized their masculine side and women their feminine. Levinson *et al.* see redressing this balance as an important part of the mid-life task. With regard to masculinity this entails resolving feelings concerning such issues as achievement and ambition, toughness and physical prowess, power and manliness. With regard to femininity the issues may revolve around questions of sensitivity, nurturance, emotionality, weakness and, for men, homosexuality. Whilst the struggles to resolve its conflicts typically meet with mixed success, the self-acceptance that both results from and is instrumental in causing one to face such contradictions within oneself is a sound basis for developing a more highly integrated personality or life structure.

4 *The Attachment/Separateness polarity.* Levinson *et al.* use the term 'attachment' broadly, to include all the forces that connect a person to his or her environment. These may be positive forces – interest, love, excitement; or negative forces – hate, confusion, fear. 'Separateness', which must be clearly distinguished from isolation or aloneness, prevails when we are primarily involved in our inner world of imagination and fantasy. Attachment is the mechanism through which we meet our needs to be engaged, involved and rooted. Separateness fosters creativity and individual growth.

During childhood the forces of attachment must be channelled in a way that enables the individual to operate in society. The forces of imagination and fantasy – of separateness – must also, however, be allowed a place since they are the routes through which creativity is nourished, individuality is sustained, and the Dream is formulated. During early adulthood, Levinson *et al.* argue, separateness is normally sacrificed in the interests of attachment. Forming a family and an occupation, struggling with external pressures and demands, fulfilling the wish to establish a niche in society, all serve to push separateness into second place. The mid-life period offers an opportunity to redress the balance. Indeed, successful resolution of the mid-life transition requires such a reparation. The reappraisal of self and reformulation of goals that characterize the era require the person to look inward 'to discover what his turmoil is about, and where it hurts' (Levinson *et al.*, 1978, p. 241). Finding a satisfactory new balance between attachment and separateness provides for the individual a better balance between the needs of the self and the needs of society. One is not sacrificed for the other.

Again Levinson *et al.*'s data fade at this point. Their subjects tended to be embarking on rather than established in the era of middle adulthood. We might conjecture about developmental tasks, but empirical evidence, at least from Levinson *et al.*'s study, is sparse. Attention now turns, therefore, to the work of Roger Gould – the second of the contemporary researchers whose ideas and propositions are considered in the present chapter. Whereas the individual life structure was the organizing concept employed by Levinson *et al.*, Gould's stages of adult development revolve around the gradual development of an adult consciousness which is grounded in reality rather than illusion.

Roger Gould's evolution of adult consciousness

Whilst Levinson and his colleagues at Yale were developing their account of adult development, Roger Gould, another researcher, was doing likewise on the other side of America – at the University of California, Los Angeles. Gould and his co-researchers initially observed patterns emerging from the life stories of psychiatric patients and subsequently tested their hypotheses in a question-naire study of more than 500 'non-patients' between the ages of 16 and 50 years (Gould, 1978).

Gould (1980) indexes adult development against the indi-vidual's changing sense of time. Until we leave our family of origin at around the age of 18 we are protected by our parents. However, we are also constrained by them, never quite believing that we will escape from our family world. Gould (1980) describes this experi-ence as, in a sense, like being in a timeless capsule: 'The future is a fantasy space that may possibly not exist' (p. 35). During the process described by Levinson as separation from parents Gould argues that we begin to glimpse an endless future. We see an infinite amount of time ahead of us provided – and this is our fear – that we are not suddenly snatched back into the restricted world of our childhood. Once into our 20s we are more confident that we have separated from our family of origin but, to incorporate Levinson's terminology again, we have not yet formed a coherent early-adult life structure:

Because of all the new decisions and novel experiences that come with setting up new adult enterprises, our time sense, when we're being successful, is one of movement along a chosen path that leads linearly to some obscure prize decades in the future. There is plenty of time, but we're still in a hurry once we've developed a clearer, often stereotyped, picture of where we want to be by then. (Gould, 1980, p. 56)

By the end of our 20s our sense of time incorporates our adult past as well as our future. We begin to become aware that our future is not infinite and our pathway is not linear – we must choose between different branches because there is not time to take them all. The sense of urgency that time is running out, which Levinson attributes to the age thirty transition, is ascribed by Gould to the decade between the mid-30s and the mid-40s. It is combined with an emotional awareness of our own mortality – a regularly cited characteristic of the mid-life transition (Jacques, 1965, 1980; Levinson *et al.*, 1978). Once attained, this awareness of our own death is never far from consciousness: 'How time is spent becomes a matter of great importance' (Gould, 1980, p. 56).

For Gould the thrust of adult development is towards a realization and acceptance of ourselves as creators of our own lives and away from the assumption that the rules and standards of childhood determine our destiny. Thus, whilst Levinson talks of the evolving life structure, Gould (1978) talks about 'the evolution of adult consciousness as we release ourselves from the constraints and ties of childhood consciousness' (p. 15). He envisages our childhood consciousness existing alongside our rational, adult view of reality. On the one hand this link with our past supports and stabilizes us, but on the other hand it also interferes with and constrains our life. Adulthood is a dynamic and changing time during which we can and must release ourselves from arbitrary internal constraints if we are to have an unfolding, creative life. These internal constraints originated as the internal standards of childhood which were instilled in us at home and school. They represent the values and assumptions of our parents and their contemporaries and must be replaced by values and assumptions more truly our own.

This process of growth or transformation occurs as we correct the false assumptions we have lived by up until then and which have restricted and restrained us unnecessarily. These false assumptions bolster the individual's illusion of safety – 'a fixture of childhood encompassing belief in omnipotent thought, omnipotent protective parents, the absoluteness of parental rules and world view, and a whole system of defenses as controlling structures against a rage reaction to separation' (Gould, 1980, p. 65).

Between the ages of 18 and 50 years the four major false assumptions which maintain this illusion surface, are challenged and are found wanting. This process can, like Levinson's model of adult development, be presented as a series of age-related stages. This time the stages are associated with the challenging of one particular false assumption as is outlined (Gould, 1978, 1980) and summarized in table 5.1.

Assumption 1: 'I will always belong to my parents and believe in their world.' (Late teens, early 20s)

This assumption is challenged as we leave home to go to college, to go to work or to get married. As with Levinson's developmental tasks the experience is profoundly contradictory. It mirrors the dynamics of Erikson's psychosocial crises – on the one hand the wish to advance and progress, and on the other hand the desire to remain in or retreat to an earlier, less threatening mode of living.

Gould identifies five components of this first major false assumption around which the characteristic conflicts of late adolescence coalesce:

(i) *'If I get any more independent, it'll be a disaster.'* This component encapsulates the fear of being unable to cope with the new-found separation from parents, the anxiety lest our newly independent selves will not be loved by misunderstanding parents and envious friends, and/or the concern lest our parents' relationship will not survive the loss of their special child.

(ii) *'I can only see the world through my parents' assumptions.'* This component contains the fear of risking being different from one's primary reference group – the family. However, the myth of family one-mindedness must be challenged if the young person is to escape what Gould describes as its powerful and constraining dynamics.

(iii) *'Only they can guarantee my safety.'* Whilst wishing to become independent the young person is either concerned lest he or she is

Table 5.1 False assumptions challenged during adulthood (Gould, 1978, 1980)

Age	False assumption and component parts
Late teens, early 20s	I will always belong to my parents and believe in their world. * If I get any more independent it'll be a disaster. * I can only see the world through my parents' assumptions. * Only they can guarantee my safety. * They must be my only family. * I don't own my body.
20s	Doing it their way with will power and perseverance will probably bring results. But when I become too frustrated, confused, or tired, or am simply unable to cope, they will step in and show me the way. * Rewards will come automatically if we do what we are supposed to do. * There is only one right way to do things. * My loved ones are able to do for me what I haven't been able to do for myself. * Rationality, commitment, and effort will always prevail over all other forces.
Late 20s, early 30s	Life is simple and controllable. There are no significant coexisting, contradictory forces within me. * What I know intellectually, I know emotionally. * I am not like my parents in ways I don't want to be. * I can see the reality of those close to me quite clearly. * Threats to my security aren't real.
35–50	There is no evil in me or death in the world. The sinister has been expelled. * My work (for men) or my relationship with men (for women) grant me immunity from death and danger. * There is no life beyond this family. * I am innocent.

unable to match the ostensibly absolute safety provided in childhood by parents, or else takes excessive risks in the seeming assumption of absolute invulnerability. In either case the lesson to be learned is that the impression we gained as children of our parents being able to provide absolute safety was an illusion.

(iv) *'They must be my only family.'* To challenge this myth we must cope with the conflicts of loyalty experienced when friends become as important or more important to us than our parents.

(v) *'I don't own my body.'* It is mainly when we choose to engage in sexual relations that this component of the false assumption is contradicted. Allowing ourselves physical pleasure is a statement of our ownership of our own body.

Assumption 2: 'Doing it their way with will power and perseverance will probably bring results. But when I become too frustrated, confused, or tired, or am simply unable to cope, they will step in and show me the way.' (The 20s)

During this period, which Gould calls the apprenticeship period of life, we experience some confirmation of this false assumption. We are often required to do things in the socially accepted way, even if we disagree with it, in order to be accepted at our work place. However, the important choices that must be made in order to establish our own life structure during our 20s do none the less provide us with experiences sufficiently powerful to challenge its validity. Gould (1980) identifies four component parts of this major false assumption – 'each causing a specific warp in our thinking and relating' (p. 68).

(i) *'Rewards will come automatically if we do what we are supposed to do.'* At the centre of this assumption is the belief that life is just and fair and that it operates an automatic payoff system. It engenders excessive expectations about life which are bound to be disappointed. Amongst those people likely to hold to this false assumption most forcibly are those who have had a particularly successful, privileged and easy childhood, and also those who have always kept to the rules – 'overconforming in order to receive rewards' (Gould, 1980, p. 69).

(ii) *'There is only one right way to do things.'* This assumption is challenged as the infallibility of our parents' way is questioned. We are reluctant to relinquish our attachment to it, however, because in so doing we relinquish the childish hope that, even though it may also be a prison, if we find their one right way 'we've found a magic key to the complex processes of reality and can guarantee our future against the terror of the unknown' (Gould, 1980, p. 69). Between what Gould calls the grinding wheels of current social expectations that we be a different kind of person and an internal imperative to be exactly like our parents we must forge a self-definition that is nobody else's 'only right way'. In so doing we may be unreasonably hard on ourselves and intolerant of others.

(iii) *'My loved ones are able to do for me what I haven't been able to do for myself.'* Termed by Gould the 'cure by love' fallacy, this assumption leads to dependency on others (for those competencies we feel to be lacking in ourselves) and to perceived power over others (with regard to those competencies we see ourselves as providing for them). To the degree that the cure-by-love myth is shared by both partners in an intimate relationship they will erect mutual conspiracies, feeling (and being seen as) superior to their partner on some issues, and inferior on others.

(iv) *'Rationality, commitment, and effort will always prevail over all other forces.'* Gould sees this final component assumption as a very cherished belief since if it were true we would be totally in control of our destiny. It must, however, be challenged if we are not to ignore the role of that which is irrational. This assumption is contradicted most forcibly in the experiences of intimacy and of power relationships such as those between employer and employee or parent and child. Dynamics set in motion largely by the invocation of the cure-by-love myth 'are unrelated to the rationally committed partnership tasks of the relationship and can't be totally understood on a conscious level' (Gould, 1980, p. 71).

During the 20s certain false assumptions must remain unchallenged if we are to fulfil the basic task of that era: becoming sufficiently independent of our parents to set up our own self-determined life structure. It is only when we reach what Gould describes as a new platform of strength at the threshold of the 30s that we are ready to handle the negation of the third major false assumption.

Assumption 3: '*Life is simple and controllable. There are no significant coexisting, contradictory forces within me.*' *(Late 20s, early 30s)*

The tasks of the 20s require us to look outwards. They are concerned with developing competency in roles beyond those defined by our family of origin. Having succeeded in this to at least some extent, we can return to our inner selves and confront aspects of ourselves that were suppressed or shelved. It is a confrontation which 'is ushered in with disillusionment, confusion about what life is all about, or a depression' (Gould, 1980, p. 72). Gould identifies four subcomponents in the major false assumption that is challenged by this self-confrontation. The payoff for working through it is a new, more direct way of dealing with reality.

(i) '*What I know intellectually, I know emotionally.*' In the return to our inner selves at this time emotions which may have been held at bay during the 20s are allowed to surface. We extend our emotional knowledge and learn how it is different from intellectual knowledge. To the extent that we can face our emotions we need no longer fear them – we 'come to see that a bit of sadness today is not the same as the endless pool of childhood sadness' (Gould, 1980, p. 72). Awareness and knowledge of our own inner complexity leaves us more self-tolerant and tolerant of others. This opening-up phase draws to our attention the limits and disadvantages of our career–family situation to date – what has been missing and what sacrifices we have made.

(ii) '*I am not like my parents in ways I don't want to be.*' Whilst struggling to maintain the illusion during our 20s of the possibility of complete independence from parental influence it was too threatening to admit to being like them in ways we did not want to be. During the 30s we must acknowledge these similarities if we are to avoid 'blind repetition of their patterns' (Gould, 1980, p. 73). Most frequently this false assumption is contradicted by our experiences of child-rearing. We find ourselves reproducing in our own parental behaviour aspects of our own parents' treatment of us which we most disliked. Unless this can be faced we 'pass on the problem to our children who have to live with our conscious repudiation and our unconscious repetition' (Gould, 1980, p. 73). Recognition of similarities between ourselves and our parents enables us to choose how to allow pertinent characteristics to be expressed – as methodical rather than rigid, as caring rather than smothering, or as self-confident rather than arrogant, for example.

(iii) *'I can see the reality of those close to me quite clearly.'* Gould sees this component of the third major false assumption being challenged primarily through the questioning of marital conspiracies formed during the 20s. Such questioning is essential for the occurrence and confirmation of a significant change in self-definition. We must recognize that what was a 'true' picture of us and of our partner is no longer the whole truth. This process of confrontation and acceptance of our own and our partner's new selves may be accompanied by high levels of marital tension.

(iv) *'Threats to my security aren't real.'* Gould lists a number of very real threats to our security that may occur during this opening-up period: career change; seeking either more intimacy or more space; returning to school; seeking more fun or bodily pleasure; settling down; having a baby; ceasing to be a baby; ceasing to fight parents when we need not; or starting to fight parents when we must. The most profound threat to our security is if we consider breaking up our marriage, especially if there are children. 'The critical issue to decide is whether the apparent enemy, the spouse, is really an enemy to our growth or a projection of our internal prohibitor' (Gould, 1980, p. 74). Gould argues that many marriages are unnecessarily dissolved when we fail to make this discrimination, and erroneously assume that our feelings of being powerless and mistreated are necessarily the other's fault.

Assumption 4: 'There is no evil in me or death in the world. The sinister has been expelled.' (35–50)

Gould describes the mid-life period between 35 and 50 years as ending the illusion of absolute safety. It is denoted by three central 'subjective shifts'. First, we discover that we are no longer young. As children begin to leave home, and the relationship with our parents, if they are still alive, begins to undergo a subtle role reversal (with their depending on us rather than vice versa), we can no longer sustain a self-image based on the conception of ourselves as young. Secondly, we question again the values, life style and life structures that we had been pursuing with full commitment. We return with the benefit of 'a ripe and mature mind' (Gould, 1980, p. 77) to the questions that we first asked and answered during late adolescence. The third subjective shift is a sense of time urgency – 'a vague but implacable sense that it is becoming time to act in some definitive and important, and therefore dangerous, way' (Gould, 1980, p. 77).

As with previous major false assumptions Gould identifies a number of component parts. He sees them as applicable to those currently in the mid-life period, but raises the question of historical and generational change when he suggests that the specific pillars propping up this assumption may possibly change for subsequent cohorts.

(i) *'My work (for men) or my relationship with men (for women) grant me immunity from death and danger.'* For men this false idea tends to take the form, 'Death can't happen to me', and for women the form 'It's impossible to live without a protector in life'. Gould (1980) describes the immunity pact many men seem to have with their work. It is a delusion that 'if we are successful we will never feel like small helpless little boys again, and the prospect of our death is banished' (p. 77). It is the delusion that success will solve all our problems. Awareness of mortality seems to weaken this pact, and as this happens the costs of our illusion of immunity become apparent. The costs are in terms of constrictions to our humanity and authenticity. This awareness can either be denied by working harder than ever before, or else it can be accepted and the challenge of finding a new balance between self and work can be undertaken. Gould describes the issue as one of deadness v. aliveness. It embodies a drive towards authenticity. 'The dams we've erected against the feared reentry of a vital passion come crumbling down, not because there's a new biological surge of instincts, but because the deterred imperative of wholeness and deep self-knowledge can wait no longer' (Gould, 1980, p. 80).

Women in the mid-life period are, like men, seeking an authenticity and wholeness that has been lacking in their lives to date. Whilst their biological role as child-bearers keeps them in touch with their own mortality, the awareness of its relevance to their own lives operates as a spur to act each on her own behalf. Whereas men's immunity pact is traditionally with work, women's has traditionally concerned their relationship with men. Whereas man's immunity pact provides them with the illusion that they can be protected from death, women's false assumption is that it is impossible to live without a man to guide them. As long as this false assumption is believed women cannot expand themselves beyond that which their protector (normally their husband) condones and supports. To do so would be to risk losing his protection. Thinking which is organized by this idea is dichotomized in that the only alternative to surrendering to a man is felt to be the total relinquishment of all intimate relationships with men and, instead, becoming one's own protector. To marry is then seen as automatically to lose one's autonomy. Whilst the women's movement propounds the falsity of this assumption, 'each woman must carry out her own transformation on the deeply embedded and often cleverly disguised version of this false idea' (Gould, 1980, p. 82).

For both men and women the rewards of dispelling their respective versions of this component of the major false assumption is androgyny – the acknowledged coexistence within the same individual of both positive masculine-stereotyped and positive feminine-stereotyped attributes.

(ii) *'There is no life beyond this family.'*   In our teens and 20s we have to dispel the myth that we must always belong to our family of origin. In mid-life we must challenge the assumption that separation and divorce are not possible – that is, 'that there is no life beyond our current husband or wife' (Gould, 1980, p. 83). If we do not challenge this belief then there is no room for the marital relationship to develop and change. Change is achieved under this false assumption not by negotiation, but by one partner 'leading the way and dragging the other' (Gould, 1980, p. 83). When the assumption is challenged there is an injection of energy into the marriage. An opportunity is created for a more satisfactory resolution of issues relating to such matters as the couple's sexual relationship, their roles within the family, and the degree of difference and aloneness that is acceptable. The risk is that irreconcilable differences and incompatibilities will emerge and the marriage will end in divorce, or will continue but be characterized by chronic hostility.

(iii) *'I am innocent.'*   This component of the false assumption is a defence against 'our deep demonic childhood badness' which we came to believe in through the experiences of infancy. To be expunged these experiences must be relabelled from the perspective of adult rather than childhood consciousness. This is often achieved by re-analysing feelings of inadequacy and finding them to reflect an overly moral labelling of what Gould refers to as vital passions, rather than inadequacy *per se*. We must relabel our inner processes so that 'we no longer interpret dissatisfaction as greed, self-concern as selfishness, sensuality as lasciviousness, pleasure as irresponsibility, curiosity as something forbidden, anger as destructiveness, love as weakness, imperfection as a fault, change as danger, or wicked thoughts as the same as wicked actions' (Gould, 1980, p. 85). This process frees us to be vital and alive, living our life freely and joyfully. It is a process of working through negative self-images.

Life after 50

Gould argues that through our negation of the four major false assumptions of our childhood consciousness we make the transition from the belief that 'I am theirs' to the recognition that 'I own myself'. With this awareness we are finally able to escape from the struggle for status. We are free to acknowledge what Gould calls our mysterious, indelible 'me' as the core of the rest of our life. This does not mean there is no more disappointment, ill health or pain to bear. It does, however, mean that those who have made contact with this inner core can face such experiences with greater strength. Their sense of meaning resides within them and it cannot be removed by misfortune. This does not happen to everyone. Old people who have not made this contact with their inner core have no recourse against the feeling that they are losing the battle with life. Finding no meaning in their own life, they attack life itself as meaningless. They have lost Erikson's struggle between integrity and despair.

Summary: recurring themes of adulthood

Many links and consistence can be identified in the accounts of adult life recounted in this and earlier chapters. For example, in Levinson *et al.*'s phases of the early adult transition and entering the adult world are tasks also located within Erikson's identity crisis – notably issues of sexual and occupational identity. Havighurst also makes reference to these tasks and, in addition identifies the development of a personal ideology as one of the developmental tasks of adolescence. For Erikson, a society's ideology is the social manifestation of the identity v. role confusion crisis. The struggles of this time can also, as argued by Gould, be seen as a challenging of the false assumption that we will always belong to our parents and believe in their world.

In Levinson *et al.*'s settling-down period (between approximately 33 and 40 years of age) there are echoes of Bühler's identification of these years as the phase of a more specified and definite self-determination of life goals. This is also consistent with Vaillant's identification of the 30s as a decade of career consolidation. Gould's analysis of the late 20s and early 30s places more emphasis on internal rather than external issues (reminiscent of Levinson *et al.*'s age thirty transition), and, with a phase beginning in the mid-30s, he goes on to discuss issues Levinson *et al.* place within the mid-life transition.

Erikson's final stage of integrity is compatible with Gould's definition of adult consciousness as the recognition that 'I own myself'. Erikson's conception of integrity as being in conflict with the antithetical outcomes of despair and disgust is consistent with Bühler's self-determination model in that both contain the concept of later life as potentially a time of continued growth and development, but with the risk of constriction and decline. Bühler uses the terms fulfilment, failure and resignation to describe the possibilities of this stage. Likewise, Havighurst's list of developmental tasks for this period contains items concerned with coming to terms with the (virtually) inevitable losses (both physical and interpersonal) of old age, and the promotion of what could, after Erikson, be called integrity rather than despair.

Links can also be made at the level of overall models rather than specific life stages. Thus, the epigenetic principle – with particular crises, tasks or preoccupations having their time of special ascendency – is found to a greater or lesser extent in all stage- or sequence-based accounts of the life course. More specifically, the notion of antithetical tasks, demands or pulls underlies the stages in both Erikson's and Levinson *et al.*'s schemas. Similarly, Bühler's expansion–restriction model is echoed in Super's life-career rainbow in that typically the number of roles occupied by an individual follows a similar trajectory – increasing, reaching a peak and then decreasing.

With regard to the end states, pinnacles or goals of development, Bühler, like Maslow, sees self-actualization, or self-fulfilment, as the pinnacle of development. Gould's adult consciousness and Erikson's integrated and wise individual also incorporate this theme. Likewise, the final stage of moral development – be it based on Kohlberg's ethic of justice or Gilligan's ethic of care – includes the global perspective that characterizes all definitions of the mature or fully developed person (cf. the examples of both Maslow and Allport). Similarly, Schaie labels the final stage of cognitive development as the reintegrative phase, and Riegel talks of mature thought incorporating a new apprehension of contradictions.

Taking a more global perspective, a number of general themes of adulthood can be identified (see, for example, Michels, 1980; Neugarten, 1977). Thus, the individual's orientation towards and perspective on time recurs and changes throughout the adult years. The relationship between oneself and significant others must regularly be addressed and adjusted. So, too, the individual's place in and responsibilities towards his or her social world and wider society must be considered and renegotiated. Successive changes and events must be incorporated into one's self-concept and sense of identity – events relating to the recurring themes of love and work: marriage, parenthood, career, retirement, and so on; and also events relating to our physical selves: indicators of physical peaks and declines, illness and death.

There is, however, another side to adult identity and maturity. In the midst of an emphasis on change and its management as a theme of adulthood we need also to ask about stability, coherence and wholeness. For definitions of maturity and adulthood incorporate a sense of integration and harmony as well as an ability to confront and handle change. Levinson et al.'s concept of the life structure captures the notion of what might be termed 'cross-sectional coherence' – that is, coherence at a particular point in time. 'Longitudinal coherence', by contrast, is captured in Cohler's (1982) concept of the personal narrative. Starting from the view that the life course is inherently unpredictable (that is, adopting Gergen's (1977, 1980) aleatory–change orientation to development), Cohler suggests that in order to maintain the coherent sense of consistent identity necessary for continued mental health, the individual weaves disparate experiences into a comprehensible story or personal narrative. This relates to the most complex of Bühler's four basic tendencies: namely, the up-holding of internal order. Individuals' personal narratives are a continuing reformulation of their life history, and, hence, are both dynamic and changing. The interpretations of events constructed at different points in the life course may vary substantially.

Since personal narratives may not be 'true' in any detached or objective sense their evaluation can be problematic from the point of view of the natural science concept of validity. Personal narratives constitute an interpretative rather than an explanatory approach to understanding, and both the requests within the present book for you to reflect on your own life course, and the provision of sufficient detail on various theories to enable you to evaluate them in relation to your own experience, represent appeals to this perspective. By this token, narratives attain their validity through shared language and modes of understanding: 'The good interpretation of an account of a life history is that which maintains internal consistency apparent to both the person and also to others hearing this account' (Cohler, 1982, p. 211). It is towards the promotion of such shared understanding that the present commentary on the life course is directed.

6

Life events, transitions and coping

Life events are bench marks in the human life cycle. They are the milestones or transition points which give 'shape and direction to the various aspects of a person's life' (Danish *et al.* 1980, p. 342). However, life events are more than markers. They are also processes having 'antecedents, durations, contexts and outcomes' (Reese and Smyer, 1983, p. 2). It is likely that the lifeline which you drew earlier was punctuated by a number of such events, experiences and turning points. Hopson (1981) reports that adults in their mid-30s can typically list more that 30 or 40 transitions or significant life events which they have experienced to date. Some of these will represent age-graded, some non-normative and some history-graded influences on the course of development. The sheer number of such marker events can itself be thought of as a history-graded influence since it is also likely that your lifeline is punctuated by more events than the lifelines of your grandparents or even your parents would have been. Technological change, greater geographic mobility, more frequent and more drastic job moves, more frequent divorce and remarriage – all this and more has contributed to a climate of social instability and a dramatic increase in the amount of change with which most people must cope during their lives. It is perhaps not surprising, therefore, that the study of significant life events and of our response to these upheavals has emerged as a field of study in its own right. In the present chapter the two concepts of life events – as markers and as processes – are discussed.

Content-free, metaphorical and/or diagrammatic representations of the human life span (for example, as a river or as a rainbow) provide us with tools for considering the life course irrespective of individual, cultural and historical variations. Once content is added to these frameworks they constitute mechanisms for systematically considering just such differences or similarities. A similar approach can be adopted with regard to life events, whether they be considered as markers or as processes. Thus we distinguish between the structural characteristics of events – that is, event dimensions which are 'common to all events over time regardless of history or content' (Danish *et al.* 1980) – and types of event. When it is types of event that are of interest then one or more of the structural characteristics can be used as the basis of event taxonomies or classifications.

Life events as markers: the description and classification of events

Reese and Smyer (1983) in a comprehensive review of the area, identify at least thirty-five dimensions which have been used in previous attempts to describe and classify life events. As pointed out elsewhere (Brim and Ryff, 1980) the way in which life events are described depends on the goals and interests of the observer or investigator. Some of the dimensions used have a theoretical origin. Others have an empirical basis – generally in factor analysis. Most dimensions, however, seem to Reese and Smyer to derive from speculation and intuition. The dimensions they identify are listed in table 6.1, grouped according to Brim and Ryff's (1980) distinction between 'event', 'perception' and 'effect' dimensions. Event dimensions describe objective characteristics of the events themselves. Perception dimensions concern the affected person's subjective impression or evaluation of the

Table 6.1   Life-event dimensions (Reese and Smyer, 1983)

Dimension	*Definition*
	'Effect' dimensions
Contextual purity	Extent to which one event influences the resolution or outcome of concurrent events.
Direction of impact	Enhancement or debilitation of the life course in response to the event.
Direction of movement	Entering or leaving a role or social field as a result of the event.
Domain	Type of functioning affected (e.g. biological, social) (also called context, life area).
Focus	Person directly affected by the event (self or other).
Impact	Amount of behavioural change in response to the event; or amount of stress engendered by the event (also called severity, stressfulness).
	'Perception' dimensions
Control	Belief that the event was chosen versus imposed, or under personal control versus uncontrolled.
Desirability	Perception of the event as desirable versus undesirable, or good versus bad.
Expectation	Extent to which the event was expected or anticipated.
Familiarity	Familiarity with an event through prior experience versus novelty of the event.
Long-range threat	Perceived severity of the negative impact over a long period.
Meaning	The person's interpretation of the event (e.g. accident versus will of God).
Perceived gain or loss	Perceived amount of gain or loss resulting from event.
Social desirability	Perceived evaluation of the event by society at large or by a smaller reference group.
Stress	Perceived stressfulness of the event.
Timeliness	Belief that the event occurred 'on time' or 'off time'.
	'Event' dimensions
Adequacy of functioning	Extent to which event reflects inferior or superior functioning of the individual (e.g. divorce might reflect inferior functioning).

(*cont.*)

Dimension	Definition
Age congruity	Typical amount of overlap in the spreads of two or more specified events. Age congruity is independent of contextual purity because an event can influence other events, whether or not they are congruous in age, without their influencing one another.
Age-relatedness	Strength of correlation with age (also called age grading, temporal predictability). Note that spread and timing can be computed even if age relatedness is weak.
Breadth of setting	Extent to which event is limited to or is independent of particular settings.
Cohort specificity	Extent to which the nature of an event depends on the individual's cohort, or generation.
Context	Area of the 'life space' in which the event occurs (e.g. family, work) (also called domain).
Duration	Amount of time required for the event to transpire (also called chronicity; chronic versus acute).
Integration	Extent to which the occurrence of one event depends on the occurrence of another. Integrated events may or may not exhibit age congruity.
Likelihood of occurrence	The probability that the event will occur for a given person (e.g. the prevalence of having Huntington's chorea is low in the population, but its likelihood is high in offspring of an affected individual).
Onset	The suddenness or gradualness of the onset of the event.
Order	The sequence in which events typically occur.
Prevalence	The number of individuals who experience a given event, proportionate to the number of individuals in the population (also called extensiveness of occurrence, generality, social distribution).
Recency	The amount of time passed since the occurrence of the event.
Reversibility	The degree to which a transition is reversible (e.g. entering the job market is reversible; but

Dimension	Definition
	marrying is irreversible because if a marriage is broken by death, for example, the survivor is a widow or widower, not a spinster or bachelor).
Sequencing	The sequence in which events occur in an individual case.
Source	The cause of an event, or the domain of the cause (e.g. heredity, physical environment) (also called domain).
Spread	The age range within which an event typically occurs.
Timing	The average age at which an event occurs (also called age grading).
Type	The nature or domain of an event (e.g. biological processes, physical-environmental events) (also called domain).

events. Effect dimensions refer to the outcomes or consequences of events.

Life-event taxonomies select one or more of these structural dimensions in order to classify events. But which dimensions should be chosen? Again, the basis can be theoretical, empirical or pragmatic but, as Reese and Smyer point out, 'the available theories are not sufficiently detailed, the available empirical evidence is fragmentary, and the available pragmatic considerations vary markedly across disciplines and across investigators within a discipline' (Reese and Smyer, 1983, p. 14). Reese and Smyer offer 'scholarly guess' or 'informed conjecture' as an alternative basis which they used to develop their own classification system.

Selecting two or more dimensions offers the possibility of defining categories by the intersection of dimensions, thus leading to more sophisticated analyses. However, only two- or, at most, three-dimensional models can be easily depicted on the printed page in full. Once we start thinking of four or more dimensions the system becomes too complex to conceptualize readily and the taxonomy's function of bringing order to chaos begins to break down. It may still, however, serve the function of providing a mechanism for describing, if not classifying, life events.

Event taxonomies: three-, two- and one-dimensional examples

Brim and Ryff (1980) provide an example of a three-dimensional taxonomy. They wanted to describe life events in a way that would be helpful to people contemplating their future. Such people, they argue, will want to know the answers to three key questions: How likely is it that a particular event will happen to me? If it does happen, when will it happen? Will I be the only person it happens to, or will there be others? From these questions Brim and Ryff derive three fundamental structural characteristics of life events which they then use as the basis of their life-events typology: the probability (or likelihood) that an event will take place; the correlation of the event with chronological age (age-relatedness); and whether the event will occur for many people or just one or a few persons (prevalence). The resulting taxonomy has eight cells as shown in table 6.2. Their hope is that such a classification system will enhance the usefulness of life events as a way of furthering our understanding of life-span development.

Reese and Smyer (1983) selected event context and event type as amongst the most salient and informative dimensions, and used these to produce a two-dimensional taxonomy. Whereas the three dimensions in Brim and Ryff's system were each merely dichotomized, Reese and Smyer distinguish between fourteen contexts and four types, producing a total of fifty-six cells. The four types they distinguished are: social-cultural, personal-psychological, biological and physical-environmental. The 14 contexts, grouped into 5 superordinate sets of contexts, are listed in table 6.3.

Such a taxonomy does make the data more manageable but may still produce a rather untidy ragbag of categories. When they classified 355 life events according to their context v. type taxonomy, Reese and Smyer found wide variation in the frequency with which categories were used. Although the miscellaneous category was used for only 3.7 per cent of the events (suggesting that their list of contexts was reasonably comprehensive), two of the contexts, namely friendships and community, were used even less often. At the other extreme, almost half the events (48.8 per cent) fell within the four categories family, work, health, and love and marriage.

136

Table 6.2 Life-event taxonomy based on probability of occurrence, correlation with age and numbers affected (Brim and Ryff, 1980)

Correlation with age	Experienced by many		Experienced by few	
	High probability of occurrence	Low probability of occurrence	High probability of occurrence	Low probability of occurrence
Strong	Learning to walk Marriage Starting to work Woman giving birth to first child	Military-service draft Polio epidemic	Coming into a large estate at 18 years old	Spina bifida School drop-out
Weak	Father's death Husband's death 'Topping out' in work career Children's marriages Moving home	War Great depression Plague Earthquake	Succeeding father in family business	Loss of limb in car accident Accident at work Death of daughter Grown children returning home to live Cured of alcoholism

Table 6.3 Life-event contexts (Reese and Smyer, 1983)

Superordinate set	Context	Comments
Family	1 Family	Context is family of origin: parents, siblings, etc.
	2 Love and marriage	Context involves date or mate.
	3 Parenting	Context refers to children, or having and rearing children.
	4 Residence	Context refers to dwelling-place.
Self	5 Health	Context is own health and biological functions.
	6 Self	Predominant reference of event is to the self.
Social relations	7 Community	Context involves community relations and functions.
	8 Friendships	Reference is to close friends, primary friendship networks.
	9 Social relations	Context refers to psychosocial relations.
Work	10 Finances	Includes all contexts related to money (including household economics).
	11 School	Context is schooling, education and training.
	12 Work	Context is related to occupation and career.
Miscellaneous	13 Law	Reference is to crime and legal matters: perpetration of crime; legal consequences (for victim of crime, context is classified elsewhere).
	14 Miscellaneous	Contexts that do not fit elsewhere in the list.

Why should there be this uneven distribution of events across categories? It may reflect real differences in the frequency of occurrence of events in different contexts. Reese and Smyer do, however, have other suggestions. It might be that the heavily used categories have been too broadly and the underused categories too finely drawn. Alternatively, or perhaps as well, 'the disproportionate distribution of events in the various contexts may be merely a reflection of the interests of the investigators we sampled' (Reese and Smyer, 1983, p. 15). The former is a theoretical and the latter an empirical question.

Reese and Smyer also found a varied distribution of events among the types as follows: social-cultural, 48.0 per cent; personal-psychological, 31.9 per cent; biological, 16.1 per cent; and physical-environmental, 4.0 per cent. They suggest that this probably reflects the interests of the researchers they covered, who tended to be social scientists rather than biological or physical scientists.

Although two dimensions have been selected as the basis of their life-events taxonomy this does not mean that other dimensions are necessarily ignored. When the objective is to compare and contrast a relatively small number of life events rather than simply to classify a large number, then other dimensions from table 6.1 can be employed as well. Thus Reese and Smyer, as an illustration of the use of their taxonomy, selected two events from each of ten contexts and rated them on ten dimensions. They selected dimensions which 'seemed hospitable to intuitive rating' (p. 15), pointing out that in an empirical study the dimensions would (or should) be selected on the basis of some theory or hunch (hypothesis).

They suggest three possible uses for their taxonomy. First, it could be used to investigate the salience of and interrelationships between various dimensions. It might then be possible to eliminate certain dimensions from consideration either because they show little or no variation across individuals or situations or because they correlate highly with other dimensions. Alternatively, it might be that certain dimensions could be combined to yield a single superordinate score. Both courses of action would aid conceptual clarity by reducing the complexity of the situation.

The ratings and/or salience of life-event dimensions need not be consistent across situations. Thus, Reese and Smyer suggest, as a second possible use of their taxonomy, the investigation of differences in dimensional values of life events as a function of such factors as age, sex, culture and history. Thirdly, they suggest the investigation of whether the salient dimensions of a particular life event change as a function of the same variables of age, sex, and so on.

A final example of a life-event taxonomy is one which utilizes only one dimension. Thus Holmes and Rahe (1967) ordered events according to their estimated stressfulness. Forty-three events so ordered comprise the 'social readjustment rating scale'. Respondents indicate the events they have experienced within (usually) the previous twelve months. The sum of the stress ratings for these events is used as an indicator of the amount of stress the person has been under. As can be seen from table 6.4, both desirable and undesirable events are included on the grounds that both can be used as a basis for predicting stress-related health problems.

Table 6.4   Life events ordered for stressfulness (Holmes and Rahe, 1967)

Rank	Life event
1	Death of spouse
2	Divorce
3	Marital separation
4	Jail term
5	Death of close family member
6	Personal injury or illness
7	Marriage
8	Fired at work
9	Marital reconciliation
10	Retirement
11	Change in health of family member
12	Pregnancy
13	Sex difficulties
14	Gain of new family member
15	Business readjustment
16	Change in financial status
17	Death of close friend
18	Change to different line of work
19	Change in number of arguments with spouse

Rank	Life event
20	Heavy mortgage repayments
21	Foreclosure of mortgage or loan
22	Change in responsibilities at work
23	Son or daughter leaves home
24	Trouble with in-laws
25	Outstanding personal achievement
26	Spouse begins or stops work
27	Begin or end school
28	Change in living conditions
29	Revision of personal habits
30	Trouble with boss
31	Change in work hours or conditions
32	Change in residence
33	Change in schools
34	Change in recreation
35	Change in church activities
36	Change in social activities
37	Moderate mortgage or loan
38	Change in sleeping habits
39	Change in number of family get-togethers
40	Change in eating habits
41	Vacation
42	Christmas
43	Minor violations of the law

Life events as processes: the dynamics of psychosocial transitions

When attention shifts from the characteristics of life events to the experiences of individuals undergoing them, then a somewhat different line of research emerges. Originating primarily in the study of people's reaction to loss or crisis, a body of research has accumulated which indicates that disruptions to our accustomed way of life trigger a predictable cycle of reactions and feelings, as shown in figure 6.1.

It is not claimed that everyone's response follows an identical path in every instance. In particular, there may be differences

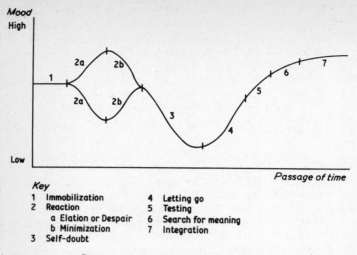

Key

1	Immobilization	4	Letting go
2	Reaction	5	Testing
	a Elation or Despair	6	Search for meaning
	b Minimization	7	Integration
3	Self-doubt		

Figure 6.1 Seven-phase model of stages accompanying transition ·(adapted from Hopson, 1981)

depending on whether or not the change is a desired and pleasurable change, such that two alternative paths through the reaction phase are noted. None the less, the cycle is sufficiently generalizable for most people to recognize it in their own experience in relation to at least some significant life events. The cycle – known as the transition cycle – is a general pattern rather than a rigid sequence. It is set in motion when 'an event or non-event results in a change in assumptions about oneself and the world and thus requires a corresponding change in one's behavior and relationships' (Schlossberg, 1981, p. 5). The inclusion of non-events in this definition is important since failure to obtain a promotion at work or to conceive a planned baby, let us say, may provoke as significant a transition as the new job or the new baby would have done. Put another way, both events and non-events can require us to modify our 'assumptive world' (Parkes, 1971) – the largely taken-for-granted assumptions we make about ourselves and our world.

Advancement through the stages of the transition cycle is rarely smooth and continuous. Taking two steps forward and one step back is how one of the key researchers in the area describes a typical progression (Hopson, 1981). Thus, an individual is likely to vacillate between different phases of the cycle. Obviously, therefore, no time units can be assigned to the horizontal dimension. Whilst individuals may typically need a certain amount of time to work through the stages (say, two years in the case of adjusting to a job promotion (Parker and Lewis, 1981), there are still likely to be significant individual differences. Likewise, an individual may cope very rapidly with one transition, and with another may never progress beyond the second or third stage. Queen Victoria is a famous example of someone who never came to terms with the death of her husband. She kept his room and his personal possessions as they had always been. She could not, or would not, 'let go' of the world of which he had been a part.

Units cannot be assigned to the vertical dimension either. The 'peak' of elation may or may not be more extreme than the 'trough' of self-doubt. The final plateau may level out either above or below the 'mood' level that pertained prior to the start of the transition. Even the labelling of this dimension is tentative. In an earlier version of the model shown in figure 6.1 the vertical dimension was identified as 'self-esteem' (Hopson and Adams, 1976). Elsewhere it has been identified as 'morale level' when talking of the response to unemployment (Harrison, 1976), or as 'competence' when discussing coping with promotion (Parker and Lewis, 1981).

Despite these caveats, however, the following stages represent a generally recognizable sequence of responses accompanying a wide range of transitions:

1 *Immobilization.* How would you feel if you were suddenly told that you had won £50,000 on a premium bond? How would you feel if you turned the corner of your road one day and found that your home had been burned to the ground? The chances are that initially you would not be able to comprehend the full implication of what had happened. Your initial response might be one of disbelief – 'This can't be true.' You might well be 'stopped dead in your tracks'. This is the stage of immobilization or shock. It is characterized by a sense of being overwhelmed, of being 'frozen up'. Its duration and intensity tend to increase with the magnitude, the suddenness and the negative valence of the transition.

2 *Reaction.* (i) *Elation or Despair:* After a greater or lesser time the sense of shock gives way to a sharp swing of mood, the direction of which depends on the nature and circumstances of the transition. For positive or desired transitions the extent of the swing may range from mild pleasure to total elation, whilst for a negative or undesired event the mood shift might be anything from slight disappointment to despair.

(ii) *Minimization:* The initial post-shock reaction will almost always be followed by some form of minimization. This might be in relation to the feelings associated with the event and/or the anticipated impact of the change. For a positive transition the feelings of elation become dampened as more ambiguous or less desirable concomitants of the transition become apparent or are confronted. Thus the joy of attaining a much sought after university place may be tempered by questions of 'Will I be able to cope?' or 'Perhaps I will miss the folk at home after all.' For a negative or undesired event the effect or importance of the event may be played down. The situation may be reassessed as being less dire than was originally thought. Thus, the person who fails to get a university place may say 'At least I won't have to take any more exams' or 'I'm just as likely to get a job without a degree.'

3 *Self-doubt.* The boundaries between the phases of the model are not distinct and the minimization of the positive aspects of a desired event may slip almost imperceptibly into a period of self-doubt. With negative events the minimization phase may not be noticeable and the individual may seem to pass almost directly from despair to self-doubt. This dip in mood is associated with the growing realization of the reality of the changes in one's life space. Originally this third phase was labelled as the period of depression (Hopson and Adams, 1976), but was altered to self-doubt (Hopson, 1981) on the realization that whilst depression was a common response it was not the only one. The underlying dimension of self-doubt might also be manifested in other ways such as by anxiety, anger or sadness. There may be fluctuations in energy level. The individual may, for example, alternate between phases of anger and phases of apathy.

4 *Letting go.* Until this point the individual has to a greater or lesser extent still been attached to the past in a way that inhibits him or her from beginning actively to cope with the new situation. At some point these attachments, or affectional bonds (Parkes,

1971), must be broken if the individual is to continue to develop and grow. The reality of the change must be accepted. The hold on the past must be relinquished.

This process of 'letting go' may be traumatic (Brammer and Abrego, 1981). There may be tears as the loss of the past is mourned. There may be anger at the injustice of the demand for change. Emerging from the experience, however, is at least some degree of commitment to 'put the past behind me' and face the future. In this sense the phase of letting go is a watershed in coping with transitions. It is the point at which we can begin to convert the tragedies and disasters in our lives into growth points.

Letting go undoubtedly requires courage. It inevitably involves a plunge into the unknown. To use the analogy offered by Levinson and his colleagues (1978), it is a phase during which we have cast ourselves adrift from the past but cannot yet see the land of the future. To use Parkes' (1971) terminology, we have severed our old affectional bonds but have not yet formed any new ones.

5 *Testing.* Once the hold on the past has been more or less relinquished the person is ready and able to explore the new terrain. New options are tentatively considered and alternative ways of behaving are tried. In effect, this is an experimental period during which new identities are tried on for size until gradually new affectional bonds or attachments to the new world are established. It may well be accompanied by rapid mood changes as plans are considered and discarded, and as hopes are raised and dashed. None the less, the 'low point' of the transition is past and, taken overall, the person's mood, morale or level of self-esteem is on the rise.

6 *Search for meaning.* 'Putting the past behind one' does not and should not imply a pretence that the disruption or the change never happened. Rather, this sixth phase in the transition cycle is characterized by a conscious striving to learn from the experience. It is a cognitive phase during which people seek to make sense of what has happened to them. It is a healthy form of reflective thinking without which the individual would not be able to develop a deep understanding of the meaning of the change in his or her life. It should not be interpreted as 'morbid dwelling on the past'.

7 *Integration.* The transition process can be said to be complete when the individual feels 'at home' in the new, post-transition reality. The new behaviours that may have been so painfully acquired, the new self-conceptions and understandings of events perhaps so agonizingly achieved, have become an integral part of the person's view of the world. The transition now becomes integrated into the life space and no longer dominates it. One is 'a student' rather than 'A STUDENT'; a person who happens to have a disability rather than 'A DISABLED PERSON', and so on. Put another way, the attainment of this status means that the stage is now set for, and the person ready to cope with, another transition of greater or lesser magnitude.

Distinction can be made between a disease and a developmental perspective on life events and transitions (Danish *et al.*, 1980). From the disease perspective, life events are viewed as pathological and the causes of dysfunctional stress. This is the assumption underlying the use of Holmes and Rahe's (1967) 'social readjustment rating scale' as a basis for predicting health problems. Interventions grounded in such a viewpoint would logically be directed at preventing the occurrence of stressful life events and transitions. Where this is not possible the intervention goal would be the elimination of stress so that the individual may return to the path of normal development (Danish, 1977), the assumption being that disruption is not conducive to such progression.

However, if you refer back to figure 6.1 (p.142) you will see that the graph shows a curve levelling out at a higher mood level than that which pertained prior to the transition. Think back to your own lifeline and you will recall being asked what positive outcomes had resulted from the troughs. Both these examples denote a developmental perspective on life events. In contrast to the disease perspective life events are here viewed as potential or possibly even necessary heralds of growth. Thus Riegel (1975) proposes that crises and catastrophes occur at the interface between four different planes of development. They result from asynchronies between the progression of four event sequences: the inner-biological, the individual-psychological, the cultural-sociological and the outer-physical. Since each developmental plane is (according to Riegel) in a constant state of change such asynchronies are inevitable. He also views such asynchronies as 'the singular cause of development' (Riegel, 1975, p. 105). Forer (1963) similarly argues that crises are necessary for personal growth.

Transitions are, however, periods of risk as well as possibility. The Chinese have two symbols for crisis – one meaning danger and the other meaning opportunity. The danger is that the individual will be unable to cope or will cope unsatisfactorily, with the risk that he or she will be 'scarred' (Murgatroyd and Woolfe, 1982) by the experience. The opportunity, of course, is for personal growth.

On the transition graph, growth is reflected in a higher mood plateau after the transition, but such a quantitative indicator may not be appropriate. Serious illness may leave us permanently impaired physically. If, however, it stimulates us to reassess our priorities and values, and appreciate anew what we had previously come to take for granted then there have been gains as well as losses. This is not to say that the illness was to be welcomed, but it does imply that there may be compensatory benefits. Likewise a day may never pass when bereaved parents do not long for their dead child, but if they have learned to cope with their sorrow and if perhaps it has brought them closer to each other then they can be said to have grown or developed. As life events are viewed from the developmental perspective as potentially having both positive and negative outcomes the goal of intervention is not the prevention of critical life events *per se*, but the enhancement of the individual's ability to grow or develop as a result of the event (Danish and D'Augelli, 1980).

Coping with life events

As with the concept of the developmental task there is implicit in the developmental perspective on life events the notion that such events can be handled with differing degrees of effectiveness. This brings us to the subject of coping, to questions concerning how individuals cope with life events and transitions, what distinguishes effective from ineffective coping, and what attributes and skills enhance our ability to cope.

Coping has been extensively studied in relation to life events and, more generally, in relation to the management of stress. By coping is meant 'efforts, both action-oriented and intrapsychic, to manage (i.e., master, tolerate, reduce, minimize) environmental and internal demands, and conflicts among them, which tax or exceed a person's resources' (Lazarus and Launier, 1978, p. 311). As Hopson (1981) reminds us, these demands may be the demands of underload as well as overload. To cope with a job where there is nothing to do may be as stressful as coping with a job where there is too much. In such instances individuals are thrown back on their own resources. Having to manage extensive 'spare time' can be one of the main stresses of retirement, hospitalization, unemployment, and so on. It is generally agreed that coping involves a complex interaction between the individual and the environment. It can involve attempts to manage the thoughts, feelings and/or behaviour of the individual. It may also be directed at managing external rather than, or as well as, internal pressures. Bronfenbrenner's (1977) conceptualization of the environment – with its micro-, meso-, exo- and macrosystems – can be invoked here. The source of the demands on the individual may lie at all or any of these different levels.

In addition to distinguishing between different sources of demands we can also distinguish between different facets of coping. Pearlin and Schooler (1978) express this neatly as a distinction between coping resources and coping responses. The former, which can be further subdivided into social resources and psychological resources, 'refer not to what people do, but to what is available to them in developing their coping repertoires' (Pearlin and Schooler, 1978, p. 5). Social resources are found in the interpersonal support network in which the individual is embedded. Psychological resources are the personal characteristics which mediate between the demands on the individual and the individual's response to those demands. Such characteristics may either mitigate or exacerbate the effect of threat or stress. If coping resources represent what the person has, then coping responses represent what the person does – people's 'concrete efforts to deal with the life-strains they encounter in their different roles' (Pearlin and Schooler, 1978, p. 5). Whilst these responses are influenced by the individual's resources it is useful to distinguish between them. We can then ask, first, what responses will make maximum use of those resources already available and, secondly, what responses might serve to enhance or increase the individual's resources.

148

Coping resources

Social resources

Social support and its relationship to personal well-being is the concern of a large and rapidly expanding literature. It is a concept with multidisciplinary roots. Moos and Mitchell (1982) identify three: sociometric analysis, social-network analysis and crisis theory. Sociometric analysis, the root of social psychology and developed by Moreno (1934), attempts to map the 'psychological geography' of groups and communities by asking individuals to plot desired or actual interactions with other people. Social anthropologists' interest in understanding patterns of interaction not based on group membership led to similar procedures. These patterns, or social networks, were seen as mechanisms intervening between the individual or family and the wider social environment. Of interest in the present discussion is the effect of such networks on people's ability to cope with life crises and transitions. The recent burgeoning of interest in this area has led to the incorporation within social-network analysis of research, pioneered by Lindemann (1979), concerning the role of members of such networks in facilitating crisis and transition management. The work of two epidemiologists, Cassel (1974) and Cobb (1976), is also significant. They emphasize the influence of environmental and situational factors on health and the ability to withstand stress. Another influential theorist is Caplan (1974a), a psychiatrist particularly interested in community health practice. The link between all these multidisciplinary perspectives is found in their ecological or interactional viewpoint on human functioning, which considers such functioning in its environmental context and with an emphasis on the interactions between the different components of that environment, including the focal person. Three aspects of social networks will be considered in the present section: their structure and function; the mechanisms through which they influence the individual's experience of and response to stress; and the determinants of an individual's social network resources.

1 *The structure and function of social networks.* Social networks can be characterized by a number of dimensions, each of which can be broken down into a number of related variables. Marsella

and Snyder (1981) distinguish between four dimensions: structure, interaction, quality and function. Structure refers to characteristics that describe the whole network or subsectors within it, and includes size (the number of people in the network); density or connectedness (the extent to which relationships exist between members of the network independently of the focal person); and stability (the degree of change in the network over time). The interaction dimension describes the relationships between pairs of network members. It is concerned with the structure of particular linkages rather than the whole network. Amongst the most typically measured interaction characteristics are: multidimensionality (the range of types of exchange that occur within the relationship); reciprocity (the extent to which the exchange is two-way); and intensity (the strength or importance of the relationship) (Moos and Mitchell, 1982). Other interaction characteristics include the degree of similarity, or homogeneity, between network members; geographic proximity of members; the duration of linkages within the network; and the frequency of contact with network members. Some of these characteristics may be applied to both whole networks and particular linkages. Quality refers to the affective nature of the relationships – their degree of friendliness, intimacy or affection, for example. Function refers to the specific purpose or support that the network provides. Overlap between Marsella and Snyder's dimensions can be seen in the fact that the provision of relationships of a particular quality or affect can be identified as one of the possible functions of social networks.

At a more general level distinction can be made between the functions of social integration and social interaction (Antonucci and Depner, 1982). The social-integration effects of social networks are those effects 'attributable to the mere existence of a social relationship' (Antonucci and Depner, 1982, p. 241). The nature of our participation in social networks is a strong determinant and reflection of our social identity. This identity is related to the roles we fulfil, our role performance and our self-concept (Hirsch, 1981). Our existence within a social network provides us with a niche in society and with guidelines and a sense of security emanating from the norms, expectations and obligations concomitant upon certain relationships. In other words, one function of such networks is that of social regulation (Moos and Mitchell,

1982). Some relationships of themselves confer the status of 'an appropriately functioning member of society' (Antonucci and Depner, 1982, p. 241). Employment, marriage and parenthood could be examples of this, at least at certain points in the life cycle under certain social conditions.

The social-interaction functions of social networks are built into Kahn and Antonucci's (1980) definition of social support as 'interpersonal transactions that include one or more of the following key elements: affect, affirmation, and aid' (p. 267). Affective transactions would involve expressions of liking, admiration, respect or love. Transactions involving affirmation would confirm the appropriateness or rightness of some action or statement. The frequently assumed network function of providing emotional support may well be achieved through transactions involving both affect and affirmation. The aid or assistance proffered by support networks may take any number of material and cognitive forms including things, money, time, advice, guidance and entitlements.

In extolling the virtues of support networks and bewailing the vices of social isolation, let us not forget that social networks can have negative (Antonucci and Depner, 1982) or stressful (Gottlieb, 1983) effects as well. The family, for example, can be a source of stress as well as support (Croog, 1970). The social-regulation function of networks can generate feelings of imprisonment as well as security. When linkages in a network are reciprocal it can be thought of as a system of both supports and demands – a system, in other words, of mutual obligations (Cobb, 1976). Whilst such a situation can be beneficial, as captured in the truism that we all need to be needed, the demands may also be perceived as burdensome. Furthermore, in entering a network we may welcome some linkages but not others. When we marry we generally join a network that includes all members of our spouse's family whether we choose to or not. Our work-place network may contain both supportive or stress-assuaging and demanding or stress-producing relationships. In addition, when support is proffered, there is no guarantee that it is effective – to offer advice when emotional support is needed is a ubiquitous pitfall of helping. Moreover, the support offered may be judged, at least by outsiders, as harmful rather than beneficial – as when parents are concerned to remove their adolescent child from a network of undesirable (by their standards) friends. In short, we must consider both the sustaining and the destructive potential of social networks and examine the balance between these forces in any particular situation.

2 *The effect of social support on the stress sequence.* To return, however, to the beneficial functions of support networks, the question of where in the sequence from stressor to health outcome they intervene has still to be addressed. Albeit somewhat simplistic, the stress sequence can be thought of as a three-stage process as shown in the horizontal sequence in figure 6.2 – a stressor provokes a reaction which results in a particular health outcome (Gottlieb, 1983). The stressor might be an acute life event such as those discussed in the first part of this chapter; it might be a continuing hardship or condition, such as raising a handicapped child or living with prolonged unemployment, which must be handled on a long-term basis; and/or it might be a series of daily tribulations such as losing things and getting stuck in traffic. It has been found (Kanner *et al.*, 1981) that such everyday nuisances are more accurate predictions of psychological symptoms than major life events – hence their inclusion as potential stressors.

The second stage in the sequence is the individual's reaction to the stressor(s). It includes the two phases of the appraisal process as identified by Lazarus (1966; Lazarus and Launier, 1978) – namely, appraisal of the meaning of the event as benign, neutral or stressful (that is, primary appraisal), followed by appraisal of the perceived coping options available (that is, secondary appraisal). The reaction phase also includes the individual's response to these appraisals – namely, the employment of emotional and behavioural coping strategies.

The final stage in the stress sequence is the health outcomes of these reactions in terms of physiological and/or psychological well-being. The latter might include affective outcomes such as feelings of depression or elation, cognitive outcomes such as level of self-esteem and/or behavioural outcomes such as the demonstration of assertiveness or passivity. Qualities such as self-esteem and assertiveness can be thought of as personal attributes as well as health outcomes. In this sense they form a part of the individual's personal coping resources and demonstrate the relation between different facets of coping.

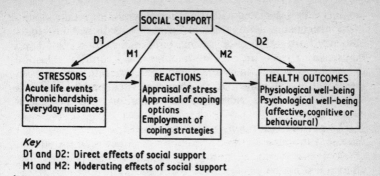

Key
D1 and D2: Direct effects of social support
M1 and M2: Moderating effects of social support

Figure 6.2 The mediation of social support in the stress sequence (adapted from Gottlieb, 1983)

Four points in the stress sequence can be identified where social support can exert its healthful (or, indeed, its adverse) influence. Two of these represent the direct effect of social support on exposure to stressors and on the individual's well-being (D1 and D2, respectively, in figure 6.2). In the first instance, the support network eradicates the stressor at least as far as the focal person is concerned. Secretaries, for example, may decide who gets to see the boss, and accountants may handle tax questions without reference to their client. Alternatively the stressor may itself be eradicated – as when the members of the support network persuade someone not to press charges relating to an offence allegedly committed by the focal individual. In the second type of direct effect the support network influences well-being rather than stressors. Thus, in a longitudinal study of Californians, Berkman and Syme (1979) found social isolation and impoverished social relations to be associated with higher mortality rates. Syme (1974) also found unmarried people to have higher mortality rates than the married. Furthermore, marital disruption can be both the precursor and the precipitator of physical and psychiatric difficulties (Bloom *et al.*, 1978). In the work place LaRocco and Jones (1978) found superior and peer support to be associated with job satisfaction. Amongst the elderly good relationships with family and friends have been found to be associated with heightened feelings of life satisfaction (Wood and Robertson, 1978). And so the examples could continue. Despite the earlier warning concerning the potential negative or stressful effects of social networks, it cannot be denied that there is substantial evidence indicating the salubrious effect of social contact *per se*.

The second two points of influence on the stress sequence represent the mediating or conditioning, rather than the direct, effect of social support. Frequently lumped together as 'buffering' effects, distinction can be made (Antonucci and Depner, 1982) between the role of social support in insulating the individual from the effects of stressors by modifying the way they are experienced or perceived (M1 in figure 6.2) and its buffering role in modifying the outcome of the stress experience (M2 in figure 6.2). Both instances constitute an interaction between support and subjective stress. Antonucci and Depner (1982) cite the example of job loss where an insulating effect of social support might be mediated through encouraging the individual to view the job loss in the most positive light (as an opportunity rather than a crisis). A buffering effect influences the impact rather than the perception of the stressor. In the job-loss example this might be achieved through help with job hunting, attempts to bolster self-esteem and generally to make the effect of the job loss less damaging to well-being.

3 *Determinants of an individual's social network resources.* Moos and Mitchell (1982) identify four key influences on the nature and amount of social network resources available to an individual: environmental factors, personal factors, life events and coping responses.

A number of relevant features of the environmental domain can be identified: its physical and organizational characteristics, its sociodemographic or suprapersonal quality, and its prevailing social norms. The physical and organizational features of a neighbourhood will facilitate and constrain different forms and amounts of interpersonal interaction. Geographic proximity, for example, facilitates interaction, and architectural factors like the relative orientation of doorways to each other effect the extent and way in which residents form social networks. The social and transport facilities of the district will also exert an influence.

Suprapersonal characteristics of neighbourhoods such as the rate of population turnover and their homogeneity with regard to social status, life stage and ethnic or religious background will be conducive towards the development of some types of networks rather than others. Value as well as structural characteristics will also influence the forms of social support available. Within any one neighbourhood there will be prevailing social norms and beliefs about appropriate and inappropriate forms of support and how such support should be proffered.

An individual's as well as a neighbourhood's sociodemographic characteristics will influence access to social support. Age, life stage, sex, marital status, social class and income level are amongst the variables that could be important. Thus a married woman in her mid-30s with two children and no paid employment is likely to have a different support network from her husband or from a woman who has no children or one who is combining motherhood with a career.

In view of their potential benefits, the creation and maintenance of effective support networks can be thought of as a coping skill. The personal resources which influence coping skills (see below) must therefore also be thought of as potential influences on the individual's support network. Again the interactive model is in operation, with the social network being both a force impinging on the individual and an outcome of the individual's coping styles and skills. For example, people with few interpersonal skills may be less active and less successful in developing opportunities for social involvement (Moos and Mitchell, 1982). They are therefore less likely to have effective social support networks.

Life events may alter the structure and supportiveness of social networks. Established networks will be disrupted by such events as retirement or house relocation. In some instances life events may trigger or mobilize support networks – as when people rally round to support the bereaved. The same events may alternatively result in the loss of support when network members fail to proffer support, possibly because of feelings of inadequacy, helplessness, embarrassment or distaste. The parents of stillborn children often find themselves bereft of support as well as their child. Friends, relatives and medical staff alike may not know what to say, and so they say nothing – either avoiding the parents or acting as if the pregnancy had never happened. It may be that support is more easily mobilized for normative, expected or 'on-time' life events, such as the death of a frail and elderly parent, than for non-normative, unexpected or 'off-time' events, such as the death of a child.

Coping responses, the final influence on social-network resources discussed by Moos and Mitchell, may be differentially effective in mobilizing social support. Individuals will engage in differing degrees of active help-seeking, and their other coping responses may either encourage or discourage others to offer support. Thus, the individual who responds to stress by maintaining 'a stiff upper lip' and carrying on as normal may communicate (accurately or not) that there is nothing the matter or that help would not be welcome.

Personal resources

A wide range of individual factors can mediate between the demands on the individual and the individual's response to those demands. Pearlin and Schooler (1978) focus on psychological or personality attributes, but here, following Schlossberg (1981), other personal characteristics are also considered under the heading of personal resources: sex and sex-role identification; age and life stage; state of health; value orientation; racial, or ethnic, and socioeconomic factors; and similar previous experience.

1 *Psychological characteristics.* The relationship between dispositional or personality characteristics and coping ability has traditionally been the main focus of research in the area (Lazarus *et al.* 1974), with situational factors and even specific coping responses being accorded relatively little attention. Whilst contemporary discussions tend to broaden this perspective, this is not to deny that more global and (possibly) stable individual psychological attributes do have an effect.

A cluster of personality characteristics has been identified as being associated with more effective coping, including self-esteem, self-efficacy, mastery, internal locus of control, self-confidence and flexibility. Of these, self-esteem is the most ubiquitous and would seem to be the most crucial – in both extreme and day-to-day conditions. Precisely what is meant by self-esteem varies across studies. It is not necessarily used as a unitary concept. Thus, Branden (1969) distinguishes two interrelated aspects – a sense of personal efficacy and a sense of personal worth. Pearlin and Schooler (1978), however, define self-esteem as 'the positiveness of one's attitude to oneself' (p. 5), seeing it as synonymous with self-worth and as distinct from mastery, 'the extent to which one regards one's life-chances as being under one's own control in contrast to being fatalistically ruled' (p. 5). This definition of mastery is, in turn, not dissimilar to the definition of internal locus of control as 'the belief that one's actions have some causal relation to one's life' (Schlossberg, 1981, p. 12). Such definitional confusion points to the interrelation between different psychological coping resources, and some authors operate at a higher level of generality by using deliberately global terms. Thus, Schlossberg (1981) utilizes the concept of psychosocial competence proposed by Tyler (1978) which subsumes, amongst other things, 'a moderately favourable self-evaluation, an internal locus of control . . . and a sense of responsibility' (Schlossberg, 1981, p. 12). Likewise, Antonovsky (1979) identifies a general attitude, called the sense of coherence, which characterizes individuals who consistently enjoy mental and physical well-being. Kobasa (1979) was interested in personality as a conditioner of the effects of stressful life events on illness onset. She compared a group of highly stressed executives who did not fall ill with a similar group who did, and found the former to show higher degrees of hardiness. Hardiness was defined as the possession of three general characteristics concerning control, commitment and challenge: (i) the belief that one can control or influence the events of one's experience; (ii) the ability to feel deeply involved in activities; and (iii) the tendency to view change as an exciting challenge to further development rather than a threat. Of the eighteen dimensions used to measure the three facets of hardiness, the four that most distinguished the high stress/low illness group from the high stress/high illness group were a sense of commitment to (or lack of alienation from) self, a sense of vigorousness (as opposed to vegetativeness) about life, a sense of meaningfulness (as opposed to nihilism) and an internal (as opposed to an external) locus of control.

Such personality characteristics are resources 'that people draw upon to help them withstand threats posed by events and objects in their environment. These resources, residing within the self, can be formidable barriers to the stressful consequences of social strain' (Pearlin and Schooler, 1978, p. 5). They have, in other words, an indirect rather than a direct effect on the stress experienced. As Witmer *et al.* (1983) point out, self-efficacy in particular is related to Lazarus's (1966; Lazarus and Launier, 1978) process of secondary appraisal whereby the individual is continually involved in cognitive judgements of personal resources, options and constraints in responding to environmental demands.

2 *Sex and sex-role identification.*   Men and women are generally socialized to adopt different attitudes and develop different strengths. To the extent that people conform to these pressures they will possess some sex-related coping resources. Thus, men's experience may lead them to be better endowed with the cluster of psychological attributes related to self-esteem that were discussed earlier. On the other hand, the encouragement of women to develop greater emotional expressiveness may enable them to handle many and diverse emotional experiences which men would find acutely distressing (Chiriboga, 1975). Androgyny can be thought of in this context as the combining of the stereotypically masculine and the stereotypically feminine personal coping resources.

The question of sex differences in coping is complicated by the different definitions of healthy adult functioning that have at times been proposed or assumed for men and women. In a now famous study by Inge Broverman and her colleagues (Broverman *et al.*, 1970), a sample of mental health professionals were asked to indicate their conceptions of a healthy male, a healthy female or a healthy adult (sex unspecified). Results indicated conceptions of a healthy adult and a healthy male to be broadly similar, and to be different from conceptions of a healthy female. In the clinicians' view, healthy women were, in comparison with men, characterized as being submissive, noncompetitive, conceited about appearance, dependent and excitable in minor crises. These findings have potentially significant implications for notions of adult development in that the traits seen as normal for women contradicted the clinicians' notions of healthy adult functioning. Since the time of Broverman *et al.*'s (1970) study there has been some easing of sex-role stereotypes. None the less, to the extent that stereotypic notions of ideal male and female functioning are taken as indicators of mental health for men and women respectively, there will be encouragement for males and females to develop and value different coping resources. It is likely that the coping resources encouraged in men will be more consistent with prevailing definitions of maturity than those encouraged in women.

3 *Age and life stage.* Both the ability to cope, and the coping resources and responses available to an individual vary with age and life stage. Thus, we would not expect a child and an adult to demonstrate the same degree of frustration tolerance, or to cope with frustration in the same way. Whereas children may be allowed to cry and stamp their feet, adults will normally be expected to show greater restraint and to engage in more constructive problem solving. Furthermore, the physical and psychosocial demands placed on individuals at different ages or life stages require different resources and responses. Thus, coping with early adult transition and the mid-life transition (Levinson *et al.*, 1978) requires in each case some unique as well as some shared resources.

It was emphasized earlier how the ability to assess a life event in a particular light is a significant component of an individual's coping resource. This is likely to vary, not only as a function of the individual's level of maturity, but also in relation to the timing of the event. One aspect of timing concerns whether an event is 'on-time' or 'off-time'. Related to, but not synonymous with, this is the way a person's age may affect his or her reaction to a crisis. Thus, a broken bone may, with justification, be viewed as potentially more serious in someone of 75 than in someone of 25 years of age.

Finally, an individual's age and life stage will influence the extraneous as well as the personal resources available. The amounts and forms of institutional and interpersonal support will vary, for example.

4 *State of health.* People's state of health will influence their internal physical resources. Individuals' appraisal of their health is, however, partly a reflection of their coping style. Thus, denial may cause people to experience themselves as more healthy than would objectively seem to be the case. Lack of faith in one's ability to influence one's life (that is, an external locus of control) may lead to passive acceptance of ill health and lack of effort to restore it. Alternatively, an unrealistically high internal locus of control

may lead one to refuse to accept the reality of restrictions imposed by a particular infirmity.

Again, the individual's state of health will influence the external resources at his or her disposal. Ill health may entitle the person to the resources of the medical profession, but preclude him or her from participating in activities which would make available the resources of friends and associates.

5 *Value orientation.* Different values will lead to the pursuit of different goals. Thus, Schein (1977) discusses different career anchors – that is, values, motives or needs which lead a person to seek out particular types of work experience and in accordance with which the attractiveness of a particular job is evaluated. For example, people with a career anchor based on technical-functional competence place highest priority on the challenge of the actual work they are doing. Their interest lies in a particular area, be it scientific investigation, marketing, teaching, or whatever. They will leave a job rather than be sidetracked into a different area or promoted into, say, a primarily managerial role. By contrast, someone who values security highly may remain in steady, low-risk work even if it has lost any intrinsic interest it initially held. Moreover, values may facilitate or inhibit coping 'dependent on the ease with which they can be translated into goals and behavior and successfully pursued' (Thurnher, 1975, p. 185). People with a career anchor grounded in creativity, for example, may have to struggle long, hard and continually at finding work consistent with their values.

A particular value orientation may facilitate coping in some situations but not in others. Schlossberg (1981) cities religious belief as 'an obvious example of a value orientation that is often said to sustain people through the trials of life' (p. 15). It may indeed be so. Religious persuasion and belief in an afterlife may ease the pain of bereavement. However, the same system of beliefs may hinder rather than help, say, a Roman Catholic's coping with divorce.

As well as values creating resources, resources or opportunities may create values. Different opportunities will be available to us at different ages or life stages, and thus, as Schlossberg (1981) points out, 'people at different stages tend to emphasise different values' (p. 15). This ties in with a society's age-grade system. Thus, a set of values based on being 'foot-loose and fancy-free' may be both easier to act out and socially more acceptable during the early 20s than the mid-40s. As was discussed in chapter 2, such factors influence what we feel is important; that is, our values.

6 *Racial and socioeconomic factors.* The value orientations, cultural norms and different opportunity structures associated with different racial or ethnic backgrounds or with different socioeconomic groups will also influence and be a part of an individual's personal coping resources. Cultures or subcultures which continue to emphasize the extended family for example may have access to greater social support in times of stress and transition (Schlossberg, 1981). Alternatively, 'racial or ethnic traditions may be an isolating factor, making adaptation more difficult'.

7 *Previous experience.* Previous experience of successfully handling a similar event or transition will generally facilitate the management of a current one. The past experience will have provided both constructive attitudes about the event (that is, the belief that it can be managed) and behavioural competencies (that is, specific coping skills) that were reinforced by the success experience (Danish and D'Augelli, 1980). Conversely, previous experience of failure may render the individual more vulnerable and less able to cope in the future (Schlossberg, 1981).

Again, the timing of an event may influence the impact it has on an individual's future coping resources. It has been suggested that a non-normative crisis such as the death of a child can inhibit the bereaved family's ability to cope with subsequent losses, whereas the experience of 'on-time' bereavements (such as, the expected death of elderly relatives) can help those involved learn how to cope more effectively with such situations (Callahan *et al.*, 1983).

Coping responses

Attention now turns to Pearlin and Schooler's second facet of coping – coping responses rather than coping resources – that is, what a person does rather than what he or she has (Pearlin and Schooler, 1978). In the face of life exigencies we might employ any number of specific responses. Thus, in response to marital difficulties we might seek advice from friends, family or professional counsellors; we might talk matters through with our spouse in an attempt to resolve our conflicts; we might change our expectations of what married life should be like; we might develop additional interests; we might separate. Pearlin and Schooler (1978) distinguish between such tactics on the basis of their more general function, of which they identify three: responses that modify the demands of the situation; responses that modify the meaning of the situation for the individual; and responses that modify the individual's ability to handle the demands of the situation.

Coping responses that fall into the first of these categories are the only ones which act directly on the situation that is making the demands. They are aimed at altering or eliminating the source of life strains, and therefore represent the most direct way of coping with them. Attempts to resolve marital conflict through negotiation between husband and wife would fall under this heading, and discussion with significant others may be a prelude to it. In their empirical study of responses to life strains Pearlin and Schooler found, however, that such direct actions constituted the minority of coping responses. They suggested four reasons why this might be the case. First, the individual may not recognize the situation as the source of the problem. Without such insight actions cannot consciously be mobilized towards altering it. Secondly, even if the source of the problem is recognized people may lack the knowledge and/or skills to change it. Thirdly, people may resist changing the situation on the ground that the resulting situation would be even worse – 'out of the frying pan into the fire', one might say. Finally, the conditions producing the demands may be resistant and difficult to change, thus undermining motivation to try.

Pearlin and Schooler (1978) found, therefore, that in their study the greater proportion of people's coping responses were concerned with controlling rather than changing the situation. One mechanism for achieving this is based on the recognition that our interpretation of a situation is often largely responsible for our evaluation of its threat or desirability. This is, of course, the basis of the difference between the disease and the developmental perspective on significant life events. Choosing between one or the other of these viewpoints is a mechanism for controlling the meaning of such events. It is analogous to a coping response in the second of Pearlin and Schooler's three categories, namely, modifying the meaning of the situation. If we can reappraise the situation by, for example, counting our blessings and recognizing that there are others worse off than ourselves, or perhaps through ignoring those parts of the situation we find unpalatable, then we may reduce the amount of stress we experience.

Pearlin and Schooler's third category of coping response constitutes an alternative, or an additional, mechanism for controlling the situation – namely modifying and thereby (it is hoped) enhancing our ability to cope with the demands. Thus, systematic planning may help us to handle a heavy work load and relaxation may help us to handle stress better generally.

With regard to the effectiveness of coping Pearlin and Schooler (1978) found that remaining involved in and committed to close interpersonal relationships mitigated against the experience of stress in the face of problems within those relationships. In more impersonal situations, however, the reverse was true, with stress being less likely to be experienced when people were able to disengage themselves from involvement. It is not, however, possible to make many general statements about the relative efficacy of Pearlin and Schooler's three different coping strategies. Arguably, the first category, being a direct rather than an indirect attack on the situation, represents (potentially) the most permanent and 'real' solution. However, as Pearlin and Schooler point out, total control over one's life events is impossible. When we talk of controlling our life we mean in large part controlling our response to life events rather than necessarily controlling the events themselves (Brammer and Abrego, 1981).

Coping skills

The greater the number and range of coping responses the individual possesses the greater is his or her range of options (Hopson and Scally, 1981) and the greater the chance of him or her coping effectively (Pearlin and Schooler, 1978). Coping responses, being what the person does rather than (although influenced by) what the person has or is, can also be thought of as skills. Skills are potentially trainable and learnable. This is the rationale underpinning Hopson and Scally's (1981) identification of 'life skills' as teachable and necessary, although not sufficient, mechanisms of self-empowerment – 'a process by which one increasingly takes greater charge of oneself and one's life'

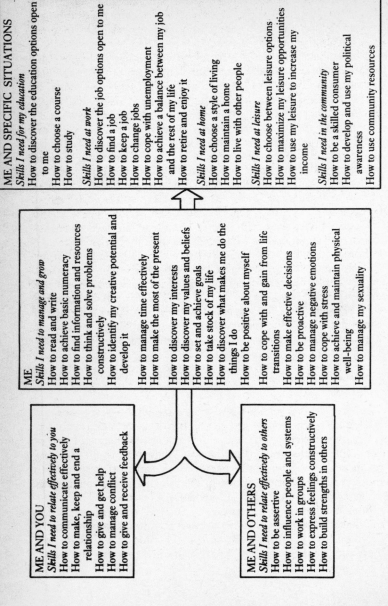

ME AND SPECIFIC SITUATIONS
Skills I need for my education
How to discover the education options open to me
How to choose a course
How to study

Skills I need at work
How to discover the job options open to me
How to find a job
How to keep a job
How to change jobs
How to cope with unemployment
How to achieve a balance between my job and the rest of my life
How to retire and enjoy it

Skills I need at home
How to choose a style of living
How to maintain a home
How to live with other people

Skills I need at leisure
How to choose between leisure options
How to maximize my leisure opportunities
How to use my leisure to increase my income

Skills I need in the community
How to be a skilled consumer
How to develop and use my political awareness
How to use community resources

ME
Skills I need to manage and grow
How to read and write
How to achieve basic numeracy
How to find information and resources
How to think and solve problems constructively
How to identify my creative potential and develop it

How to manage time effectively
How to make the most of the present

How to discover my interests
How to discover my values and beliefs
How to set and achieve goals
How to take stock of my life
How to discover what makes me do the things I do
How to be positive about myself

How to cope with and gain from life transitions
How to make effective decisions
How to be proactive
How to manage negative emotions
How to cope with stress
How to achieve and maintain physical well-being
How to manage my sexuality

ME AND YOU
Skills I need to relate effectively to you
How to communicate effectively
How to make, keep and end a relationship
How to give and get help
How to manage conflict
How to give and receive feedback

ME AND OTHERS
Skills I need to relate effectively to others
How to be assertive
How to influence people and systems
How to work in groups
How to express feelings constructively
How to build strengths in others

Figure 6.3   Basic life skills (Hopson and Scally, 1981)

(Hopson and Scally, 1981, p. 57). Whilst recognizing that the development of any skills can potentially facilitate the individual's self-empowerment, they have attempted to define those skills that are most crucial. These skills, detailed in figure 6.3, can be subdivided into four areas: skills the individual needs to survive and grow generally; skills needed to relate effectively within one-to-one personal relationships; skills needed to relate effectively to others within society; and skills needed in specific situations. In similar vein, Brammer and Abrego (1981) delimit the basic coping skills necessary for managing transitions effectively.

Hopson and Scally (1981) discuss how the skills in their chart can be introduced and taught in schools and colleges. They give details of relevant teaching resources and materials, and have published three sets of material specially designed for teaching (and learning) a selection of these skills (Hopson and Scally, 1980b, 1982, 1985). The teaching of coping skills is concerned with modifying coping resources as well as coping responses. Implicit in such programmes is also the assumption that the relevant personal characteristics (for example, self-esteem) are not immutable. They may be relatively stable, but they are not necessarily static. In discussing such issues we are moving on to the topic that is the main concern of the final chapter of this book – namely, intervening in the life course.

7

Intervention

Life-span developmental psychology was defined in chapter 1 as the description, explanation and modification of the life course. Intervention is concerned with the third of these goals. It is concerned with change – with promoting, facilitating or preventing it. It is not, however, concerned with any old change or, usually, with change *per se*. It is generally concerned with particular types of change for particular purposes. The present chapter first raises some of the intervention implications of adopting a life-span perspective on development. It then considers the sources of help an individual might call upon. Thirdly, it notes a number of key dimensions in relation to which interventions can be described and analysed; and, fourthly, intervention taxonomies are considered. Finally, the book ends as it began – with an invitation to the reader to engage in some personal reflection. This time, before a final request for consideration of the lifeline, it takes the form of a hypothetical situation in which the reader is asked to intervene and to ponder upon the nature of and possible interventions in relation to the categories discussed earlier in the chapter.

Intervention implications of the life-span perspective

The life-span approach to development encompasses wide-ranging, contextually analysed change processes occurring across the whole of a person's life – the total life span, total life space approach as Super (1980) describes it. Such an emphasis has a number of intervention implications, some already alluded to at various points in the present book, but usefully summarized by Lerner and Ryff (1978). These can be thought of as the basic assumptions of life-span interventions.

Lerner and Ryff (1978) identify two major issues which characterize the life-span approach to intervention: first, the assumption that the effect of any particular intervention procedure will vary across individuals and, secondly, the consequent belief that the interventionist must select from an array of possible procedures the one which is most appropriate for that particular intervention goal under those particular conditions. The responses to or effects of a particular procedure are recognized as being moderated by 'the entire range of personological, cultural, and historical differences manifest in each individual' (p. 14). It is virtually impossible, therefore, to offer fixed recommendations about ideal interventions. There is no single or unequivocal answer to the question of which behaviours should be the targets for intervention, or to the question of which theories, perspectives or data concerning a particular issue are most useful. These questions must always be asked in the context of specific situations and persons. Given the assumed absence of unequivocal solutions, the life-span perspective encourages interventionists to adopt a professional-role definition which departs from that of the typical 'expert' role towards one which is negotiated between interventionist and client. As Lerner and Ryff (1978) put it, 'rather than rely on the merits of their own intuitive frameworks, scientists could wisely benefit from listening to the developmental needs voiced by those they study' (p. 16).

The assumption of life-long change that characterizes the life-span approach to intervention means that disruption is not seen as inherently undesirable. Nor does it take the intervenor by surprise, contravening some assumption of stability. A developmental perspective on life events implies interventions encouraging people to view change positively. Demystifying adulthood and questioning our age-related stereotypes is itself an intervention, an attempt to modify our attitudes towards and hence our experience of the life course.

Lerner and Ryff (1978) emphasize the importance of charting developmental sequences and behaviour-change processes across the whole life span in order to facilitate a preventive rather than an a-posteriori treatment approach to intervention – such a goal being another implication of the life-span perspective. To the extent that the life course or, at least, potential crises and dysfunctions, can be predicted there is a possibility of early intervention so that developmental problems can be avoided. For example, the knowledge that continued cognitive activity can help mitigate intellectual decline in old age indicates to interventionists the likely benefit of providing adult education programmes – for example, the University of the Third Age, a programme of university-level study specifically directed at those of retirement age.

Reliable, generalizable maps of life-span changes may, however, be elusive or even non-existent – this was the basis of Gergen's (1980) questioning of prediction and control as appropriate functions of social theory in the field of life-span development. We need, therefore, more abstract analyses of life-span changes which can serve as a basis for assessing the likely accuracy of our predictions concerning the probable effect of any planned intervention. An example of such a theory–intervention interface is to be found in Baltes *et al.*'s (1980) distinction among age-graded, history-graded and non-normative systems of influence on the life course (Baltes and Danish, 1980). Such a conceptualization serves to remind us that in designing interventions we need to consider the joint impact of all such influence systems. Furthermore, since the distinguishing feature of non-normative influences is that they are neither age-graded nor history-graded in any systematic way (that is, they are the least predictable influence, at least as far as timing is concerned), it follows that these will be the most difficult to approach from a preventive rather than an a-posteriori treatment orientation.

If, as has been suggested, the impact of a non-normative influence system relative to other influence systems tends to increase throughout the life course (Baltes *et al.*, 1980), then we can expect the difficulty of designing preventive interventions to increase in tandem. This, combined with the basic assumption of life-long change, leads to another characteristic of the life-span developmental approach to intervention: namely an emphasis on the development of generic skills and on the provision of resources for dealing with the unexpected. This is the rationale underlying the concept of life skills (for example, Brammer and Abrego, 1981; Hopson and Scally, 1981) and the arguments in favour of teaching such skills both within schools and elsewhere. From such a perspective, there will, for example, be an emphasis on teaching people the principles of effective time management rather than, or in addition to, giving assistance with the specific problems of work overload. Likewise, generic models, such as that depicting the individual's relatively predictable response to significant life events – that is, the transition cycle (Hopson, 1981) – may be presented to and discussed with clients in order to facilitate their management of a variety of normative and non-normative events, both anticipated and unexpected.

Adoption of a life-span development orientation to intervention also encourages confrontation of the ethical issues and value systems which underly any intervention attempt (Lerner and Ryff, 1978). This arises out of the conceptual and value-laden nature of the concept of development. The decision to intervene is always based, if only implicitly, on the belief that one way of being (namely, that which the intervention seeks to achieve) is preferable to another way of being (namely, that which the client is currently living). The interventionist is, in Chandler's (1980) words, 'a moralist and proselytizer for a conversionary cause' (p. 83). The inevitability of such directiveness enhances the need for consideration of the ethics of intervention, and for 'reflective scrutiny' (Chandler, 1980) of the motives for and values underpinning any intervention attempt.

The potential for ethical doubts and conflicting value systems is readily apparent when, for example, the resulting quality of life is added to the preservation of life as a criterion for evaluating the worth of some of the technical advances in medical science. Thus the lead character in Brian Clark's play *Whose Life is it Anyway?* questions the value of his existence after being totally paralysed in an accident, and successfully challenges the right of the medical profession to keep him alive against his wishes. Such dilemmas tend to be most apparent at the very beginning and the very end of the life span. The lives of many very low-birth-weight babies can now be saved, but the risk of handicap is sometimes high. In extreme old age, or under conditions of extended illness, it may still be possible to maintain low levels of biological life. Is, however, life worth preserving at all costs? If not, who has the right to decide to allow somebody to die? Given that on such issues views are likely to vary, whose opinion should take priority? These are questions of values rather than of logic, and there are, as yet, not guiding principles to which interventionists and, in particular, behavioural as opposed to medical scientists can turn (Baltes and Danish, 1980).

The general model of development which is adopted will also have intervention implications (Montada and Schmitt, 1982). Thus, adherence to the view that development is primarily a maturational process points to something of a non-interventionist policy by suggesting 'that one not overstress the growing organism, but wait for the naturally occurring maturational process to take place' (p. 13). The suggestion that descriptions of development constitute 'the "natural course" of ontogenetic development' (p. 9) also encourages the assumption that later acquisitions or stages are in some sense better and more valuable than earlier acquisitions or stages. Whilst the error of assuming descriptions of the typical life course to be synonymous with development was pointed out in chapter 1, such descriptions have still been used as the basis of guidelines for practical decisions and goal-setting. Descriptive age norms and developmental tasks are frequently used to define socialization goals and to evaluate achievement and development. Thus Havighurst (1972) writes:

> some developmental tasks may be located at the ages of special sensitivity for learning them. When the body is ripe, and society requires, and the self is ready to achieve a certain task the teachable moment has come. Efforts at teaching, which would have been largely wasted if they had come earlier, give gratifying results when they come at the *teachable moment*, when the task should be learned. For example, the best times to teach reading, the care of children, and adjustment to retirement from one's job can be discovered by studying human development, and finding out when conditions are most favorable for learning these tasks. (p. 7)

Taking a life-span perspective can also encourage the consideration of the possible long-term implications, as well as the more immediate side effects, of any intervention decision (Brandtstädter, 1980). For example, mandatory retirement practices may demand a reduction in achievement-striving which casts doubt on the ethical justification of attempts earlier in the life course to encourage and maximize commitment to just such efforts. Can organizations, and societies, really justify the encouragement of competitive career advancement and commitment to upward career mobility if this is likely to be followed by a period of retirement bereft of social status and achievement opportunities? Such questions require that in planning interventions with younger age groups the possible developmental consequences for older age groups also be considered. Furthermore, expanding one's span of attention to the whole of the life course also encourages the notion of early preparation for later life tasks.

The typical commitment of adherents of a life-span perspective to contextual evaluation renders questionable the ethics of intervening in the life course of an individual without consideration of the social context in and with which he or she operates (see, for example, Horowitz and Paden, 1973). An individual may be affected not only by intervention efforts occurring earlier in his or her own life course, but also by interventions aimed at different age cohorts or at other aspects of social structure such as sex, social class or occupation (Baltes and Danish, 1980). Thus, encouraging women to return to paid employment once their children are grown, or to develop in some other way a sense of personal identity that is not inextricably bound up with their families, may make them less available, when they become grandparents, as a childcare resource on which their children can make substantial demands.

Finally, Lerner and Ryff (1978) suggest that the life-span perspective may stimulate 'a reordering of the description, explanation, intervention sequence' (pp. 15–16) such that, to use a phrase coined by Brandtstädter (1980), intervention practice becomes the touchstone of developmental psychological theory rather than vice versa. Whilst, argues Brandtstädter (1980), the first and basic aim of intervention should remain the solution (by alleviation or prevention) of developmental problems, we should not (and here he cites Baltes and Willis, 1977) 'overlook the knowledge-generation potential of intervention' (Brandtstädter, 1980, p. 22). When the primary goal is intervention the criteria on which an option is selected concern utility rather than 'truth' – that is, the extent to which particular strategies 'lead to socially relevant implementations and possess the potential for optimization of developmental processes' (Lerner and Ryff, 1978, p. 16). Thus, research becomes problem-driven, with descriptive and explanatory frameworks following rather than preceding concern with enhancing human lives and development.

Brandtstädter (1980), whilst supporting such activity, also offers some cautionary words. First, it is questionable whether interventions resting on shaky knowledge bases should be undertaken:

> to design large-scale intervention programs on the basis of theoretical and technological assumptions that are not yet sufficiently corroborated through previous research is to play a questionable game of chance. Theories and technologies should therefore be tested in low-risk situations before they are 'applied' in high-risk environments. (Brandtstädter, 1980, p. 22)

Secondly, Brandtstädter points to the usual impossibility in intervention research – for practical, methodological and ethical reasons – of employing experimental-type research designs with adequate control groups for the drawing of unambiguous theoretical conclusions. Finally, he points to the typical complexity of treatments in practical intervention programmes which mean that 'the results observed in evaluation research generally cannot be related to theoretical hypotheses in a stringent and clear-cut way. In applied intervention research, action programs, not theories are put to the test' (p. 23). Similarly, Reese and Overton (1980), in a brief discussion of the ethics of intervention, save their greatest concern for the ethics of intervention research:

> Interventions often come to an end because of political or other expediencies, and one would be justified in asserting that 'at least they had a few good years.' However, when the intervention is terminated because a research project has been completed, the ethics of the entire intervention must be questioned. (p. 44)

This, of course, applies to all intervention research, not only that carried out from a life-span perspective.

Sources of help

It is tempting to think of intervention in the life course as the province of various professional groups, but this is only one of several sources of help, and is frequently the source of last resort. There is substantial evidence (for example, Gottlieb, 1976; Gurin *et al.*, 1960; Roberts *et al.*, 1966; Ryan, 1969) that most people draw first upon their own resources and those of kith and kin before approaching official sources of assistance. It is important not to emphasize professional help to the exclusion of these other resources. As Cowen (1982) writes: 'Help is where you find it' (p. 385). Golan (1981), in an amalgam of several classifications of sources of help (for example, Caplan, 1970; Lieberman, 1975), identifies five potential sources of assistance available to a person in need or distress: the self; the natural help system (that is, family, friends and neighbours); the mutual help system (both formal and informal); the 'nonprofessional' support system (including voluntary organizations, community caregivers and paraprofessionals); and, finally, the professional help system (people who are, because of their specific training and particular discipline, designated as qualified to help troubled individuals and families with psychological and/or social problems in living). The sources of help available to an individual are a component of that individual's coping resources as defined in the previous chapter – namely, what is available to the individual in developing his or her coping repertoire. In distinguishing between these sources it is important to recognize that only rarely is just one form of help utilized: 'What we usually find is a weaving back and forth, an intricate combination of asking for and getting aid that merges into a pattern of multiple needs (or multiple aspects of the same need) attended to by various sources within the community' (Golan, 1981, p. 242).

The self as a source of help

Much of the section in chapter 6 on personal resources for coping is concerned with the self as a source of help in managing life events and transitions. Here, if you like, the individual is intervening in his or her own life. Most individuals will attempt to reach their own decisions and solve their own problems, either with or without the help of others. Furthermore, intervention by others is frequently directed at developing and mobilizing the resources and skills of self-dependence within the individual. Thus, others may teach the person generalizable problem-solving skills rather than offer him or her specific solutions to a current problem. In this way the individual becomes more able, it is hoped, to resolve future difficulties without recourse to intervention from others. It is also a case of practice making perfect: successful coping through one's own actions promotes self-direction and self-dependence (Perlman, 1957) and enhances self-esteem and self-worth (Oxley, 1971).

The natural help system

The previous chapter's section on social resources was concerned largely with the natural help system available to individuals through family, friends and neighbours, and mediated via social-support networks. The kith and kin system, as Caplan (1974b) calls it, it is probably the first outside help to which an individual turns in times of difficulty or uncertainty. Golan (1981) adds 'informal caregiver' to Caplan's term, distinguishing between the 'generalists' who are known for their overall wisdom and knowledge of the system and the 'specialists' who have already coped successfully with particular misfortunes.

The mutual help system

The distinguishing features of mutual help systems are a shared belief in the efficacy of peer help and a focusing of attention on a core problem area which all members have experienced or are experiencing and which binds them together. It is likely that the members of a mutual help system will be at different stages in relation to the life event or experience which links them. Thus, new members will be able to look to the system for details of how others have coped with a similar situation. They can look to and identify with individuals within the system as role models and as a source of hope for the future. Although these new members of mutual help systems may gain a great deal, it has been suggested (Riessman, 1965) that it is the helper who gains most. Thus, Skovholt (1974) identified four benefits that the helper might receive from helping: (1) an increased sense of interpersonal competence from having successfully helped another; (2) an enhanced sense of personal adequacy from having given as well as received help; (3) further self-insight gained through the process of working with others on their problems; and (4) the gratitude and social approval of those who have been helped.

Despite such common factors, there may be many differences between particular mutual help systems. Although operable between dyads, mutual-help systems more usually involve groups of individuals with varying purposes and varying degrees and types of structure and formal organization. Thus, Silverman (1978) distinguishes between four main activities of mutual help groups: fund raising, political action, consumer activity and personal help. Bean (1975) identifies three main types of mutual-help groups based on the nature of the members' predicament. First, there are groups organized around the experiencing of a particular crisis or transition. For example, all members may have experienced the death of a child or a particular type of surgery, such as amputation or colostomy. Alternatively they may be undergoing a particular transition such as divorce or the birth of a first child. The purpose of the mutual help system is generally to offer information and support during the crisis period. It is not normally expected that individuals will remain within the system on a long-term basis, although they may change their role to becoming a helper rather than a client. Alternatively their activity may shift away from the giving and/or receiving of personal help towards the more outward-looking activities of fund raising, political action and consumer advocacy.

Bean's second type of mutual-help group is for people with a permanent, fixed, stigmatized condition, for example homosexuality. It is likely that as well as helping members cope with the stigma and maintain a positive self-image, such groups will also campaign to attack prejudice and change the social attitudes which stigmatize them. Finally, Bean's third category of mutual help organizations are for people caught in a habit, addiction or self-destructive way of life. The most obvious examples would include people with drink- or drug-dependency problems, but

organizations such as Weight Watchers and Gamblers Anonymous would also fall into this category. The main focus is on
helping members behave differently and maintain a life style
which enables them to avoid returning to their addictive or
self-destructive habits.

Mutual help organizations also differ considerably with regard
to their attitude towards and their relationship with professional
sources of help. Some have been established and are organized by
members of the professional help system, whilst others have been
set up in opposition to such systems and in response to their
perceived inadequacies and limitations. Some groups consciously
exclude the involvement of professionals, whilst in other instances
professionals may act, if not as direct leaders, then as consultants.

The nonprofessional help system

Golan (1981), focusing specifically on sources of help during
times of transition, distinguishes between three categories of
nonprofessional help: voluntary workers, community care-givers
and paraprofessionals.

Voluntary work tends, like mutual help, to be organized around
specific problems, situations or categories of people. Unlike the
mutual help system, however, there is no necessity for the helpers
to have experienced the same situation as the client, nor the
expectation that they obtain the same therapeutic gain from the
encounter as, say, the ex-alcoholic may gain from helping others
with drink-related problems. Thus, prison visitors need not have
served time themselves. Nor would they look to the prisoner for
the same type of support as they were offering him or her. This is
not to say that there are no rewards for voluntary work. Indeed, if
such workers gained nothing from the experience then the system
would not survive.

Community care-givers provide help and support to people in
need either as a part of their professional role or as an adjunct to it.
Teachers, police officers and the clergy, for example, may all fulfil
such a function. They work in direct contact with various client
groups in a number of types of relationships. Although they may
be professionals in their own right, the formal qualifications of
community care-givers as defined by Golan (1981) are not specifically related to the field of helping. They will often operate as

referral agencies, bringing clients to the attention of other sources of help and vice versa.

Paraprofessionals are personnel working within organizations that offer a helping service, but whose training is either more general or more specific, or at a lower level than those categorized as professional helpers. They frequently work in conjunction with or under the direction of members of the professional help system who, in turn, may rely heavily on their contribution. Often paraprofessionals will be concerned with work 'where the need is for relatively concrete, immediate intervention to carry out specific, defined activities aimed at restoring the person's equilibrium' (Golan, 1981, p. 250). In some instances voluntary workers and community care-givers come into the category of paraprofessionals.

The professional help system

At the far extreme of Golan's (1981) continuum of sources of help lie those individuals whose training and employment confers on them community or institutional sanction and responsibility for offering help to various client groups. Psychiatrists, clinical psychologists, trained counsellors, social workers and psychiatric nurses are amongst those in this category. Each group has its own professional identity, particular area of competence and modes of intervention.

The vast majority of research on the helping process has been conducted with members of the professional help system and their clients, despite this system being responsible for only a small proportion of the help sought or received for psychological or psychosocial problems. None the less, the facets of helping interventions discussed in the remaining sections of this chapter can generally be applied to other sources of help as well. Thus, help emanating from the self, and from the natural, mutual and 'nonprofessional' help systems can be thought of in relation to parameters such as those discussed in the following section.

Dimensions of intervention

Baltes (1973), defining intervention as programmatic attempts at alteration, selected several intervention parameters to indicate the diversity of possible intervention actions. Thus, target behaviours include cognition, language, intellectual achievement, social interactions, motivational states, personality traits and attitudes. The setting for the intervention might be the laboratory, the family, the classroom, the hospital, the community or the environment. The intervention mechanisms could range through psychotherapy, counselling, training, environmental change, health delivery and economic support. Such examples are illustrative rather than exhaustive. The lists are limited only by our imagination and inventiveness.

In order to grasp the issues involved in intervention more than a lengthy list of specific options is required. A shift of attention from the specific to the general is needed. It is at the level of generic strategies rather than concrete modes of intervention (to use Baltes and Danish's (1980) distinction) that generalizable, transferable and manageable frameworks will emerge. Generic strategies can be discussed in relation to a number of parameters, the most frequently used of which are considered below: intervention goal, timing in relation to the target issue, level of analysis, level of intervention and style of delivery.

The intentions or goals of intervention

If, as has been claimed, intervention is not directed at change *per se*, then it must be goal-directed. A number of classifications of intervention goals have been offered (for example, Baltes, 1973; Caplan, 1964; Danish *et al.*, 1980; Horowitz and Paden, 1973). Although the terminology varies and sometimes the same term relates to different categories, each of these systems encompasses some or all of the following four subdivisions: treatment, prevention, adjustment and optimization.

Treatment is the first intervention goal which comes to most people's minds. Treatments are interventions designed to alleviate or correct existing illnesses or problems. The second intervention goal, namely *prevention*, is now widely recognized. Here the aim is to avoid problems, 'to counteract the harmful circumstances before they have a chance to produce illness or dysfunctioning' (Baltes and Danish, 1980, pp. 59–60). Thirdly, there are interventions aimed at *adjustment*. These are designed to help the individual come to terms with an illness, a disability or other changed circumstances. A final possible intervention goal is the *optimization* of individual functioning as opposed to merely the avoidance of malfunctioning. This assumes that there is more to good health than the absence of disease. Whereas an emphasis on prevention sees the world as being full of danger, an emphasis on optimization sees it as being full of opportunity. Optimization stands out from the other generic intervention goals as being concerned with the promotion of health rather than the easement of illness. That is, it is premised upon a developmental rather than a disease conception of human functioning (Danish *et al.*, 1980).

Interventions undertaken in accordance with a developmental perspective are designed to enhance the individual's ability to grow or develop (Danish and D'Augelli, 1980). In several classifications of intervention, goals optimization is not accorded its own category. This is likely to be a result of the (often implicit) adoption of a disease conception of intervention. As a discipline, life-span developmental psychology is concerned with the promotion of positive mental health. This makes the developmental conception the appropriate paradigm, and optimization the preferred intervention goal.

Timing of interventions

Developmental interventions typically occur in relation to life events which, in turn, can be viewed as comprising a period of anticipation, a period of actual occurrence of the event and an aftermath (Danish *et al.*, 1980). Intervention can, in other words, occur before, during or after the event. The timing of an intervention and its goals are related. A particular timing will delimit the possible intervention goals. Interventions occurring before the onset of a particular life event will frequently be concerned with prevention. Those occurring during a life event will generally be concerned with treatment and those occurring afterwards with adjustment. Thus, pre-marriage counselling will attempt to forestall the occurrence of marital difficulties; marriage-guidance counselling is generally undertaken in response to problems that have already arisen; and support groups for the separated and divorced will probably include amongst their goals facilitating adjustment to the marital break-up.

With regard to the intervention goal of optimization the question of timing is rather more complex. Its basis in a developmental conception of human functioning means that it can be thought of as a particular way of facilitating prevention, treatment or adjustment. This makes optimization a possible goal irrespective of the timing of an intervention in relation to a critical life event.

Levels of analysis

Psychology has traditionally focused its attention on the individual. From this perspective the source of illness or other dysfunctioning is located within the individual. Social problems are seen as arising out of the inability of certain individuals to fit into the structure of society or to be comfortable being different (Rappaport, 1977). Given an interactive, contextual world view this can, at most, be thought of as representing only a partial analysis of the problem. Other levels of analysis must be considered. Thus, Rappaport (1977) identifies four levels of analysis of social problems. As well as the individual level he discusses small group, organizational, and institutional and community levels of analysis. These last three levels relate to Bronfenbrenner's microsystems and mesosystems. A further level of analysis may be derived from Bronfenbrenner's work, one which is compatible with an emphasis on the exosystem.

The levels of analysis and the parallel levels of intervention are cumulative. Thus, analysis at, let us say, the institutional level does not preclude analysis and, indeed, intervention at the small-group or individual level. None the less, each level of analysis is characterized by different values and goals. The assumptions of the individual level of analysis have already been noted. The small-group level of analysis looks to interpersonal rather than intrapersonal sources of problems. Group rather than individual deficits and difficulties are emphasized. This perspective leads to a focus on the family rather than individual therapy, for example, and to an emphasis on such strategies as team building and interpersonal-communication training within organizations.

Analysis at the organizational level begins from the assumption that the way in which organizations function and are structured may result in problems for individuals. For example, ineffective channels of communication may mean that an individual cannot perform his or her job adequately. The solution is not, or not only, individual training or interpersonal-skills training. It is also a problem of organizational design.

At the institutional and community level of analysis the emphasis is on broad social analysis. Social problems are seen as the products of our social institutions rather than the fault of individuals, groups or specific organizations. Blame is laid at the door of housing policy rather than particular housing departments, for example, or the structure of the National Health Service may be criticized rather than particular hospitals, staff groups or patients.

Finally, at the more abstract level analysis looks beyond institutions and communities to the way our thinking is influenced by such factors as the structure of a society's language and the mores of its operation. Thus, the sexist nature of the English language is seen as at least partly responsible for the sexism shown and experienced by individuals. For example, the practice of using the masculine pronoun generically implies, even if it does not explicitly intend, that women are a deviation from the norm.

Levels of intervention

Many psychologists are faced with a dilemma. They experience a discrepancy between, on the one hand, the intervention need which they perceive and, on the other hand, the intervention role for which they have been trained and which is expected of them. By tradition psychologists have adopted both an individual level of analysis and an individual level of intervention. They have looked for within-individual variables to account for problems and difficulties and have looked to changes in individuals to effect a solution. They have worked, and continue to work, directly with those whose life-span development they seek to promote. Thus, clinical psychologists, educational psychologists and careers counsellors, for example, have spent most of their time working with individual patients, school-children and school-leavers respectively. The model of intervention is the one-to-one helping relationship.

However, focusing exclusively on the psychological dynamics of individual clients represents incomplete problem analysis from an interactive world view. The previous section suggested four other levels of analysis. Moreover, the efficacy of individually based therapy has been questioned – see Oatley (1984) for a discussion of the evidence. In addition, it has long been recognized that there are insufficient resources to fulfil the requirements of an individually orientated treatment practice (Albee, 1959).

There have been several appeals for the 'reconstruction' of various aspects of psychological practice (Armistead, 1974; Gillham, 1978; McPherson and Sutton, 1981) along less myopic lines. These appeals have typically endorsed the attempts of community psychology (Bender, 1976; Rappaport, 1977) to fuse two traditions – the psychological and the sociological/political. They include, amongst other things, a plea for interactive, multiple-level problem analysis and an expansion of the psychologists' professional role.

Alternative possible levels of intervention mirror the alternative possible levels of analysis outlined above. Whilst different levels of analysis may suggest particular interventions as optimum, it is not, essential that there always be parity between levels of analysis and intervention. Cognizance should also be taken of the intervenor's skills and of what is permissible and/or achievable in a particular situation. That is, the feasibility of goals (Brandtstädter, 1980) warrants consideration. If, for example, a client's problem stems from inadequate housing provision (that is, it is a social- and community-level problem) it is still justifiable to treat the client's consequent depression. The criticism of such practice is that it treats the symptoms not the cause and it encourages the acceptance of inequity. Labelled the elastoplast of society, such interventions may be seen as covering up, hiding and thereby avoiding the 'real' problem. However, it could equally well be argued that it is unethical not to treat an individual's symptoms when it is known that this may be possible. Furthermore, interventions directed at the individual level can help to address the root cause if, for example, they are concerned with supporting the individual's efforts to press for more adequate housing.

Recognizing multiple levels of problem location does none the less imply some expansion of psychologists' traditional roles. A number of not dissimilar forms of such expansion have been proposed (for example, Bender, 1976; Caplan, 1970). Lawton (1985) distinguishes between client work, worker work and community work. In addition to working directly with clients either individually or in groups, psychologists need to operate in relation to at least two other categories of personnel. First, they should work with others such as teachers, social workers and nurses who themselves work directly with clients. That is, they should involve themselves with nonprofessional, paraprofessional and other professional helpers. These groups should become psychologists' clients. Secondly, they need to expand their administrative and consultancy function, working at the level of policy-making and programme-planning. One major difficulty is that at present the professional training of psychologists – especially in the clinical and educational fields – does little to facilitate such role development.

Styles of delivery

Styles of delivery refer to the ways in which services (interventions) are delivered to the target population. They represent a link between the theoretical and assumptive bases of intervention and specific intervention techniques. Rappaport (1977; Rappaport and Chinsky, 1974) distinguishes between the waiting-mode and the seeking-mode styles of delivery. The former is reactive, epitomized by the traditional relationship between doctor and patient, lawyer and client, or other expert and service recipient. Its main characteristics include the expert or other authority who waits and is approached by the client for diagnosis and treatment. By contrast, seeking-mode interventions actively search out potential clients.

The style of delivery that is adopted will have a number of professional role implications for the intervenor. It can influence or logically be determined by the setting, level, target population, timing and goal of intervention. Thus, with regard to intervention setting, services offered in the waiting mode are usually located in the expert's office. For seeking-mode interventions excursions must generally be made into the potential client's territory. In an attempt to reach more clients a college counselling service may move its location from, say, the student health centre to the students' union. However, this alone would be insufficient to reach all those who might benefit from its services. Potential clients would still have to define themselves as such and take the initiative in approaching the counsellor's office. It is still a waiting-mode style of delivery. Bringing intervention into the classroom by, for example, including self-development programmes as an integral part of the college curriculum might provide one way of breaking out of the waiting-mode straightjacket. In this way individuals who would benefit from personal counselling might be identified or identify themselves. It is a way of seeking out clients.

The seeking-mode style of delivery is particularly well suited to preventive interventions. In the reactive waiting mode the expert responds to requests for treatment or for prevention. The seeking mode has the potential for dealing with issues before they are forced on the expert's or, indeed, the client's attention. It can also attempt to reach those who, for whatever reason, do not approach services operating through the waiting-mode style of delivery. As a consequence of this strategy of searching out clients the inter-venor may well be taking responsibility for defining the client population, whereas with the waiting mode the clients are gener-ally self-defined. It is possible that some clients will reject their label. Moves to add fluoride to drinking water in order to mitigate tooth decay in children represent attempts at preventive interven-tion using a seeking-mode style of service delivery. The compul-sory wearing of seat belts in cars is another example. Such interventions may be seen as violations of individual freedom. Those resisting such interventions are, in effect, objecting to being defined as clients. Simply prescribing or selling fluoride tablets for those children whose parents ask for them would constitute preventive intervention using a waiting-mode style of delivery.

Seeking-mode interventions are often associated with what Rappaport (1977) calls a 'new attitude' to the role of the profes-sional. This attitude is largely concerned with crossing traditional professional boundaries and role definitions. If the co-operation and support of new groups of clients is to be gained the nature of the helper–client relationship may need to be fundamentally changed. Not only will seeking-mode interventions typically take place outside the expert's office, but they may also be delivered by any number of persons either professional or nonprofessional. The traditional expert, rather than delivering the service directly, is more likely to assume the role of consultant, programme initiator and/or evaluator. Seeking-mode interventions are more likely than waiting-mode interventions to be directed at other than the individual client. Initiatives for training teachers or other professional groups in counselling skills, for example, are more likely to emanate from counsellors than from the teachers themselves. In other words, the counsellors will probably need to seek out these new client groups rather than simply wait to be approached by them. Furthermore, style of delivery may influence level of intervention – or vice versa, since it may be that intervention level is selected prior to style of delivery.

Intervention taxonomies

Using one or more parameters, interventions can be classified into different types. Thus Rappaport (1977; Rappaport and Chinsky, 1974) proposes that every model for mental-health delivery can be divided into two basic components irrespective of its content – a conceptual component and a style-of-delivery component. The former refers to 'that aspect of the model which dictates the empirical data base, theoretical notions and basic assumptions for understanding human behaviour' (Rappaport, 1977, p. 72). The style-of-delivery component has already been discussed and refers to 'that segment of the model which dictates how the service called for by the conceptual component will be offered to the target population' (Rappaport, 1977, pp. 72–3).

Danish *et al.* (1980) also propose a two-dimensional classification of intervention approaches. Deriving their typology of intervention approaches from Rappaport and Chinsky's (1974) schema, they accept the conceptual component as one crucial parameter, but argue that for the life-events perspective which they adopt the timing of an intervention is more salient than the style of delivery.

The conceptual component of an intervention model is a theory of human behaviour. Paramount amongst such theories has been the medical model which employs disease notions to understand problems in living (that is, sees them as similar to physical illness) and/or emphasizes a repairing rather than a preventive strategy. However, there are many other possible conceptual components. Rappaport suggests as alternatives a behavioural conceptualization of human behaviour, a social-learning conceptualization, a neurological conceptualization and a sociological conceptualization. These are only some of the possible options and herein lies the disadvantage of employing this parameter. Rappaport says only that the conceptual component is crucial. He does not classify or offer a typology of different conceptual components. He does not, in other words, indicate which are the key discriminating dimensions in theories of human behaviour. Danish *et al.* do, however, suggest an appropriate way of distinguishing conceptual components. They adopt a life-events perspective as a way of facilitating interventions with a developmental conceptual component, and this leads them to distinguish between a developmental and a disease theory of human functioning. They divide their second dimension, the timing of an intervention, into three categories according to whether the intervention occurs before, during or after the target life event. A six-cell typology of intervention approaches is the result. Table 7.1 gives examples falling within each category. Caplan's (1964) alternatives of primary prevention, secondary prevention (that is, early treatment) and tertiary prevention (the latter called remedial services by Danish *et al.*, 1980) constitute interventions based on a disease model of human functioning. Enhancement efforts, support groups and counselling are compatible with a developmental approach.

Generally the parameters in such intervention taxonomies are selected pragmatically (Baltes, 1973), reflecting the particular interests of the researcher or interventionist involved. The resulting schema may provide useful heuristic devices, but are arbitrary bases for considering the implications of particular approaches since they offer different starting points and different assumptions

Table 7.1 Intervention taxonomy based on conceptual component and timing (Danish *et al.*, 1980)

	Timing of intervention in relation to event		
Conceptual component of intervention	Before	During	After
Disease	Primary prevention	Secondary prevention	Remedial services
Developmental	Enhancement efforts	Support groups	Counselling

as to which are the most crucial or fundamental intervention parameters. However, a typology of helping models proposed by Brickman *et al.* (1982) (see, alternatively, Karuza *et al.*, 1982) does, whilst endowed with a basic simplicity, allow for systematic consideration of a wide range of intervention parameters. For this reason Brickman *et al.*'s typology is considered here in some detail.

In helping relationships questions of power and control are never far from the surface (Rogers, 1978). Who, for example, decides the goals of an intervention? Who decides the mechanisms by which goals shall be addressed? Does the helper/intervenor really know best, or should clients be encouraged to make these decisions themselves? After all, self-determination is one of the generally agreed hallmarks of a developing person. Both inside and outside helping relationships individuals may or may not be held responsible for causing their problems. Likewise, they may or may not be held responsible for finding and effecting a solution. Brickman *et al.* (1982) propose that such implicit or explicit assumptions concerning the locus of responsibility for causing and for solving problems are amongst the key determinants of the form a helper's help takes. Depending on the attributions made, helpers offer material aid, instruction, exhortation, discipline, emotional support or some other form of help.

By distinguishing between attributions of responsibility for causing problems and attributions of responsibility for finding solutions four alternative general models of helping are derived, as shown in table 7.2. First, general characteristics of the resulting typology will be discussed. Then attention will turn to the four models it points to.

Two of the taxonomy's helping models (labelled in table 7.3 the moral and medical models) are 'symmetrical' models in that the individual is held responsible in these models for respectively both and neither problem and solution. In the compensatory and enlightenment models attributions of responsibility for causing and solving problems are vested in different parties. In the former it is assumed that whilst individuals may not be responsible for the problematic situations in which they find themselves, they are responsible for doing something about it. In the latter model these assumptions are reversed. Individuals are held to be responsible for their problems but to be unable to effect a solution without

187

Table 7.2 Intervention typology based on attributions of responsibility for causing and solving problems (Brickman *et al.*, 1982)

Attribution to self of responsibility for problem	Attribution to self of responsibility for solution	
	High	Low
High	Moral model	Enlightenment model
Low	Compensatory model	Medical model

some form of outside help. A number of corollaries, as summarized in table 7.3, arise from the adoption of any particular model. These relate to the assessment made of the client and the appropriate response or form of help. Thus, the categorization accorded an individual – as lazy, sick, underprivileged, and so on – and the assistance offered are seen as functions of the attributions concerning the locus of responsibility for the cause and the solution of problems. As Brickman *et al.* point out these attributions are made both by those experiencing the problem and by those offering the help. This raises the subsidiary question of whether in any particular instance the attributions made by the helper and those made by the client coincide. Thus, counsellors often find clients wanting unequivocal advice whereas their own preference is for clients to make their own decisions and choices, thereby accepting responsibility for themselves. The confrontation and resolution of such differences may constitute an important part of the early stages of helping.

A number of Brickman *et al.*'s central hypotheses concerning the implications of each model are discussed below.

The moral model derives its name from its use, historically, to argue that others should feel 'neither obligated to help (since everyone's troubles are of their own making) nor capable of helping (since everyone must find their own solutions)' (Brickman *et al.*, 1982, p. 370). Under the moral model it is assumed, for example, that the unemployed could find jobs if only they tried

Table 7.3 Corollaries for helping and coping of attributions of responsibility for causing and solving problems (Brickman *et al.*, 1982)

	Attribution to self of responsibility for solution	
Attribution to self of responsibility for problem	High	Low
High	*Moral model*	*Enlightenment model*
Perception of self	Lazy	Guilty
Actions expected of self	Striving	Submission
Others besides self who must act	Peers	Authorities
Actions expected of others	Exhortation	Discipline
Implicit view of human nature	Strong	Bad
Potential pathology	Loneliness	Fanaticism
Low	*Compensatory model*	*Medical model*
Perceptions of self	Deprived	Ill
Actions expected of self	Assertion	Acceptance
Others besides self who must act	Subordinates	Experts
Actions expected of others	Mobilization	Treatment
Implicit view of human nature	Good	Weak
Potential pathology	Alienation	Dependency

hard enough. It is assumed that it is their own fault that they are unemployed and that the effort they have expended in trying to get work has been inadequate and/or misdirected. They are categorized as lazy. The only form of help deemed appropriate is for others to encourage or exhort the individual to change, improve and try harder, with reminders of how we are responsible for our own fate and have a 'moral duty' to help ourselves. In other words, the moral model places a strong emphasis on the self as a source of help.

The *medical model* is so called because historically it has been medical practice that best represents the assumption that people are responsible for neither the origin of nor the solution to their problem – or illness, as it would probably be called. The illness is not the patient's 'fault' nor is he or she responsible for prescribing the solution. The individual is, however, normally expected to take responsibility for following the expert's advice and trying to get well.

The assumptions underpinning this model are found not only in the medical world. Its criteria are also fulfilled by extreme reactive or mechanistic views of the person. Here it is the view that since human behaviour is determined by rewards and punishments (that is, by factors external to the individual) it is inappropriate to blame people for their problems or give them credit for finding solutions.

Under the *compensatory model* people are seen as having to compensate by their own effort for handicaps, obstacles or disadvantages imposed on them by their situation. Thus, whilst individuals may not be seen as responsible for their inability to obtain a job, for example, they are considered to be responsible for managing and coping with this situation. They are, in other words, responsible for their response to, if not the fact of, their unemployment.

Helpers operating under the assumptions of this model see their help as compensating for resources or opportunities that their clients deserve or need but do not have. It is with the recipient of help, however, that responsibility for effectively using this help is located. The compensatory model is the model of helping people to help themselves. Rather than helpers simply providing what they believe the clients need, as under the medical model, under the compensatory model helpers assist clients to obtain the resources for themselves. Thus, it seeks to empower individuals and, as it were, promote their own development. It is an attempt to move the source of an individual's help away from the 'professional' end of Golan's (1981) continuum of sources.

Finally, there is the *enlightenment model* under which 'people are blamed for causing their problems, but not believed to be responsible for solving them' (Brickman *et al.*, 1982, p. 273) This model derives its name from the consequent efforts of those offering help to enlighten their clients as to what is really the problem and what they must do to deal with it. In other words, clients must first be made to see and accept the error of their ways and secondly to realize that they cannot solve their problems themselves but must follow the instructions of those who can help them. Great power accrues to those who are seen as being able to offer help once clients accept the premises of this model. Clients view themselves as their own worst enemy but as being powerless to do anything about it on their own. Rather, they see themselves as dependent on others for assistance and, lacking a sense of self-efficacy, may experience low self-esteem. Self-esteem may rise again when, once 'cured', clients seek with determination and possibly with fanaticism to enlighten others. The assumptive base of the enlightenment model is found in some religious movements and mutual help systems. Considerable commitment to the authority of the group and/or its leaders is actively encouraged. This allows for a high degree of social control, which may be efficient in terms of facilitating achievement of the organization's goals, but which disregards personal autonomy and overrides dissent.

As outlined above each of the four alternative models of helping is something of a caricature. It should be noted that table 7.3 allocates relative rather than absolute levels of responsibility. In practice responsibility is generally shared to some degree. Also, the appropriateness of applying the different models may change over time. Thus, immediately following a sudden trauma it may be appropriate for a helper to assume responsibility for the client, gradually relinquishing this hold as the client emerges from the state of shock (to use the language of transition management). Likewise, it may be appropriate if a helper initially accepts a client's denial of any culpability with regard to, for example, a marital breakdown, in the interests of understanding the client's point of view and building a sound relationship. At some point, however, the client's role in precipitating the breakdown will need to be confronted.

Whilst bearing these subtleties in mind, the generalized consequences, advantages and dangers of adopting each of the different models can be identified. Attributions of responsibility to the self for causing problems (viz. the moral and enlightenment models) engenders guilt, whilst attributions of responsibility to others for finding solutions (viz. the medical and enlightenment models) engenders dependency. Application of the enlightenment model is, therefore, especially likely to result in clients having very negative self-images. It makes clients see themselves as doubly inadequate: first, because they allowed the problem to develop in the first place, and secondly, because of their perceived inability to do anything about it.

The medical model, like the enlightenment model, tends to foster dependency in that people are not encouraged to believe that they can do much for themselves. It may, however, make it easier for them to seek help in that their need for help is not seen as evidence of personal culpability or blame. They are likely to be classified as 'sick' rather than 'criminal'. Modern medical practice can deviate from the assumptions of this model. Biofeedback techniques, for example, may be used in preference to drugs for controlling high blood pressure, thereby giving the individual responsibility for controlling his or her condition. The natural childbirth movement is, amongst other things, an attempt to return control over managing birth to the mother rather than vesting it entirely in the medical practitioner. Interventionists who operate under the assumptions of the medical model will sometimes feel threatened by such movements, seeing them as challenges to their expertise.

Models which credit individuals with the responsibility for dealing with their problems encourage an active stance by arguing that if we do not like things the way they are we should do something about it ourselves rather than wait for someone else to take the initiative. When this attitude is combined with the assumption of the moral model, that individuals are also responsible for having got themselves into the difficult situation in the first place, then unsuccessful attempts at coping can precipitate a deep sense of failure and be very damaging to self-esteem. An emphasis on self-reliance and self-responsibility can also be conducive to isolation and loneliness.

The compensatory model 'allows people to direct their energies outward, working on trying to solve problems or transform their environment without berating themselves for their role in creating, or in permitting others to create, these problems in the first place' (Brickman *et al.*, 1982, p. 372). Taken to its extreme, the compensatory model is a reactive model – one is continually responding to problems not of one's own making. This can impose pressures on the lives of helpers and actors – seeing the same problem cropping up time and time again, feeling that as soon as one hurdle is surmounted there is another to be faced. If responsibility for solving problems is expanded to mean not simply coping with the immediate problem but attempting to prevent the problem recurring in the future, then this vicious cycle can be broken. It also implies accepting some responsibility for avoiding problems in the future if not for causing the problems of the present. As such it represents a move towards the assumptions of the moral model. This again emphasizes how these models are frequently abstractions. The attributions of responsibility change depending on how the problem is defined.

It is generally possible to consider any one problem from the perspective of more than one of the four models of helping presented in this section. Unemployment has already been used to exemplify the attributions made under the moral and the compensatory models. The problem of alcoholism is one that can be viewed from the perspective of any one of the four models. Under the medical model it would be seen as a physiologically based illness. Treatment would probably include medication. Certainly it would be under the control and direction of a professional expert. Interpretation of alcoholism under the assumptions of the enlightenment model is a harsh judgement. The individual is not allowed to plead excuses but rather must accept that it is his or her own weakness that has allowed the problem to get out of hand. Furthermore, individuals must accept their own inability to cope with the problem. Claims to the contrary will be disbelieved. Clients must accept that they need the support and guidance of others – possibly ex-alcoholics who have been through the same process. It may also be argued that this support and contact must continue if any success is to be maintained. Without such contact the individual is in danger of regressing to former habits. Pressure of work, the demands of a specific personal relationship or some other external stress may, under the compensatory model, be credited as having driven the person to drink. The individual is expected, however, to become actively involved in changing the situation and/or modifying his or her response to it. Finally, under the moral model individuals would probably be told to pull themselves together and be reminded of family or other responsibilities that are being neglected whilst they allow themselves to succumb to their desire for excessive alcohol.

Unfortunately from the point of view of convenience and

simplicity, it is not possible to identify one interpretation as the 'right' one. Cases vary. Difficulties arise when actors and/or helpers will admit of only one interpretation. The chances of this occurring are increased if the premises of such judgements are not made explicit. The models of helping presented by Brickman *et al.* and discussed in this section offer, via their characteristic of distinguishing between responsibility for causing problems and responsibility for finding solutions, a simple framework for articulating the bases of these judgements and reflecting on their validity in any particular instance. They provide a mechanism for making explicit the assumptions and values on which any intervention is based.

An intervention parable

In the present chapter a number of dimensions implicit in any attempt by an individual to intervene in his or her own life course or that of another have been identified. These dimensions can be brought together in a story depicting an attempt by one person to help another.

Imagine you are sitting quietly by the bank of a river when suddenly you see someone struggling in the water and being carried downstream by the current. You jump into the river, pull the victim out and administer artificial respiration. All at once you see two more people in the water in imminent danger of drowning. Again you dive in, this time rescuing one with each arm. When, a few minutes later, there are four people floating downstream you are unable to save them all. No one else who is with you on the river bank can swim and two of the victims slip away as you try to drag them to the shore.

This story represents a situation where someone (that is, you) intervenes in the life course of others. It has been employed in at least two textbooks (Egan and Cowan, 1979; Rappaport, 1977) to illustrate different intervention strategies and options. A number of relevant questions can be asked about this story. What intervention strategies have you been using so far? What alternatives may be open to you? What are the assumptions and values underpinning different options?

In terms of the categories used in this chapter you have been operating in the waiting mode, intervening at the individual level, with the goal of treating a problem that has already arisen. Whilst you may not have initially made any attribution of responsibility concerning the cause of the problem, by diving in to save the various individuals you have yourself assumed responsibility for effecting a solution. As more and more people float downstream you may well conclude that someone is pushing them in or that there has been some other large-scale disaster. In other words, you may eventually conclude that the drowning individual is not responsible for having caused his or her problem.

In the longer term there are a range of additional interventions open to you. Teaching individuals to swim and training more people in the skills of life saving would reduce the scale of any future such incident – more people could then save themselves or be saved. However, such strategies are still designed to treat a problem – although, arguably, teaching people to swim has a preventive component as well. It should preclude their getting into difficulties as well as enabling them to extricate themselves from an otherwise dangerous situation. None the less, a more effective strategy may be to move upstream and find out why and how people are getting into the water in the first place. It may be that they are voluntarily throwing themselves into the water – in which case, why? Do they realize what they are letting themselves in for? If they do, then what right have we to intervene? What are our responsibilities in such a situation? But, perhaps, rather than jumping they are being pushed. If so, can this be stopped? An environmental intervention may be in order. There may be a footbridge that needs repair or a fence that needs to be built. Such strategies would be directed at prevention rather than treatment. Additional interventions can doubtless be imagined. This example, it is hoped, serves to demonstrate that any one set of symptoms can be responded to in a variety of ways. The principles of intervention outlined in the present chapter are designed to help the would-be intervenor map out alternatives and conceptualize and evaluate strategies already in operation.

Finally, this book will end where it began – with your own lifeline. If you look again at this graph you can reflect on some further questions which are relevant to the subject matter of the present chapter. For example, what sources of help were offered or sought at various points in your life course? What sources of help do you tend to concentrate on? On the basis of what assumptions was help proffered or accepted? How did this influence its effectiveness? At a more general level it has been my hope that you have seen yourself in at least some of the pages of the present book. I can only reiterate the opening sentence – namely, that life-span developmental psychology is about all of us. It is not merely the study of other people.

Acknowledgements

The author and publisher would like to thank the following for permission to reproduce copyright material:
Figure 1.1 from D. E. Super (1980) 'A life-span, life-space approach to career development', *Journal of Vocational Behaviour*, 16, 282–98. Reprinted by permission of Academic Press, Inc. Figure 1.2 from G. Egan and M. A. Cowan (1979) *People in Systems: A Model for Development in Human Service Professions and Education*, Brooks/Cole Publishing Co. Reprinted by permission. Figure 1.3 from R. L. Kahn and T. C. Antonucci (1980) 'Convoys over the life course: attachment, roles and social supports', in P. B. Baltes and O. G. Brim (eds) *Life-Span Development and Behavior*, Vol. 3, Academic Press, Inc. Reprinted by permission. Figure 2.2 from P. B. Baltes *et al.* (1980) 'Life-span developmental psychology', *Annual Review of Psychology*, 31, 65–110. Reprinted by permission of Annual Reviews, Inc. Figure 3.1 from K. F. Riegel (1973) 'Dialectical operations: the final period of cognitive development', *Human Development*, 16 (5), 346–70. Reprinted by permission of S. Karger, AG, Basel. Figure 3.2 from K. W.

Schaie (1977–8) 'Toward a stage theory of adult cognitive development', *Journal of Aging and Human Development*, 8 (2), 129–38. Reprinted by permission of Baywood Publishing Co., Inc. Figure 5.1 from D. J. Levinson *et al.* (1978) *The Seasons of a Man's Life*, A. A. Knopf. Reprinted by permission. Figure 6.1 from B. Hopson (1981) 'Response to the papers by Schlossberg, Brammer and Abrego', *Counseling Psychologist*, 9 (2), 36–9. Copyright © 1981 by Division 17, Division of Counseling Psychology of the American Psychological Association. Reprinted by permission of Sage Publications, Inc. Figure 6.2 from B. H. Gottlieb (1983) 'Social support strategies: Guidelines for mental health practice'. Copyright © by Sage Publications, Inc. Reprinted by permission of Sage Publications, Inc. Figure 6.3 from B. Hopson and M. Scally (1981) *Lifeskills Teaching*, McGraw Hill. Reprinted by permission. Table 1.1 from *Adolescents: Behavior and Development* by Boyd R. McCandless. Copyright © 1970 by the Dryden Press, Inc. Reprinted by permission of CBS College Publishing. Tables 6.1 and 6.3 from H. W. Reese and M. A. Smyer (1983) 'The dimensionalization of life events', in E. J. Callahan and K. A. McCluskey (eds) *Life-Span Developmental Psychology: Nonnormative Life Events*, Academic Press, Inc. Reprinted by permission. Table 6.2 adapted from O. G. Brim and C. D. Ryff (1980) 'On the properties of life events', in P. B. Baltes and O. G. Brim (eds) *Life-Span Development and Behavior*, Vol. 3, Academic Press, Inc. Reprinted by permission. Table 7.1 from S. J. Danish *et al.* (1980) 'Developmental interventions', in P. B. Baltes and O. G. Brim (eds) *Life-Span Development and Behavior*, Vol. 3, Academic Press, Inc. Reproduced by permission. Table 7.3 from P. Brickman *et al.* (1982) 'Models of helping and coping', *American Psychologist*, 37(4), 368–84. Reprinted by permission of American Psychological Association, Inc.

Suggestions for further reading

1 Development across the life span

(i) Books

Rapaport, R. and Rapaport, R. (1980) *Growing Through Life*, London, Harper & Row.

Salmon, P. (1985) *Living in Time: a New Look at Personal Development*, London, Dent.

(ii) Articles

Baltes, P. B., Reese, H. W. and Lipsitt, L. P. (1980) 'Life-span developmental psychology', *Annual Review of Psychology*, 31, 65–110.

Clausen, J. A. (1972) 'The life course of individuals', in Riley, M. W., Johnson, W., Foner, A. (eds) *Aging and Society*, vol. 3: *A Sociology of Age Stratification*, New York, Russel Sage Foundation.

Runyan, W. M. (1978) 'The life course as a theoretical orientation: sequences of person-situation interaction', *Journal of Personality*, 46, 569–93.

2 Research

(i) Methodology

Baltes, P. B., Reese, H. W. and Nesselroade, J. R. (1977) *Life-Span Developmental Psychology: Introduction to Research Methods*, Belmont, California, Wadsworth.

(ii) Handbooks on ageing

Birren, J. E. and Schaie, K. W. (eds) (1977) *Handbook of the Psychology of Aging*, New York, Van Nostrand Reinhold.

Birren, J. E. and Sloane, R. B. (eds) (1980) *Handbook of Mental Health and Aging*, Englewood Cliffs, NJ, Prentice-Hall.

Poon, L. W. (ed.) (1980) *Aging in the 1980s: Psychological Issues*, Washington, DC, American Psychological Association.

(iii) Empirical studies (with particular reference to adulthood)

(a) Review
Schaie, K. W. (ed.) (1983) *Longitudinal Studies of Adult Psychological Development*, London, Guilford Press.

(b) Individual studies
Nicholson, J. (1980) *Seven Ages*, Glasgow, Fontana.

Sheehy, G. (1974) *Passages: Predictable Crises of Adult Life*, New York, E. P. Dutton.

Vaillant, G. E. (1977) *Adaptation to Life: How the Brightest and Best Came of Age*, Boston, Little, Brown.

3 Intervention

Hopson, B. and Scally, M. (1981) *Lifeskills Teaching*, London, McGraw-Hill.

Murgatroyd, S. and Woolfe, R. (1985) *Coping with Crisis: Understanding and Helping People in Need*, London, Harper & Row.

References and name index

Albee, G. W. (1959) *Mental Health Manpower Trends*, New York, Basic Books. *182*

Allport, G. W. (1964) *Pattern and Growth in Personality*, New York, Holt, Rinehart & Winston. *26, 29, 35–7*

Ambron, S. R. and Brodzinsky, D. (1982) *Lifespan Human Development*, 2nd edn, New York, Holt, Rinehart & Winston. *24*

Antonovsky, A. (1979) *Health, Stress and Coping*, San Francisco, Jossey-Bass. *157*

Antonucci, T. C. and Depner, C. E. (1982) 'Social support and informal helping relationships', in Willis, T. A. (ed.) *Basic Processes in Helping Relationships*, New York, Academic Press. *150–1, 154*

Arenberg, D. and Robertson-Tchabo, E. A. (1977) 'Learning and aging', in Birren, J. E. and Schaie, K. W. (eds) *Handbook of the Psychology of Aging*, New York, Van Nostrand Reinhold. *59*

Aries, P. (1962) *Centuries of Childhood*, New York, Vintage. *45*

Arlin, P. K. (1975) 'Cognitive development in adulthood: a fifth stage?', *Developmental Psychology*, 11, 602–6. *42, 64–5*

Arlin, P. K. (1977) 'Piagetian operations in problem finding', *Developmental Psychology*, 13, 297–8. *42, 64–5*

Armistead, N. (ed.) (1974) *Reconstructing Social Psychology*, Harmondsworth, Penguin. *182*

Baer, D. M. (1970) 'An age-irrelevant concept of development', *Merrill-Palmer Quarterly*, 16, 230–45. *12*

Baltes, P. B. (1968) 'Longitudinal and cross-sectional sequences in the study of age and generation effect', *Human Development*, 11, 145–71. *19, 21–2*

Baltes, P. B. (1973) 'Strategies for psychological intervention in old age: a symposium', *Gerontologist*, 13, 4–38. *177–8, 186*

Baltes, P. B. (ed.) (1978) *Life-Span Development and Behavior*, vol. 1, New York, Academic Press. *24*

Baltes, P. B. (1979) 'Life-span developmental psychology: some converging observations on history and theory', in Baltes, P. B. and Brim, O. G. (eds) *Life-Span and Development Behavior*, vol. 2, New York, Academic Press. *23, 48*

Baltes, P. B. (1983) 'Life-span and developmental psychology: observations on history and theory revisited', in Lerner, R. M. (ed.) *Developmental Psychology: Historical and Philosophical Perspectives*, Hillsdale, New Jersey, Lawrence Erlbaum. *23*

Baltes, P. B. and Brim, O. G. (eds) (1979, 1980, 1982, 1983, 1984, 1985) *Life-Span Development and Behavior*, vols 2–7, New York, Academic Press. *24*

Baltes, P. B., Cornelius, S. W. and Nesselroade, J. R. (1978) 'Cohort effects in behavioral development: theoretical and methodological perspectives', *Minnesota Symposium on Child Psychology*, 11, 1–63. *19*

Baltes, P. B. and Danish, S. J. (1980) 'Intervention in life-span development and aging: issues and concepts', in Turner, R. R. and Reese, H. W. (eds) *Life-Span Developmental Psychology: Intervention*, New York, Academic Press. *168, 170–1, 178*

Baltes, P. B., Reese, H. W. and Lipsitt, L. P. (1980) 'Life-span developmental psychology', *Annual Review of Psychology*, 31, 65–110. *24, 28, 47–8, 168*

Baltes, P. B. and Schaie, K. W. (eds) (1973) *Life-Span Developmental Psychology: Personality and Socialization*, New York, Academic Press. *24*

Baltes, P. B. and Willis, S. L. (1977) 'Toward psychological theories of aging and development', in Birren, J. E. and Schaie, K. W. (eds) *The Handbook of the Psychology of Aging*, New York, Van Nostrand Reinhold. *28, 172*

Bean, M. (1975) 'Alcoholics Anonymous, Part II', *Psychiatric Annals*, 5(3), 7–57. *175*

Bee, H. L. and Mitchell, S. K. (1984) *The Developing Person: A Life-Span Approach*, 2nd edn (1st edn 1980), San Francisco, Harper & Row. *24, 53, 90*

Bender, M. P. (1976) *Community Psychology*, London, Methuen. *182*

Berkman, L. F. and Syme, S. L. (1979) 'Social networks, host resistance, and mortality: a nine-year follow-up study of Alameda county residents', *American Journal of Epidemiology*, 109, 186–204. *153*

Bijou, S. W. (1968) 'Ages, stages, and the naturalization of human development', *American Psychologist*, 23, 419–27. *38, 41*

Birren, J. E. (1969) 'The concept of functional age: theoretical background', *Human Development*, 12, 214–15. *53*

Birren, J. E., Kinney, D. K., Schaie, K. W. and Woodruff, D. S. (1981) *Developmental Psychology: A Life-Span Approach*, Boston, Mass., Houghton-Mifflin. *24*

Birren, J. E. and Schaie, K. W. (eds) (1977) *Handbook of the Psychology of Aging*, New York, Van Nostrand Reinhold. *56*

Block, J. and Haan, N. (1971) *Lives Through Time*, Berkeley, California, Bancroft Books. *24, 44, 90*

Bloom, B. L., Asher, S. J. and White, S. W. (1978) 'Marital disruption as a stressor: a review and analysis', *Psychological Bulletin*, 85, 867–94. *153*

Botwinick, J. (1977) 'Intellectual abilities', in Birren, J. E. and Schaie, K. W. (eds) *Handbook of the Psychology of Aging*, New York, Van Nostrand Reinhold. *62*

Botwinick, J. (1978) *Aging and Behaviour*, 2nd edn, New York, Springer. *58–9*

Botwinick, J. and Storandt, M. (1974) *Memory, Related Functions and Age*, Springfield, Illinois, C. C. Thomas. *59*

Bower, T. (1977) *The Perceptual World of the Child*, London, Open Books. *56*

Brainerd, C. J. (1978) 'The stage question in cognitive-developmental theory', *Behavioral and Brain Sciences*, 1(2), 173–82. *38, 41*

Brammer, L. M. and Abrego, P. J. (1981) 'Intervention strategies for coping with transitions', *Counseling Psychologist*, 9(2), 19–36. *145, 163, 165, 169*

Branden, N. (1969) *The Psychology of Self-Esteem*, New York, Bantam Books. *156*

Brandtstädter, J. (1980) 'Relationships between life-span development theory, research and intervention: a revision of some stereotypes', in Turner, R. R. and Reese, H. W. (eds) *Life-Span Developmental Psychology: Intervention*, New York, Academic Press. *171–2, 182*

Brickman, P., Rabinowitz, V. C., Karuza, J., Coates, D., Cohn, E. and Kidder, L. (1982) 'Models of helping and coping', *American Psychologist*, 37 (4), 368–84. *187–90, 192*

Brim, O. (1975) 'Macro-structural influences on child development and the need for childhood social indicators', *American Journal of Orthopsychiatry*, 45, 516–24. *9*

Brim, O. G. and Ryff, C. D. (1980) 'On the properties of life events', in

Baltes, P. B. and Brim, O. G. (eds) *Life-Span Development and Behavior*, vol. 3, New York, Academic Press. *28, 132, 136–7*

Bronfenbrenner, U. (1977) 'Toward an experimental ecology of human development', *American Psychologist*, 32, 513–31. *9, 11–12, 148*

Broverman, I. K., Broverman, D. M., Clarkson, F. E., Rosenkrantz, P. S. and Vogel, S. R. (1970) 'Sex role stereotypes and clinical judgements of mental health', *Journal of Consulting and Clinical Psychology*, 34 (1), 1–7. *158*

Bühler, C. (1933) *Der menschliche Lebenslauf als Psychologiches Problem*, Leipzig, Hirzel. *78*

Bühler, C. (1935) 'The curve of life as studied in biographies', *Journal of Applied Psychology*, 19, 405–9. *79*

Bühler, C. and Massarik, F. (eds) (1968) *The Course of Human Life: A Study of Goals in the Humanistic Perspective*, New York, Springer. *78, 81, 105*

Buss, A. R. (1973) 'An extension of developmental models that separate ontogenetic changes and cohort differences', *Psychological Bulletin*, 80, 466–79. *19*

Buss, A. R. (1974) 'A general model for interindividual differences, intraindividual differences, and intraindividual changes', *Developmental Psychology*, 10 (1), 70–8. *19*

Buss, A. R. (1979) 'Dialectics, history, and development: The historical roots of the individual-society dialectic', in Baltes, P. B. and Brim, O. G. (eds) *Life-Span Development and Behavior*, vol. 2, New York, Academic Press. *93*

Callahan, E. J., Brasted, W. S. and Granados, J. L. (1983) 'Fetal loss and sudden infant death: grieving and adjustment for families', in Callahan, E. J. and McCluskey, K. A. (eds) *Life-Span Developmental Psychology: Nonnormative Life Events*, New York, Academic Press. *161*

Callahan, E. J. and McCluskey, K. A. (eds) (1983) *Life-Span Developmental Psychology: Nonnormative Life Events*, New York, Academic Press. *24*

Caplan, G. (1964) *Principles of Preventive Psychiatry*, New York, Basic Books. *178, 186*

Caplan, G. (1970) *The Theory and Practice of Mental Health Consultation*, New York, Basic Books. *173, 182*

Caplan, G. (1974a) *Support Systems and Community Mental Health*, New York, Behavioral Publications. *149*

Caplan, G. (1974b) 'Support systems', in Caplan, G. (ed.) *Support Systems and Community Mental Health*, New York, Behavioral Publications. *174*

Cassel, J. (1974) 'Psychosocial processes and stress: theoretical formulations', *International Journal of Health Services*, 4, 471–82. *149*

Chandler, M. J. (1980) 'Life-span intervention as a symptom of conversion hysteria', in Turner, R. R. and Reese, H. W. (eds) *Life-Span*

Developmental Psychology: Intervention, New York, Academic Press. *169*

Charles, D. C. (1970) 'Historical antecedents of life-span developmental psychology', in Goulet, L. R. and Baltes, P. B. (eds) *Life-Span Developmental Psychology: Research and Theory*, New York, Academic Press. *23*

Chiriboga, D. (1975) 'Perceptions of well-being', in Lowenthal, M. F., Thurnher, M. and Chiriboga, D., *Four Stages of Life: A Comparative Study of Women and Men Facing Transitions*, San Francisco, Jossey-Bass. *158*

Chodorow, N. (1978) *The Reproduction of Mothering*, Los Angeles, University of California Press. *74*

Clark, B. (1979) *Whose Life is it Anyway?* London, French. *169*

Cobb, S. (1976) 'Social support as a moderator of life stress', *Psychosomatic Medicine*, 38, 300–14. *149, 151*

Cohen, L. B. and Salapatek, P. (eds) (1975a) *Infant Perception: From Sensation to Cognition*, vol. 1: *Basic Visual Processes*, New York, Academic Press. *56*

Cohen, L. B. and Salapatek, P. (eds) (1975b) *Infant Perception: From Sensation to Cognition*, vol. 2: *Perception of Space, Speech and Sound*, New York, Academic Press. *56*

Cohler, B. J. (1982) 'Personal narrative and the life course', in Baltes, P. B. and Brim, O. G. (eds) *Life-Span Development and Behavior*, vol. 4, New York, Academic Press. *129, 130*

Collins, W. A. (eds) (1982) *The Concept of Development: The Minnesota Symposium on Child Psychology*, vol. 15, Hillsdale, New Jersey, Lawrence Erlbaum. *27*

Corso, J. F. (1971) 'Sensory processes and age effects in normal subjects', *Journal of Gerontology*, 26, 90–105. *56*

Corso, J. F. (1975) 'Sensory processes in man during maturity and senescence', in Ordy, J. M. and Brizzie, K. R. (eds) *Neurobiology of Aging*, New York, Van Nostrand Reinhold. *53*

Cowen, E. L. (1982) 'Help is where you find it: four informal helping groups', *American Psychologist*, 37 (4), 385–95. *173*

Craig, G. J. (1983) *Human Development*, 3rd edn, Englewood Cliffs, New Jersey, Prentice-Hall. *24*

Craik, F. I. M. (1977) 'Age differences in human memory', in Birren, J. E. and Schaie, K. W. (eds) *Handbook of the Psychology of Aging*, New York, Van Nostrand Reinhold. *58–9, 60*

Croog, S. H. (1970) 'The family as a source of stress', in Levine, S. and Scotch, N. A. (eds) *Social Stress*, Chicago, Aldine. *151*

Danish, S. J. (1977) 'Human development and human services: a marriage proposal', in Iscoe, I., Bloom, B. L. and Spielberger, C. C. (eds) *Community Psychology in Transition*, New York, Halstead. *146*

Danish, S. J. and D'Augelli, A. R. (1980) 'Promoting competence and enhancing development through life development intervention', in Bond, L. A. and Rosen, J. C. (eds) *Competence and Coping During Adulthood*, Hanover, New Hampshire, University Press of New England. *147, 161, 179*

Danish, S. J., Smyer, M. A. and Nowak, C. (1980) 'Developmental intervention: enhancing life-event processes', in Baltes, P. B. and Brim, O. G. (eds) *Life-Span Development and Behavior*, vol. 3, New York, Academic Press. *131–2, 146, 178, 179, 185, 186*

Datan, N. (1983) 'Normative or not? Confessions of a fallen epistemologist', in Callahan, E. J. and McCluskey, K. A. (eds) *Life-Span Developmental Psychology: Nonnormative Life Events*, New York, Academic Press. *47*

Datan, N. and Ginsberg, L. H. (eds) (1975) *Life-Span Developmental Psychology: Normative Life Crises*, New York, Academic Press. *24*

Datan, N. and Reese, H. W. (eds) (1977) *Life-Span Developmental Psychology: Dialectical Perspectives on Experimental Research*, New York, Academic Press. *24*

Dewald, P. A. (1980) 'Adult phases of the life cycle', in Greenspand, S. I. and Pollock, G. H. (eds) *Psychoanalytic Contributions Toward Understanding Personality Development*, vol. 3: *Adulthood and the Aging Process*, Washington, DC, National Institute of Mental Health. *100*

Dewey, J. and Bentley, A. F. (1949) *Knowing and the Known*, Boston, Beacon. *8*

Egan, G. and Cowan, M. A. (1979) *People in Systems: A Model for Development in the Human-Service Professions and Education*, Monterey, California, Brooks/Cole. *9, 194*

Engen, T. (1977) 'Taste and Smell', in Birren, J. E. and Schaie, K. W. (eds) *Handbook of the Psychology of Aging*, New York, Van Nostrand Reinhold. *57*

Erber, J. T. (1974) 'Age differences in recognition memory', *Journal of Gerontology*, 29, 177–81. *60*

Erikson, E. H. (1959) 'Identity and the lifecycle', *Psychological Issues*, 1 (1), 1–171. *35, 83*

Erikson, E. H. (1963) *Childhood and Society*, rev. edn (1st edn 1950), New York, W. W. Norton (Harmondsworth, Penguin, 1965). *83, 88–9*

Erikson, E. H. (1980) *Identity and the Life Cycle: A Reissue*, New York, W. W. Norton. *83–4, 87, 88–90, 92, 100*

Fakouri, M. E. (1976) '"Cognitive development in adulthood: a fifth stage?": a critique', *Developmental Psychology*, 12, 472. *65*

Forer, B. (1963) 'The therapeutic value of crisis', *Psychological Reports*, 13, 275–81. *147*

Fozard, J. L. (1980) 'The time for remembering', in Poon, L. W. (ed.) *Aging in the 1980's: Psychological Issues*, Washington, DC, American Psychological Association. *59*

Fozard, J. L., Wolf, E., Bell, B., McFarland, R. A. and Podolsky, S. (1977) 'Visual perception and communication', in Birren, J. E. and Schaie, K. W. (eds) *Handbook of the Psychology of Aging*, New York, Van Nostrand Reinhold. *56*

Garn, S. M. (1975) 'Bone loss and aging', in Goldman, R. and Rockstein, M. (eds) *The Physiology and Pathology of Human Aging*, New York, Academic Press. *55*

Gergen, K. J. (1977) 'Stability, change and chance in understanding human development', in Datan, N. and Reese, H. W. (eds) *Life-Span Developmental Psychology: Dialectical Perspectives on Experimental Research*, New York, Academic Press. *38, 44, 76, 129*

Gergen, K. J. (1978) 'Toward generative theory', *Journal of Personality and Social Psychology*, 36 (11), 1344–60. *3, 76–7*

Gergen, K. J. (1980) 'The emerging crisis in life-span developmental theory', in Baltes, P. B. and Brim, O. G. (eds) *Life-Span Development and Behavior*, vol. 3, New York, Academic Press. *3, 4, 76, 129, 168*

Gillham, W. (ed.) (1978) *Reconstructing Educational Psychology*, London, Croom Helm. *182*

Gilligan, C. (1982) *In a Different Voice*, Cambridge, Mass., Harvard University Press. *72, 74*

Golan, N. (1981) *Passing Through Transitions: A Guide for Practitioners*, New York, Free Press. *173–4, 176–7, 190*

Gollin, E. S. (ed.) (1981) *Developmental Plasticity: Behavioral and Biological Aspects of Variations in Development*, New York, Academic Press. *9*

Gottlieb, B. H. (1976) 'Lay influences on the utilization and provision of health services: a review', *Canadian Psychological Review*, 17, 126–36. *173*

Gottlieb, B. H. (1983) *Social Support Strategies: Guidelines for Mental Health Practice*, Beverly Hills, California, Sage. *151–3*

Gould, R. L. (1978) *Transformations: Growth and Change in Adult Life*, New York, Simon & Schuster. *2, 24, 103, 107, 117–20*

Gould, R. L. (1980) 'Transformational tasks in adulthood', in Greenspan, S. I. and Pollock, G. H. (eds) *The Course of Life: Psychoanalytic Contributions Toward Understanding Personality Development*, vol. 3: *Adulthood and the Aging Process*, Washington, DC, National Institute for Mental Health. *103, 107, 117–27*

Goulet, L. R. and Baltes, P. B. (eds) (1970) *Life-Span Developmental Psychology: Research and Theory*, New York, Academic Press. *24*

Groffmann, K. J. (1970) 'Life-span developmental psychology in Europe: past and present', in Goulet, L. R. and Baltes, P. B. (eds) *Life-Span Developmental Psychology: Research and Theory*, New York, Academic Press. *23*

Guilford, J. P. (1956) 'The structure of the intellect', *Psychological Bulletin*, 53, 267–93. *65*

Gurin, G., Veroff, J. and Feld, S. (1960). *Americans View their Mental Health: A Nationwide Interview Survey*, New York, Basic Books. *173*

Haan, N. (1972) 'Personality development from adolescence to adulthood in the Oakland Growth and Guidance Studies', *Seminars in Psychiatry*, 4 (4), 399–414. *19*

Haan, N. and Day, D. (1974) 'A longitudinal study of change and sameness in personality development: adolescence to later adulthood', *International Journal of Aging and Human Development*, 5, 11–39. *44*

Harris, D. B. (ed.) (1957) *The Concept of Development*, Minneapolis, University of Minnesota Press. *27*

Harrison, R. (1976) 'The demoralising experience of prolonged unemployment', *Department of Employment Gazette*, 1–10. *143*

Hartley, J. T., Harker, J. O. and Walsh, D. A. (1980) 'Contemporary issues and new directions in adult development of learning and memory', in Poon, L. W. (ed.) *Aging in the 1980s: Psychological Issues*, Washington, DC, American Psychological Association. *59, 60*

Havighurst, R. J. (1953) *Human Development and Education*, New York, Longmans, Green, (reissued 1961). *94*

Havighurst, R. J. (1956) 'Research on the developmental task concept', *School Review*, 64, 215–23. *95*

Havighurst, R. J. (1972) *Developmental Tasks and Education*, 3rd edn (1st edn 1948), New York, David McKay. *39–40, 94, 100, 105, 170*

Havighurst, R. J. (1973) 'History of developmental psychology: socialization and personality development through the life span', in Baltes, P. B. and Schaie, K. W. (eds) *Life-Span Developmental Psychology: Personality and Socialization*, New York, Academic Press. *23, 90*

Havighurst, R. J. (1982) 'The world of work', in Wolman, B. B. (ed.) *Handbook of Developmental Psychology*, Englewood Cliffs, New Jersey, Prentice-Hall. *94*

Hirsch, B. J. (1981) 'Social networks and the coping process: creating personal communities', in Gottlieb, B. H. (ed.) *Social Networks and Social Supports*, Beverly Hills, California, Sage. *150*

Holland, J. (1973) *Making Vocational Choices*, Englewood Cliffs, New Jersey, Prentice-Hall. *16*

Holmes, T. H. and Rahe, R. H. (1967) 'The social readjustment rating scale', *Journal of Psychosomatic Research*, 11, 213–18. *140, 146*

Honzik, M. P. (1984) 'Life-span development', *Annual Review of Psychology*, 35, 309–31. *24*

Hopson, B. (1981) 'Response to the papers by Schlossberg, Brammer and Abrego', *Counseling Psychologist*, 9 (2), 36–9. *131, 142–4, 148, 169*

Hopson, B. and Adams, J. (1976) 'Towards an understanding of transition: defining some boundaries of transition dynamics', in Adams, J., Hayes, J. and Hopson, B. (eds) *Transition: Understanding and Managing Personal Change*, London, Martin Robertson. *143–4*

Hopson, B. and Scally, M. (1980a) 'Change and development in adult life: some implications for helpers', *British Journal of Guidance and Counselling*, 8 (2), 175–87. *50*

Hopson, B. and Scally, M. (1980b) *Lifeskills Teaching Programmes*, no. 1, Leeds, Lifeskills Associates. *165*

Hopson, B. and Scally, M. (1981) *Lifeskills Teaching*, London, McGraw-Hill. *29, 38, 163–5, 169*

Hopson, B. and Scally, M. (1982) *Lifeskills Teaching Programmes*, no. 2, Leeds, Lifeskills Associates. *165*

Hopson, B. and Scally, M. (1985) *Lifeskills Teaching Programmes*, no. 3, Leeds, Lifeskills Associates. *165*

Horowitz, F. D. and Paden, L. Y. (1973) 'The effectiveness of environmental intervention programmes', in Caldwell, B. M. and Ricuiti, H. N. (eds) *Review of Child Development Research*, vol. 3, Chicago, University of Chicago Press. *171, 178*

Jacques, E. (1965) 'Death and the mid-life crisis', *International Journal of Psychoanalysis*, 46, 502–14. *108, 118*

Jacques, E. (1980) 'The mid-life crisis', in Greenspan, S. I. and Pollock, G. H. (eds) *The Course of Life: Psychoanalytic Contributions Toward Understanding Personality Development*, vol. 3: *Adulthood and Aging*, Washington, DC, National Institute of Mental Health. *108, 118*

Jahoda, M. (1950) 'Toward a social psychology of mental health', in Senn, M. J. E. (ed.) *Symposium on the Healthy Personality*, New York, Josiah Macy Jr Foundation. *35*

Jahoda, M. (1958) *Current Concepts of Positive Mental Health*, New York, Basic Books. *29*

Jourard, S. M. (1974) *The Healthy Personality: An Approach from the Viewpoint of Humanistic Psychology*, New York, Macmillan. *29*

Jung, C. G. (1972) 'The transcendent function', in Read, H., Fordham, M., Adler, G. and McGuire, W. (eds) *The Structure and Dynamics of the Psyche*, 2nd ed, vol. 8 of *The Collected Works of C. G. Jung*, London, Routledge & Kegan Paul. *4, 108*

Kagan, J. (1980) 'Perspectives on continuity', in Brim, O. J. and Kagan, J. (eds) *Constancy in Human Development*, Cambridge, Mass, Harvard University Press. *42–3, 49*

Kahn, R. L. and Antonucci, T. C. (1980) 'Convoys over the life course: attachment, roles and social support', in Baltes, P. B. and Brim, O. G. (eds) *Life-Span Development and Behavior*, vol. 3, New York, Academic Press. *10, 11, 151*

Kalish, R. A. (1982) *Late Adulthood: Perspectives on Human Development*, 2nd edn, Monterey, California, Brooks/Cole. *59*

Kanner, A. D., Coyne, J. C., Schaeffer, C. and Lazarus, R. S. (1981) 'Comparison of two modes of stress management: daily hassles and uplifts versus major life events', *Journal of Behavioral Medicine*, 4, 1–39. *152*

Kaplan, B. (1983) 'A trio of trials', In Lerner, R. M. (ed.) *Developmental Psychology: Historical and Philosophical Perspectives*, Hillsdale, New Jersey, Lawrence Erlbaum. *2, 27–9, 38*

Karp, D. A. and Yoels, W. C. (1982) *Experiencing the Life-Cycle: A Social Psychology of Aging*, Springfield, Illinois, C.C. Thomas. *9, 23, 45*

Karuza, J., Zevon, M. A., Rabinowitz, V. C. and Brickman, P. (1982) 'Attributions of responsibility by helpers and recipients', in Willis, T. A. (ed.) *Basic Processes in Helping Relationships*, New York, Academic Press. *187*

Kastenbaum, R. (1979) *Growing Old: Years of Fulfilment*, London, Harper & Row. *55*

Kenshalo, D. R. (1977) 'Age changes in touch, vibration, temperature, kinesthesis, and pain sensitivity', in Birren, J. E. and Schaie, K. W. (eds) *Handbook of the Psychology of Aging*, New York, Van Nostrand Reinhold. *57–8*

Kleemeier, R. W. (1959) 'Behavior and the organization of the bodily and the external environment', in Birren, J. E. (ed.) *Handbook of Aging and the Individual*, Chicago, University of Chicago Press. *54*

Kobasa, S. C. (1979) 'Stressful life events, personality and health: an inquiry into hardiness', *Journal of Personality and Social Psychology*, 37, 1–11. *157*

Kohlberg, L. (1963) 'The development of children's orientation toward a moral order: sequences in the development of moral thought', *Vita Humana*, 6, 11–33. *70*

Kohlberg, L. (1969) *Stages in the Development of Moral Thought and Action*, New York, Holt, Rinehart & Winston. *70*

Kohlberg, L. (1973a) 'Continuities in childhood and adult moral development revisited', in Baltes, P. B. and Schaie, K. W. (eds) *Life-Span Developmental Psychology: Personality and Socialization*, New York, Academic Press. *70–1, 74*

Kohlberg, L. (1973b) 'Stages and aging in moral development – some speculations', *Gerontologist*, 13, 497–502. *38–40*

Kohlberg, L. (1978) 'Revisions in the theory and practice of moral development', in Damon, W. (ed.) *Moral Development: New Directions for Child Development*, San Francisco, Jossey-Bass. *70, 72*

Kohlberg, L. and Turiel, E. (eds) (1973) *Recent Research in Moral Development*, New York, Holt, Rinehart & Winston. *71*

LaRocco, J. M. and Jones, A. P. (1978) 'Coworker and leader support as moderators of stress-strain relationships in work situations', *Journal of Applied Psychology*, 63, 629–34. *153*

Lawton, A. (1985) 'Youth counselling', *British Journal of Guidance and Counselling*, 13 (1), 35–48. *182*

Lazarus, R. S. (1966) *Psychological Stress and the Coping Process*, New York, McGraw-Hill. *152, 158*

Lazarus, R. S., Averill, J. R. and Opton, E. M. (1974) 'The psychology of coping: issues of research and assessment', in Coehlo, G. V., Hamburg, D. A. and Adams, J. E. (eds) *Coping and Adaptation*, New York, Basic Books. *156*

Lazarus, R. S. and Launier, R. (1978) 'Stress-related transactions between persons and environments', in Pervin, L. A. and Lewis, M. (eds) *Perspectives in Interactional Psychology*, New York, Plenum. *148, 152, 158*

Lerner, R. M. (1976) *Concepts and Theories of Human Development*, Reading, Mass., Addison-Wesley. *7, 18*

Lerner, R. M. and Ryff, C. D. (1978). 'Implementation of the life-span view of human development: the sample case of attachment', in Baltes, P. B. (ed.) *Life-Span Development and Behavior*, vol. 1, New York, Academic Press. *167–9, 171–2*

Levinson, D. J., Darrow, D. N., Klein, E. B., Levinson, M. H. and McKee, B. (1978) *The Seasons of a Man's Life*, New York, A. A. Knopf. *4, 24, 72, 90, 94, 100, 103–9, 111, 113–16, 118, 145, 159*

Lieberman, M. (1975) 'Group therapies', in Usdin, G. (ed.) *Overview of the Psychotherapies*, New York, Brunner-Mazel. *173*

Lindemann, E. (1979) *Beyond Grief: Studies in Crisis Intervention*, New York, Jason Aronson. *149*

Loevinger, J. (1976) *Ego Development: Conceptions and Theories*, San Francisco, Jossey-Bass. *4*

McCandless, B. R. (1970) *Adolescence: Behavior and Development*, Hinsdale, Illinois, Dryden Press. *13*

McCandless, B. R. and Evans, E. D. (1973) *Children and Youth: Psychosocial Development*, Hinsdale, Illinois, Dryden Press. *4, 7, 13, 24, 54, 75, 78*

McCluskey-Fawcett, K. A. and Reese, H. W. (eds) (1984) *Life-Span Developmental Psychology: Historical and Generational Effects*. New York, Academic Press. *24*

McPherson, I. and Sutton, A. (1981) (eds) *Reconstructing Psychological Practice*, London, Croom Helm. *182*

Marsella, A. J. and Snyder, K. K. (1981) 'Stress, social supports and schizophrenia disorders: toward an interactional model', *Schizophrenia Bulletin*, 7, 152–63. *149*

Maslow, A. H. (1968) *Toward a Psychology of Being*, 2nd edn, New York, Van Nostrand Reinhold. *26, 30, 34*

Maslow, A. H. (1970) *Motivation and Personality*, 2nd edn, New York, Harper & Row (1st edn 1954). *26, 29–35*

Michels, R. (1980) 'Adulthood', in Greenspan, S. I. and Pollock, G. H. (eds) *Psychoanalytic Contributions Toward Understanding Personality development*, vol. 3: *Adulthood and the Aging Process*, Washington, DC, National Institute of Mental Health. *129*

Mischel, T. (ed.) (1969) *Human Action: Conceptual and Empirical Issues*, New York, Academic Press. *44*

Montada, L. and Schmitt, M. (1982) 'Issues in applied developmental psychology: a life-span perspective', in Baltes, P. B. and Brim, O. G. (eds) *Life-Span Development and Behavior*, vol. 4, New York, Academic Press. *170*

Moos, R. H. and Mitchell, R. E. (1982) 'Social network resources and adaptation: a conceptual framework', in Willis, T. A. (ed.) *Basic Processes in Helping Relationships*, New York, Academic Press. *149, 150, 154–5*

Moreno, J. (1934) *Who Shall Survive: A New Approach to the Problem of Human Interrelations*, Washington, DC, Nervous and Mental Disease Publishing. *149*

Mortimer, J. T., Finch, M. D. and Kumka, D. (1982) 'Persistence and change in development: the multidimensional self-concept', in Baltes, P. B. and Brim, O. G. (eds) *Life-Span Development and Behavior*, vol. 4, New York, Academic Press. *42, 49*

Murgatroyd, S. and Woolfe, R. (1982) *Coping with Crisis: Understanding and Helping People in Need*, London, Harper & Row. *147*

Nesselroade, J. R. and Baltes, P. B. (1974) *Adolescent Personality Development and Historical Change: 1970–72*, Monographs of the Society for Research in Child Development, 39. *44*

Nesselroade, J. R. and Reese, H. W. (eds) (1973) *Life-Span Developmental Psychology: Methodological Issues*, New York, Academic Press. *24*

Neugarten, B. L. (1965) 'A developmental view of adult personality', in Birren, J. E. (ed.) *Relations of Development and Aging*, Springfield, Illinois, C. C. Thomas. *108*

Neugarten, B. L. (1977) 'Adaptation and the life cycle', in Schlossberg, N. K. and Entine, A. D. (eds) *Counseling Adults*, Monterey, California, Brooks/Cole. *44, 51, 129*

Neugarten, B. L. and associates (1964) *Personality in Middle and Late Life*, New York, Atherton Press. *44*

Neugarten, B. L. and Datan, N. (1973) 'Sociological perspectives on the life cycle', in Baltes, P. B. and Schaie, K. W. (eds) *Life-Span Developmental Psychology: Personality and Socialization*, New York, Academic Press. *50*

Nicholson, J. (1980) *Seven Ages*, Glasgow, Fontana. *14, 24*

Nunnally, J. C. (1973) 'Research strategies and measurement methods for investigating human development', in Nesselroade, J. R. and Reese, H. W. (eds) *Life-Span Developmental Psychology: Methodological Issues*, New York, Academic Press. *18–19*

Oates, J. (ed.) (1979) *Early Cognitive Development*, London, Croom Helm. *56*

Oatley, K. (1984) *Selves in Relation: An Introduction to Psychotherapy and Groups*, London, Methuen. *182*

Oden, M. H. and Terman, L. M. (1968) 'The fulfillment of promise – 40 year follow-up of the Terman Gifted Group', *Genetic Psychology Monographs*, 77, 3–93. *90*

Olweus, D. (1977) 'A critical analysis of the "modern" interactionist position', in Magnusson, D. and Endler, N. S. (eds) *Personality at the Crossroads: Current Issues in Interactional Psychology*, Hillsdale, New Jersey, Lawrence Erlbaum. *8*

Overton, W. F. and Reese, H. W. (1973) 'Models of development: methodological implications', in Nesselroade, J. R. and Reese, H. W. (eds) *Life-Span Developmental Psychology: Methodological Issues*, New York, Academic Press. *7*

Oxley, G. (1971) 'A life-model approach to change', *Social Casework*, 52 (10), 627–33. *174*

Parker, C. and Lewis, R. (1981) 'Beyond the Peter Principle: managing successful transitions', *Journal of European Industrial Training*, 5 (6), 17–21. *143–5*

Parkes, C. M. (1971) 'Psycho-social transitions: a field for study', *Social Science and Medicine*, 5, 101–15. *55, 142*

Pearlin, L. I. and Schooler, C. (1978) 'The structure of coping', *Journal of Health and Social Behaviour*, 19, 2–21. *148, 156–8, 161–3*

Perlman, H. (1957) *Social Casework: A Problem-Solving Process*, Chicago, University of Chicago Press. *174*

Pervin, L. A. and Lewis, M. (1978) 'Overview of the internal-external issue', in Pervin, L. A. and Lewis, M. (eds) *Perspectives in Interactional Psychology*, New York, Plenum Press. *7–8*

Phillips, J. L. (1981) *Piaget's Theory: A Primer*, San Francisco, W. H. Freeman. *63*

Piaget, J. (1932) *The Moral Judgement of the Child*, New York, Macmillan. *70*

Piaget, J. (1970) 'Piaget's theory', in Mussen, P. (ed.) *Carmichael's Manual of Child Psychology*, vol. 1, 2nd edn, New York, Wiley. *63*

Pick, A. D. (ed.) (1979) *Perception and Its Development: A Tribute to Eleanor J. Gibson*, New York, John Wiley. *56*

Ponzo, Z. (1978) 'Age prejudice of "Act your age"', *Personnel and Guidance Journal*, 57, 140–4. *52*

Rappaport, J. (1977) *Community Psychology: Values, Research and Action*, New York, Holt, Reinhart & Winston. *180, 182–5, 194*

Rappaport, J. and Chinsky, J. M. (1974) 'Models for delivery of service from a historical and conceptual perspective', *Professional Psychology*, 5, 42–50. *183, 185*

Rappaport, L. (1972) *Personality Development: The Chronology of Experience*, Glenview, Illinois, Scott, Foresman. *102*

Reese, H. W. (1976) 'Conceptions of the active organism', *Human Development*, 19, 108–19. *8*

Reese, H. W. and Overton, W. F. (1970) 'Models of development and theories of development', in Goulet, L. R. and Baltes, P. B. (eds) *Life-Span Developmental Psychology: Research and Theory*, New York, Academic Press. *7–8, 27*

Reese, H. W. and Overton, W. F. (1980) 'Models, methods and ethics of intervention', in Turner, R. R. and Reese, H. W. (eds) *Life-Span Developmental Psychology: Intervention*, New York, Academic Press. *172*

Reese, H. W. and Smyer, M. A. (1983) 'The dimensionalization of life events', in Callahan, E. J. and McCluskey, K. A. (eds) *Life-Span Developmental Psychology: Nonnormative Life Events*, New York, Academic Press. *131–3, 135–6, 138–9*

Reinert, G. (1979) 'Prolegomena to a history of life-span developmental psychology', in Baltes, P. B. and Brim, O. G. (eds) *Life-Span Development and Behavior*, vol. 2, New York, Academic Press. *23*

Reinert, G. (1980) 'Educational psychology in the context of the human life span', in Baltes, P. B. and Brim, O. G. (eds) *Life-Span Development and Behavior*, vol. 3, New York, Academic Press. *10, 95*

Riegel, K. F. (1973) 'Dialectic operations: the final period of cognitive development', *Human Development*, 16, 346–70. *65–7*

Riegel, K. F. (1975) 'Adult life crises: a dialectic interpretation of development', in Datan, N. and Ginsberg, L. H. (eds) *Life-Span Developmental Psychology: Normative Life Crises*, New York, Academic Press. *66, 146–7*

Riegel, K. F. and Meacham, J. A. (1978) 'Dialectics, transaction, and Piaget's theory', in Pervin, L. A. and Lewis, M. (eds) *Perspectives in Interactional Psychology*, New York, Plenum Press. *8*

Riegel, K. F. and Riegel, R. M. (1972) 'Development, drop and death', *Developmental Psychology*, 6, 306–19. *49*

Riessman, F. (1965) 'The "helper" therapy principle', *Social Work*, 10, 27–32. *175*

Roazen, P. (1976) *Erik H. Erikson*, New York, Free Press. *93*

Roberts, J., Prince, R., Gold, B. and Shiner, E. (1966) *Social and Mental Health Survey: Summary Report*, Montreal, Mental Hygiene Institute. *173*

Rockstein, M. (1975) 'The biology of aging in humans: an overview', in Goldman, R. and Rockstein, M. (eds) *The Physiology and Pathology of Aging*, New York, Academic Press. *55*

Rogers, C. R. (1961) *On Becoming a Person*, London, Constable. *29*

Rogers, C. R. (1978) *Carl Rogers on Personal Power*, London, Constable. *187*

Rossman, I. (1977) 'Anatomic and body composition changes with aging', in Finch, C. E. and Hayflick, L. (eds) *Handbook of the Biology of Aging*, New York, Van Nostrand Reinhold. *55*

Rowan, J. (1976) *Ordinary Ecstasy*, London, Routledge & Kegan Paul. *34*

Runyan, W. M. (1978) 'The life course as a theoretical orientation: sequences of person–situation interaction', *Journal of Personality*, 46, 569–93. *2*

Ryan, W. (ed.) (1969) *Distress in the City: Essays on the Design and Administration of Urban Mental Health Services*, Cleveland, Ohio, Case Western Reserve University Press. *173*

Sameroff, A. J. (1982) 'Development and the dialectic: the need for a systems approach', in Collins, W. A. (ed.) *The Concept of Development: The Minnesota Symposia on Child Development*, vol. 15, Hillsdale, New Jersey, Lawrence Erlbaum. *8*

Sampson, E. E. (1977) 'Psychology and the American ideal', *Journal of Personality and Social Psychology*, 35, 767–82. *35*

Schaie, K. W. (1965) 'A general model for the study of developmental problems', *Psychological Bulletin*, 64, 92–107. *19–20*

Schaie, K. W. (1977–8) 'Toward a stage theory of adult cognitive development', *Journal of Aging and Human Development*, 8 (2), 129–38. *65–6, 68–9*

Schaie, K. W. (1980) 'Intelligence and problem solving', in Birren, J. E. and Sloane, R. B. (eds) *Handbook of Mental Health and Aging*, Englewood Cliffs, New Jersey, Prentice-Hall. *62–3*

Schaie, K. W. and Baltes, P. B. (1975) 'On sequential strategies and developmental research', *Human Development*, 18, 384–90. *19*

Schaie, K. W. and Parnham, I. A. (1976) 'Stability of adult personality traits: fact or fable?', *Journal of Personality and Social Psychology*, 34, 146–58. *44*

Schein, E. H. (1977) 'Career anchors and career paths: a panel study of management school graduates', in Van Maanen, J. (ed.) *Organizational Careers: Some New Perspectives*, London, John Wiley. *160*

Schell, R. E. and Hall, E. (1983) *Developmental Psychology Today*, 4th edn, New York, Random House. *24*

Schlossberg, N. K. (1981) 'A model for analyzing human adaptation to transition', *Counseling Psychologist*, 9 (2), 2–18. *10, 142, 156–7, 160–1*

Schlossberg, N. K., Troll, L. E. and Leibowitz, Z. (1978) *Perspectives on Counseling Adults: Issues and Skills*, Monterey, California, Brooks/Cole. *51–2*

Schonfield, A. E. D. (1980) 'Learning, memory and aging', in Birren, J. E. and Sloane, R. B. (eds) *Handbook of Mental Health and Aging*, Englewood Cliffs, New Jersey, Prentice-Hall. *59*

Schonfield, D. and Robertson, E. A. (1966) 'Memory storage and aging', *Canadian Journal of Psychology*, 20, 228–36. *60*

Silverman, P. R. (1978) 'Mutual help: an alternative network', in *Women in Midlife – Security and Fulfillment*, Select Committee on Aging, US House of Representatives, Washington, DC, US Government Printing Office. *175*

Skovholt, T. M. (1974) 'The client as helper: a means to promote psychological growth', *Counseling Psychologist*, 4 (3), 58–64. *175*

Smith, A. D. (1980) 'Age difference in encoding, storage, and retrieval', in Poon, L. W., Fozard, J. L., Cermak, L. S., Arenberg, D. and Thompson, L. W. (eds) *New Directions in Memory and Aging: Proceedings of the George Talland Memorial Conference*, Hillsdale, New Jersey, Lawrence Erlbaum. *59*

Staude, J. R. (1981) *The Adult Development of C. J. Jung*, Boston, Routledge & Kegan Paul. *98*

Stevens-Long, J. (1979) *Adult Life: Developmental Processes*, California, Mayfield. *54*

Super, D. E. (1976) 'Vocational guidance: emergent decision-making in a changing society', in *Proceedings of the Eighth Seminar of the International Association for Educational and Vocational Guidance*, Lisbon, Sociedade Portuguesa de Psicologia. *4*

Super, D. E. (1980) 'A life-span, life-space approach to career development', *Journal of Vocational Behavior*, 16, 282–98. *4–6, 167*

Syme, S. L. (1974) 'Behavioral factors associated with the etiology of physical disease: a social epidemiological approach', *American Journal of Public Health*, 64, 1043–5. *153*

Terman, L. M. and Oden, M. H. (1959) *Genetic Studies of Genius*, vol. 5: *The Gifted Group at Mid-Life: Thirty-Five Years' Follow-Up of the Superior Child*, Stanford, California, Stanford University Press. *44*

Thurnher, M. (1975) 'Continuities and discontinuities in value orientations', in Lowenthal, M. F., Thurnher, M. and Chiriboga, D., *Four Stages of Life: A Comparative Study of Women and Men Facing Transitions*, San Francisco, Jossey-Bass. *160*

Troll, L. E. and Nowak, C. (1976) '"How old are you?" The question of age bias in the counseling of adults', *Counseling Psychologist*, 6, 41–4. *52*

Turner, J. (1984) *Cognitive Development and Education*, London, Methuen. *25*

Turner, J. S. and Helms, D. B. (1979) *Life Span Development*, Philadelphia, W. B. Saunders, *24, 90*

Turner, R. R. and Reese, H. W. (eds) (1980) *Life-Span Developmental Psychology: Intervention*, New York, Academic Press. *24*

Tyler, F. (1978) 'Individual psychosocial competence: a personality configuration', *Educational and Psychological Measurement*, 38, 309–23. *157*

Vaillant, G. E. (1977) *Adaptation to Life: How the Best and Brightest Come of Age*, Boston, Little, Brown. *19, 24, 72, 90–1, 106*

Van den Daele, L. D. (1976) 'A Cook's tour of development', *Journal of Genetic Psychology*, 128, 137–43. *26*

Walsh, D. A. (1983) 'Age differences in learning and memory', in Woodruff, D. S. and Birren, J. E. (eds) *Aging: Scientific Perspectives and Social Issues*, 2nd edn, Monterey, California, Brooks/Cole. *59*

Waugh, N. C. and Norman, D. A. (1965) 'Primary memory', *Psychological Review*, 72, 89–104. *60*

Wechsler, D. (1955) *The Measurement and Appraisal of Adult Intelligence: Manual for the Wechsler Adult Intelligence Scale*, New York, Psychological Corporation. *61*

Welford, A. T. (1959) 'Psychomotor performance', in Birren, J. E. (ed.) *Handbook of Aging and the Individual*, Chicago, University of Chicago Press. *55*

Welford, A. T. (1977) 'Motor performance', in Birren, J. E. and Schaie, K. W. (eds) *Handbook of the Psychology of Aging*, New York, Van Nostrand Reinhold. *55*

Welford, A. T., (1980) 'Sensory, perceptual, and motor processes in older adults', in Birren, J. E. and Sloan, R. B. (eds) *Handbook of Mental Health and Aging*, Englewood Cliffs, New Jersey, Prentice-Hall. *56–7*

Wetherick, N. E. (1978) 'In defence of circularity', *Behavioural and Brain Science*, 1 (2), 205. *41*

Whitbourne, S. K. and Weinstock, C. S. (1979) *Adult Development: The Differentiation of Experience*, New York, Holt, Rinehart & Winston. *60, 101–2*

Willis, S. L. and Baltes, P. B. (1980) 'Intelligence in adulthood and aging: contemporary issues', in Poon, L. W. (ed.) *Aging in the 1980's: Psychological Issues*, Washington, DC, American Psychological Association. *62*

Witmer, J. M., Rich, C., Barcikowski, R. S. and Mague, J. C. (1983) 'Psychosocial characteristics mediating the stress response: an exploratory study', *Personnel and Guidance Journal*, 62, 73–7. *158*

Wohlwill, J. F. (1973) *The Study of Behavioral Development*, New York, Academic Press. *38*

Wohlwill, J. F. (1980) 'Cognitive development in children', in Brim, O. G. and Kagan, J. (eds) *Constancy and Change in Human Development*, Cambridge, Mass., Harvard University Press. *42–3, 49*

Wood, V. and Robertson, J. (1978) 'Friendship and kinship interaction: differential effects on the elderly', *Journal of Marriage and the Family*, 40, 367–75. *154*

Woodruff, D. S. and Birren, J. E. (1972) 'Age changes and cohort differences in personality', *Developmental Psychology*, 6, 252–9. *44*

Subject index

normative age-graded influences, 47,
48–9, 168
normative history-graded influences,
47, 48, 49, 168
norms, 14–15

ordered-change concept of
development, 38–41
age-linked social role, 39, 40
biological concept of stage, 38–9
developmental task concept, 39–40
sociocultural concept of stage, 39,
40

pain threshold, 58
paraprofessionals, 177
perception, 56–8
person–environment relationship, 3,
6–7
aleatory-change orientation and,
45–6
interactional model, 8
transactional model, 8–9
physical changes, 54–8, 75
appearance, 54–5
perception, 56–8
psychomotor performance, 55–6
positive mental health, 29
potential, developmental, 2, 3
problem-finding stage of cognitive
development, 65
professional help system, 177
psychomotor performance, 55–6
psychosocial development (Erikson),
83–94, 98, 127, 128, 129
adulthood and, 108
age boundaries, 85, 90
autonomy v. shame/doubt, 85,
86–7, 88
basic trust v. basic mistrust, 85, 86,
88
career consolidation stage and, 90
criticism of theory, 93–4
cultural manifestations, 84
ego integrity v. despair/disgust, 85,
92, 128
generativity v. stagnation, 85, 90–2
identity v. role confusion, 85, 88–9,
128

industry v. inferiority, 85, 88
initiative v. guilt, 85, 87–8
intimacy v. isolation, 85, 89–90
stages of individual development,
84, 85

research, developmental, 12–23
age-associated changes and, 12–13,
14, 18, 19, 21–2
ahistorical, 15–16
cohort-sequential study
(longitudinal sequence), 21, 22
cross-sectional study, 15, 19, 20, 24
cross-sequential method, 22
design, 18–23
dimensions of, 13–18
explanatory, 15
general developmental model and,
19
historical, 15
longitudinal study, 15, 18, 20, 24
manipulative, 16–17
naturalistic, 16
norms and, 14–15
theoretical grounding, 17
time-lag method, 21
time-sequential study
(cross-sectional sequence), 21,
22

seeking mode, 183, 184
self-actualizing person (Maslow), 29,
30–5, 102, 129
characteristic traits of S-A people,
31–2
deficiency motivation/growth
motivation, 34
hierarchy of needs, 30–1, 35
self-empowerment, 29
self-fulfilment model, 80–1, 82
sequential research designs, 21–2
settling-down period, 104, 106, 128
smell, 57
social networks, 149
coping responses and, 156
determinants of individual's
resources, 154–6
environmental factors and, 154–5
life events and, 155–6

natural help system and, 174
negative effects, 151–2
personal factors, availability of
  resources and, 155
quality dimension, 150
social-integration effects, 150–1
stress sequence and, 152–4
  direct effects, 153
  insulating/buffering effects, 154
structure, 150
well-being, influence on, 153–4
social readjustment rating scale, 146
social support: *see* social networks
social support convoy, 10–11
sociometric analysis, 149
stability orientation, 41–4, 49–50
  ipsative stability, 43
  level invariance, 42–3
  normative stability, 43
  process stability, 43
  structural invariance, 42
stress sequence, 152, 153
  appraisal reactions, 152, 153
  coping resources, 152
  employment of coping strategies,
    152, 153
  health outcome, 152, 153
  stressors, 152, 153
subdisciplines, 23
symbolic interactionism, 9

taste, 57
theory
  functions of, 3–4, 76–8
  interventions and, 168
thirties
  adult consciousness during, 120,
    123–4

age thirty transition, 128
time-lag study, 21
time-sequential study, 21, 22
touch, 57–8
transition cycle, 141, 142–3
  immobilization stage, 143
  integration, 146
  letting go, 144–5
  minimization stage, 144
  post-shock reaction, 144
  search for meaning, 145
  self-doubt, 144
  testing, 145
transitions, psychological, 141–7, 169
  developmental perspective, 146–7
  disease perspective, 146
  model of stages: *see* transition cycle
twenties, adult consciousness during,
  119–22, 123–4

vision, 56–7
voluntary work, 176

waiting mode, 183–4
Wechsler Adult Intelligence Scale
  (WAIS), 61
West Virginia conferences, 23–4
women
  appearance and, 55
  developmental tasks of early
    adulthood, 113
  mid-life search for authenticity,
    125–6
  moral reasoning, 72, 74–5
  sex/sex-role related coping
    resources, 158–9